Submarine Torpedo Tactics

SUBMARINE TORPEDO TACTICS

An American History

Edward Monroe Jones *and*
Shawn S. Roderick

McFarland & Company, Inc., Publishers
Jefferson, North Carolina

ALSO OF INTEREST
Crossing the Zorn: The January 1945 Battle at Herrlisheim as Told by the American and German Soldiers Who Fought It, edited by Edward Monroe-Jones (McFarland 2010)

LIBRARY OF CONGRESS CATALOGUING-IN-PUBLICATION DATA

Monroe-Jones [sic], Edward.
    Submarine torpedo tactics : an American history / Edward Monroe Jones and Shawn S. Roderick.
        p.   cm.
    Includes bibliographical references and index.

    ISBN 978-0-7864-9646-4 (softcover : acid free paper) ∞
    ISBN 978-1-4766-1758-9 (ebook)

    1. Torpedoes—United States—History. 2. Submarines (Ships)—United States—History. 3. Submarine warfare—United States—History. 4. Fire control (Naval gunnery)—History. I. Roderick, Shawn S., 1976– II. Title.
V850.J65 2014
359.9'34—dc23   2014039833

BRITISH LIBRARY CATALOGUING DATA ARE AVAILABLE

© 2015 Edward Monroe Jones and Shawn S. Roderick. All rights reserved

No part of this book may be reproduced or transmitted in any form or by any means, electronic or mechanical, including photocopying or recording, or by any information storage and retrieval system, without permission in writing from the publisher.

Cover design by Laurie Berg © 2015

Printed in the United States of America

McFarland & Company, Inc., Publishers
    Box 611, Jefferson, North Carolina 28640
    www.mcfarlandpub.com

Table of Contents

Acknowledgments vii
Preface 1
Introduction 3

1. The Torpedo Is Born   7
2. First World War Fire Control Techniques   16
3. Between the Wars   28
4. An Analysis of the Fire Control Problem   53
5. The Second World War   70
6. The Era of the GUPPY   98
7. From *Tang* to *Nautilus*   122
8. A Most Unusual Torpedo   135
9. *Skipjack*, the Convergence of *Nautilus* and *Albacore*   142
10. The *Sturgeon*-Class Submarine   151
11. The *Los Angeles*–Class Submarine   159
12. The Ballistic Missile Submarine   170
13. The *Seawolf* and *Virginia* Submarines   183
14. The Future of American Submarines   194

Appendix A—A Glossary of Submarine Fire Control Terminology   201
Appendix B—A Evolution of Submarine Torpedo Fire Control Equipment   205
Chapter Notes   207
Bibliography   217
Index   219

Acknowledgments

Appreciation and gratitude are extended by the authors to the following individuals who provided invaluable assistance and encouragement in the writing of this book:

Naval Undersea Museum Curator Mary Ryan and the library staff for their assistance and support in conducting research pertinent to this work, in particular Registrar/Collections Manager Jennifer Heinzelman, whose help in locating rare documents and artifacts was invaluable.

Irmgard Diekmann for the translation of documents pertaining to the Kriegsmarine, Howaldswerke and G7 German torpedo.

Direktor, Deutsches Schiffahrtsmuseum, Dr. Dirk J. Peters for providing information on the Type XXI submarine.

Damien D. Jones, who provided computer technical guidance and who integrated photographs, illustrations and text into a comprehensive flow of information.

Laurie Berg of Graphics Ranch in Seabeck, Washington, who provided illustrations, photograph enhancements and charts.

Archivist Wendy S. Gulley of the Submarine Force Museum, who graciously provided a photograph of the damaged USS *Nautilus*.

Naval History and Heritage Command staff members, who provided assistance to the author in researching files of equipment relating to torpedo fire control.

Robert Paul, who provided amplifying information on specifics of the Fleet Type boat.

Rob Brennan, who instructed the author in computer manipulation of data.

Kristen Bernacchi of the Submarine League and journal *Submarine Review*, who encouraged the authors to write the history of submarine torpedo fire control as an informative, interesting and entertaining journey.

Acknowledgments

Gerry Patten, Lcdr., USN (Ret.), prior executive officer under Cdr. James Osborn of USS *Tunny* (SSG-282), who provided the authors with insights into the rigors of Regulus I patrols.

Susan Todd Brook of the Naval Institute Press, who granted permission to the authors to reprint portions of the Institute's Oral History Program.

Preface

Because of our knowledge of American submarine history and technology, many questions from the public are referred to our small group of active and retired submarine officers at the Submarine Research Center. The most frequently asked questions involve the aiming of torpedoes to hit targets that are moving and often submerged. These "How do they do it?" questions cannot be answered without knowing when, in the one hundred fifty years that naval submarines have been in operation, the question applies. Invariably, the inquiring person has little or no knowledge of how submarines and their torpedoes work, so the answer expands into rather lengthy correspondence.

It seemed appropriate to organize a formal description of torpedo tactics and fire control in terms that might be understood by those having a curiosity about the subject, but having no real background concerning those things that run under water to strike a moving target. In so writing, it became apparent to us that the subject did not lend itself to any quick answers. Without regard to how many words and diagrams it might take, the authors conducted the research to fill in the gaps of their personal knowledge of the subject. Technical manuals and our personal experience in torpedo fire control provided the explanation of the "Hows." Biographical descriptions and recorded interviews introduced us to insights of naval personnel whose brilliant minds solved seemingly incomprehensible problems. Their story became the focus of our research. Some were the captains of submarines on war patrol whose logs recorded the teamwork of torpedo tactics. Others were scientists and system engineers who designed electronic equipment of unmatched complexity.

Most of the research was conducted in the library and archives of the Naval Undersea Museum in Keyport, Washington. The Submarine Force Museum at Groton, Connecticut, the Naval History and Heritage Com-

Preface

mand at the Naval Shipyard in Washington, D.C., and the National Archives in College Park, Maryland, were all most kind in guiding our research.

Although there is an abundance of information about torpedoes available in bookstores, our research failed to find any on torpedo fire control beyond specific United States Navy technical manuals designed for crew members of operating submarines and relevant Naval schools. Thus, our effort to reduce a somewhat complicated subject to a description understandable to anyone is singular and introductory in published form.

The authors could not ignore the unique character of the submariner, who is generally brilliant, courageous and blessed with a sense of humor that manifests itself in mischief and skullduggery. It seemed appropriate to include a few examples that can only be described as schoolboy pranks. We do so with the respect and reverence for all those submariners who have sacrificed so much in the tradition of the American Submarine Force.

Introduction

The April 1904 issue of *Popular Mechanics* (Vol. 6, No. 4) ran an article titled "The Torpedo: War's Deadliest Weapon." It said in part, "It [the torpedo] is the deadliest, most stealthful, most ingenious instrument of war. It is the most wonderful mechanical ingenuity [*sic*] of any machine ever constructed by man." Despite the quaint grammar, the writer's enthusiasm accurately reflects the fear-tinged wonder that the torpedo inspired at the turn of the twentieth century. Although we may have become accustomed to marvelous scientific advances since the invention of the torpedo, there remains a mystery as to how these sophisticated weapons managed to hit their mark. The torpedo, by its very nature, is an immoral thing when one considers the stealth by which it deals out its destruction. It is an extension of the submarine, which lurks beneath the waves to deal out its deadly payload without notice to its intended victim.

And yet, one cannot help contemplate how the captain of a submarine can calculate the intricate and variable quantities involved in hitting a moving target with a projectile that having once left the submarine, must find the proper course to intercept a ship at a point, not where the ship is, but where it will be when the torpedo intersects its course. This is the Torpedo Fire Control Problem, which in modern-day parlance is termed Target Motion Analysis. Those who have a curiosity to know how torpedoes find their targets will discover the solutions simple and interesting. Likewise, the history of how seemingly difficult calculations were reduced to quick answers is a history of tricks and gadgets of amazing ingenuity. Imagine what it was like to be in the conning tower of a Second World War American submarine during an attack. The following description is typical.

The captain stands near the attack periscope. He is aware of a potential target still at some distance from his submarine. Hanging in the balance is the safety of his boat, his crew and the mission of the submarine. The

Introduction

aggressive commander is the one who has confidence in his weapons. He expects that his torpedoes will perform as they were designed, but through experience he often has the uneasy feeling that the next one he shoots may not run hot, straight and normal. Once leaving the torpedo tube, his weapons must quickly gain the speed, depth and course his skill and fire control system have determined will result in a hit. Dependability of his weapon and reliability of his calculations will either mean the destruction of the target, or the probable demise of his submarine and its crew.

Beneath the surface, the submarine has only its periscope to give glimpses of surface ships, and below periscope depth has only sound as its source of target movements. At one end of the conning tower, a cylindrical tube capped at the ends with hard-steel hemispheres, is the helmsman; at the other end is a small chart table where an officer keeps a running plot of the attack. On one side of the periscopes is the torpedo data computer, manned by another officer. The captain has taken several short periscope observations. He says, "Up scope," and the hissing of compressed air accompanies the sliding of the silver shaft. "Bearing, mark," he says, then quickly follows with, "Range mark." An instant later he claps the handles to the shaft. It is the signal for the quartermaster to lower the periscope. At the same time the periscope assistant reads the range from the stadimeter. "Twelve hundred yards," he reports to the torpedo data computer operator, who cranks in the new range. By this time the muzzle doors to the forward torpedo tubes are open and the captain says, "Tubes one, two and three, spread M.O.T., aft, forward, set depth 9 feet, high speed." The quartermaster repeats into his sound-powered telephone the message to the torpedomen at the forward tubes. He switches the firing panel indicators to "standby" and reports to the captain that tubes one, two and three show "ready" lights. The captain says, "Final bearing and shoot." The periscope is raised, the captain adjusts the cross hairs to the target and says, "Bearing mark." Again the scope comes down as the torpedo data computer operator reports, "Set." The assistant torpedo data computer operator looks to his panel for the red correct-solution light, which tells him that the spread has been set into the torpedoes. It lights and he says, "Shoot." The firing button is pushed and the boat shudders as the first torpedo starts its run to the impact point. The final phase of the attack has taken less than ten minutes.

Now the submarine begins a series of maneuvers that will hide it from reprisal attacks by enemy surface ships. The hunter becomes the hunted,

Introduction

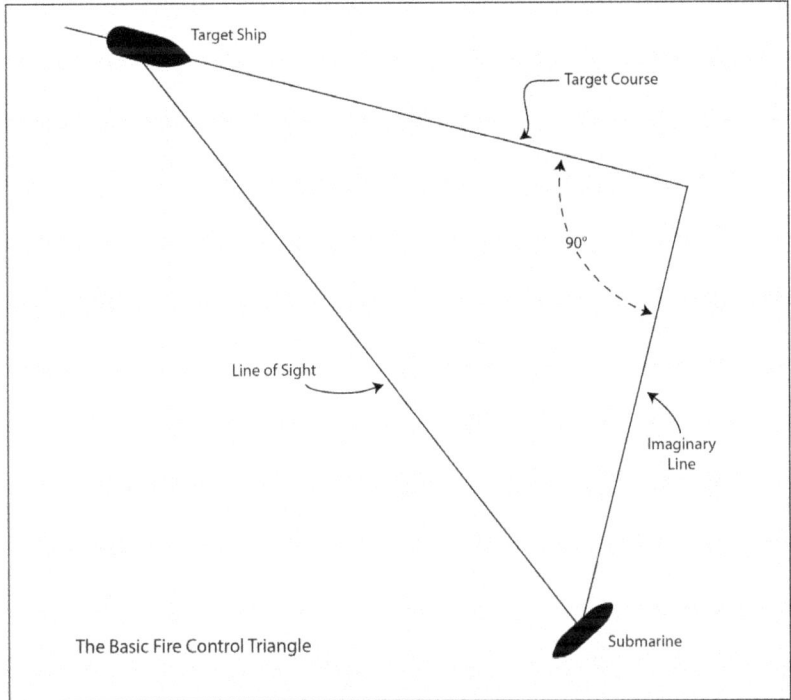

The Basic Fire Control Triangle

The basic torpedo fire control problem consists of a triangle formed by the line of sight, the target ship course and an imaginary line perpendicular to the target ship course (Submarine Research Center).

but if the captain's calculations have been correct, those on the surface will be occupied by the chaos his torpedoes have wrought.

An attacking submarine must send its weapons to hit targets that may be using torpedo evasion tactics. The problem facing the submarine captain is not only how to hit the target, but how to anticipate the moves of the other captain who seeks to foil the submarine's maneuvers.

To begin the study of how torpedoes find their mark, an examination of the following illustration is helpful: The attacking submarine places itself in a position relative to a target ship from which it may launch a torpedo with pre-set depth and course, at a range within the run capability of the torpedo. Since the torpedo contains a gyro, which will keep it on a desired course, it is not necessary for the submarine to point itself toward the target. The problem of getting close enough to the target and setting

Introduction

the correct inputs for depth and torpedo course is one of target information acquisition and mathematical application. In its simplest form, the problem is one of a right triangle in which the line of sight from the submarine to the target ship represents the hypotenuse, the target's course represents the first leg, and an imaginary line from the submarine to a point perpendicular to the target's course represents the second leg. The triangle thus formed is as follows:

The distance from the target ship to the intersection of the imaginary 90-degree line is a function of target speed. With this basic model in mind, further complexities of torpedo tactics can be understood with little difficulty. Fundamental to all target motion analysis is the simple equation, distance equals time times speed, or $D = T \times S$.

When one examines the broader nature of torpedo tactics, the environment of the men who conduct them should not be ignored. While soldiers live in the harsh elements, fight freezing winters and scorching summers, and come face to face with their enemy in close-quarter combat, the submariner lives in comparative comfort and fights a sterile battle of mathematical problem-solving without having to come to grips with the reality of a torpedo's destructive power. Submarines may become victims of the enemy's efforts, but most often death to a submarine and its crew comes from the uncompromising sea, which treats each submarine with the same ruthless impartiality of indifferent hydrostatic pressure.

While the tactics of torpedo attack occupy center stage in this work, many vitally related systems are necessarily described, particularly sonar, equipment silencing, high-speed underwater propulsion, and hull strength integrity. Of greatest importance are the men who gave so much to the development of submarines.

1

The Torpedo Is Born

In 1864 an Italian inventor named Giovanni de Ciotta was introduced to an English engineer by the name of Robert Whitehead. The Englishman was in charge of a factory called Technical Stabilimento Tecnico Fiumano, commonly referred to as "Fiume."[1] The young Italian inventor presented an unworkable idea to the factory's lead engineer, but Whitehead was not impressed with Ciotta's technical ability in the design of an underwater, self-propelled vehicle. However, he saw in the crude drawings the potential for a military weapon and he agreed to split with Ciotta any profit that might be produced by their mutual effort. It took over two years for Whitehead to design and produce a prototype torpedo.

The revolutionary new weapon not only ran submerged, but was powered by an inboard pneumatic engine of Whitehead's own design. It was driven by compressed air contained in a chamber within the body shell of the torpedo. Thus, in the year 1866 the first Whitehead torpedo was invented. It had the ability to maintain a reasonably steady depth at a speed of 6 knots with a range of 220 yards.[2]

With a single propeller, the body of the torpedo tended to roll. It would take some time before this problem was corrected by the rather complex mechanical design of contra-rotating propellers, one drive shaft within the other. This was the work of Robert Wilson and John Ericsson, both of whom were brilliant engineers.[3]

Over the next decade Whitehead manufactured succeeding torpedoes, each time improving its power source, depth control and steering. Many attempts by other inventors resulted in more failures than successes. Most, as seen from today's perspective, were so impractical as to be ludicrous and without enough merit to be lifted from the drawing board. Some of the early attempts at torpedo invention consisted of shore-controlled cables that so severely limited range as to render the torpedo useless. Rudders were manipulated by men standing on a pier with lengthy lines connected to rudder bars. The men furiously jerked on these strings as the torpedo wobbled to and fro. When the strings reached their limit, so did the torpedo.

Depth control was simple. It consisted of rigid rods attached vertically from the torpedo to floats. Stealth was a concept far in the future.

One inventor, Louis Brennan, also stood on a pier with a length of wire to his torpedo. This wire was rigid and was axially driven by a pier-mounted electric motor. The wire was fixed to the torpedo's propeller and so the weapon had ample propulsive power with a range of about a hundred yards.[4] Also included in those well-intentioned experiments was a rocket propelled torpedo which proved to be uncontrollable.[5]

The motive power for the Sims Edison torpedo was electricity supplied by a dynamo on shore. The heavy transmission cable ran underwater from the torpedo to shore. The cable was coiled in a compartment within the torpedo and was payed out as the torpedo advanced. It was not only propelled, but steered by electricity. Once again, its range was a function of the wire's length.[6]

In the Nordenfelt electrical torpedo, the motive power was supplied by storage cells. The storage battery and motor were within the torpedo, which was steered by a balanced rudder that was manipulated from shore through a flexible line.[7]

These early designs suffered from one common defect: they were attached in some way to a controller on shore. The automotive torpedo was without any connection to shore and was referred to as a "fish" torpedo because it was able to swim on its own. Developing such a torpedo required sophisticated engineering and continuing experiments.

The first U.S. Navy torpedo of a Whitehead design had a small, two-cylinder engine. It was not a very successful weapon as the engine type failed to produce enough speed through the water. The U.S. Naval Torpedo Station, established in 1869 on Goat Island in Narragansett Bay near Newport, Rhode Island, continued to experiment with propulsion alternatives.

In 1898 Califf described the most successful torpedo of the day:

> The Howell torpedo, the invention of Capt. Howell of the U.S. Navy, has much the general appearance of the Whitehead, and is its principal rival. The shell is of brass, the outer parts of steel or phosphorous bronze. The propelling power is stored in a steel flywheel, driven at high velocity of rotation before the torpedo is launched. The flywheel is geared directly to the propeller shaft. The degree of submersion is controlled by hydrostatic

pressure. After launching, it automatically takes the depth for which set, which it maintains.[8]

The flywheel system of propulsion was quickly abandoned. The Whitehead torpedo continued to be the most reliable weapon in several features, one of which was his revolutionary propulsion system. In the 1890s Whitehead perfected a compressed air turbine for his torpedo's propulsion.

This development replaced unreliable reciprocating-type engines. The Navy quickly followed suit, but the design was still handicapped by its limited range, which was dependent upon the size and compression limits of the air flask.

The compressed air–driven turbine continued to undergo design changes as inventors tried to get higher speeds and longer ranges. Other inventors worked on the problems of automatic depth and course control. As long as these two aspects of torpedo design eluded the inventors, its viability as a weapon would be in question.

The problem of depth control was attacked by several engineers including Whitehead. In 1913 Corbin described the development of Whitehead's hydrostatic depth-keeping device:

> A hydrostatic membrane or valve is attached to a spring which acts upon rods indirectly connected to the horizontal rudder. If the torpedo descends too low, this valve operates the rudder and steers it upwards, or if too high in the water it is steered downwards. Indeed, this arrangement works too well, for it would bring a too deeply submerged torpedo up so quickly that it would jump clean out of the water. Therefore, this valve is made to work in conjunction with a pendulum placed so as to swing to one end or the other as the nose is pointed upwards or downwards. When the hydrostatic valve tends to throw the torpedo upwards too quickly, the pendulum swings toward the stern of the torpedo and that swing checks its too rapid rise. Thus, the partnership between the hydrostatic valve and the pendulum results in the torpedo assuming and keeping to any predetermined level under water.[9]

Whitehead continued to improve the depth-keeping mechanism by refining the dampening weights within his balance chamber. This was important in maintaining a constant depth near the surface, where wave action tended to upset the sensitive hydrostatic valve with a resulting broach of the surface. This breakthrough became his patented "secret chamber" which successfully controlled a torpedo's running depth, even when close to the surface.[10]

In the meantime, another inventor stumbled upon a method for controlling a torpedo's course. As described earlier, John Howell was an experimenter of torpedo propulsion systems. While working in 1870 on a large flywheel, which was intended to act as the torpedo's propulsion system, he discovered that the flywheel resisted attempts to change its pre-set orientation. The stability of the spinning wheel acted similarly upon the torpedo when the wheel was rigidly fixed within it. Improvements were made upon this idea and the torpedo gyroscopic steering system was born. The gyro was improved by adding transverse azimuth dampening pendulums to eliminate small deviations in course.[11]

Whitehead took the initial work of Howell one step further by purchasing the improved gyro of inventor L. Obry. In 1907, Commodore Murray F. Suetter of the Royal Navy described the Obry gyro as follows:

> This apparatus for automatically controlling the direction of their locomotive torpedoes was invented by Mr. L. Obry of Trieste, who sold his invention to Mr. Whitehead and the latter then developed it for his torpedo. The instrument is now generally spoken of as the "gyroscope" or "Obry." ... In skillful hands 95 percent of launchings should result in hits. The apparatus consists of a heavy flywheel supported in gimbals, a method that gives the wheel a very delicate suspension as friction is practically non-existent.... The U.S. Navy's Mark II gyroscope has a flywheel spun by air impulse and its parts are so arranged that it can be adjusted without disturbance to its position in the torpedo.[12]

Depth and course mechanisms had only to be adjusted and improved.

In the last decade of the 19th century, Germany awakened to the advent of the torpedo. The Ministry of Marine was so impressed by its possibilities that its warship building program was interrupted. Adjustments were made to its building schedule and more emphasis was placed on the submarine as a possible weapon platform of the future. Torpedo development took a high priority and the "C" series culminated in the C74 and C79, which were derivatives of the original Whitehead 1876 design. By 1906 these were being manufactured in Friedricksort and had 45-centimeter (diameter) bodies of corrosion-resistant phosphorbronze. The improved model for U-boat use was 7 meters long and was 50 centimeters in diameter. This was the first of the "G" series.[13] This advanced torpedo had twin gyros. The redundancy provided improved reliability and the gyros were actuated in tandem as torpedoes' ranges increased. By 1916 the G7 had a range of 30 km at a speed of 45 knots or 100 km at 30 knots. U-boats of the First World War at first carried C74s and C79s, but these were quickly replaced

1—The Torpedo Is Born

with the superior G7s.[14] This weapon was used as Germany's standard torpedo for the rest of the First World War and with modifications became its major submarine weapon of the Second World War.[15]

In America, the E.W. Bliss Company contracted with engineer Frank McDowell Leavitt to build a torpedo using many of the concepts devised by Robert Whitehead. The resulting Bliss-Leavitt torpedo series was manufactured for the U.S. Navy until 1921. The first signature torpedo was the Mark 3, the specifications for which were published by the Navy in 1903. The initial specifications called for an automobile torpedo 5 meters in length and 45 centimeters in width. Point number 17 of the specifications included the condition, "The torpedoes to be furnished under the contract of which these specifications shall form a part, shall have separate warheads and exercise heads complete for each torpedo and shall be equipped with steering gear." It also stated that "the air flask shall have an elastic limit of 90,000 pounds, air pressure up to 2,250 pounds with a test pressure of 3,000 pounds.... The turbine engine shall be designed for a range of 1,200 yards at not less than a speed of 35 knots ... it shall be fitted with a Leavitt electric gyroscope or Navy gyroscope so arranged as to allow a wide angle of fire up to 140 degrees each side."[16]

The resulting Mark 4 Bliss-Leavitt torpedo had a range of 2,000 yards and a speed of 29 knots.[17] It was the first Navy torpedo to be specially designed for submarines. Wildenberg and Polmar describe the importance of the Mark 7 as follows: "The extended range of these 5 meter long torpedoes provided the impetus to develop a torpedo director for use with a periscope that could solve the problem of how much lead was needed to hit a moving target."[18]

Referring to the basic torpedo fire control triangle defined in the Introduction, the distance of the leg created by the target ship's advance is a function of its speed. To determine the target's speed it is necessary to know the range to the target as expressed in the triangle's hypotenuse. Knowing the range or distance to the target and the target's course expressed in angle-on-the-bow, the submarine can determine the target's speed by its rate of bearing change (AOB). From speed information, the time it will take for the target to reach the impact point can be calculated. Wildenberg and Polmar use the term "lead," that is, the distance traveled by the target ship from the moment the torpedo is fired to the moment it strikes the target. The solution to this problem involves some accurate information, arithmetic calculations and application of simple trigonometry. In its simplest form, *distance* is equal to *time* times *speed* (rate) or D=RT. Normally, only the trigonometric sine of the angle formed by the target's relative bearing (hypotenuse) and target ship's course comes into play in the effort to learn the distance from the submarine to the target ship's track. This distance is the target's closest point of approach (CPA) to the submarine, assuming that the target stays on course and speed and the submarine remains stationary. But the captain needs to maneuver as close to the target's track as possible. He needs to know not only the distance to the track, but the optimum course for the submarine to take in order to obtain the best firing position. The answer to this problem will be discussed in subsequent chapters.

The competent captain soon learns to juggle these relationships in his mind and to make reasonably accurate assessments of his best course and speed to intercept the target.

In an effort to reduce the fire control problem's complexity, mechanical devices had been used on surface ships that made the torpedo fire control problem more manageable. The destroyer class of Navy ship had been built for the purpose of attacking ships with torpedoes as its primary weapon. Tubes were mounted on trainable pedestals so that the weapons could be launched from the destroyer's beam quadrant. To accommodate quick fire control problem-solving, the device was aligned with the bore of the multi-tube mounts. Wildenberg and Polmar describe the device as follows:

> In the early days of torpedo warfare the torpedo fire triangle could be solved by mechanical torpedo directors. These were simple mechanical devices that automatically provided an aiming point for the proper release of the torpedo. They were made of metal and had sliding arms that could create a miniature model of the space and velocity triangle. A ruled bar, called the speed to torpedo bar, was aligned with the torpedo tube. It had an adjustable slide that could move back and forth on a scale graduated in knots to represent the running speed of the torpedo. Another ruled bar called the target speed bar, swiveled about a pivot that represented the impact point. It also had an adjustable slide that could be used to set the estimated speed of the target.
> The last element was the slotted sighting bar that swiveled from a pedestal on top of the torpedo speed bar. It was connected to the target speed bar via a pin running within the slot. When the slide bars on both speed bars were adjusted, the sighting bar was aligned with the sighting line required to produce a hit. Once the director was adjusted, the trainer

in charge of the torpedo tube looked down the sight line and waited for the target to come into view, at which point the torpedo would be fired.[19]

The Mark 4 torpedo had a range and speed sufficient to warrant the use of the surface ship mechanical fire control device in submarines. The D Class submarines were only 134.8 feet in length. They displaced from 288 tons to 337 tons.[20] The torpedo fire director as used on surface ships during the decade preceding the First World War presented engineering difficulties if it were to be installed in the D Class submarines. The USS *Salmon*, D-3, had been commissioned on September 8, 1910, and represented the latest type boat in the submarine fleet. She had three compartments consisting of a torpedo room, a control room and an engine room. Separating the three compartments were two watertight bulkheads. The doors through these bulkheads had eight dogging levers so that if one compartment was flooded crewmembers had a chance of survival in the remaining dry two compartments.

Two periscopes occupied the forward end of the control room. A radio mast was at the after end. The bridge ladder was on the port side adjacent to the periscopes. All in all, the control room was cramped in its original design and the installation of a surface-type torpedo director, which would have to be aligned and attached to the attack periscope, was impossible without adding space to the control room. The decision was made to lengthen the control room by moving the forward bulkhead a distance into the torpedo room.[21]

The D Class submarines were so modified contrary to the opinion of some involved naval architects. The modification destroyed the balance of compartmental watertight integrity and so compromised the ability of the boats to survive a flooding.

Since several boats of the class were later lost at sea, the efficacy of the modification remains in question as to the importance of the early torpedo aiming device. First World War German U-boats gained great success by relying on the skill of the captain to mentally solve the torpedo fire control problem.

The submarine version of the torpedo director was engineered by the Electric Boat Company. It was smaller than the surface model, but still was bulky. Even with the two feet of additional space made by pushing the forward bulkhead into the torpedo room, the instrument hardly fit. Since the approach officer had to have unencumbered space at the periscope's eye piece, the director's sliding arms had to be mounted under and forward of the periscope. The director was attached to the periscope's base plate so that it could be slid in place and clamped securely. An officer stood forward of the periscope on the starboard side of the director and manipulated the arms as the captain announced the target's bearing, angle-on-the-bow (course), estimate of target speed and estimate of range. Once the firing data had been translated into the director's sliding arms, the captain could either swing the submarine to bring the cross hairs of the periscope onto the target or could take a course that would intersect a desired point of impact. Both options provided a zero gyro angle. In the former option he would immediately fire his torpedo. In the latter option he would wait until the target's motion brought it across the cross hairs before firing his weapon."[22]

It was said earlier in this work that improvements in torpedo capability and fire control techniques went hand in hand. Perhaps it was more like a race between two runners with each surging ahead at different times. In this case, the capability of the torpedo outpaced the fire control system, since a gyro angle could be pre-set into the torpedo, but the submarine's captain was constrained to swing his ship to line up his tubes with the desired course of the torpedo. At this point of pre–First World War development the Mark 4's gyro had to remain on zero.

In Europe and particularly in England, strides were being made in ways to heat a torpedo's compressed air and thereby produce more energy for propulsion. W.G. Armstrong developed a combustion chamber where air was mixed with fuel, then ignited by an electrical spark.[23] While it was a large step forward, the extreme heat was a significant danger. Gesztesy in Germany improved the chamber by adding water as a coolant.[24] Califf described the first attempts at using superheated steam: "The propulsion turbine driven by superheated steam will give the torpedo a speed of about 22 knots for 400 yards, and an extreme range of about 1000 yards at slower speeds."[25] The concept of the steam-driven torpedo was adopted by others who redesigned the mixture of fuel, water and air as well as the torpedo's ignition system.

Just prior to the opening of the First World War, the United States submarine force consisted of coastal defense submarines and by definition

1—The Torpedo Is Born

were limited to the role of defense rather than offense. While the Mark VII steam torpedo was then being manufactured by both the Bliss-Leavitt Company and the Naval Ordnance Facility in Newport, Rhode Island, the K Class submarine fell short of making optimal use of this excellently designed weapon. With a 3000-yard range and speed of 33 knots, its potential far outpaced the weapon platforms that would carry it.

2

First World War Fire Control Techniques

The young Imperial German Navy began with two Nordenfeldt-type submarines. In 1890 and in 1902 it produced its ultra-secret, all-electric Howald submarine with a single bow torpedo tube.[1] In 1906 the German Navy ordered its first U-boat, the U-1, powered by a kerosene engine with direct reduction drive. Although Britain awoke rather late to the potential of the submarine, in 1901 it began building a submarine component to its fleet with the purchase of five Holland submarines built in the United States. By the summer of 1914 not one of the world's leading naval powers lacked some form of submarine. The exact role of the new weapon had yet to be defined. One English admiral, Sir Arthur Wilson, had suggested as early as 1902 that the crews of captured submarines should be hanged as pirates. He went on to describe submarines as "underhanded, unfair and damned un–English."[2] Opinion changed rapidly. Only a few years later Admiral Sir John Fisher wrote, "I don't think it is even faintly realized the immense impending revolution which the submarine will affect as offensive weapons of the war."[3]

The immediate effect of German submarines on the British Grand Fleet was the withdrawal of all British battleships and battle cruisers into the bay of Scapa Flow. Thus, even before the Germans had fired their first torpedo the threat of the submarine caused alarm and dread in the British Navy.

The British continued to regard the submarine as a sneaky, underhanded weapon even as the First World War began. For this reason Britain failed to immediately begin a submarine building program of its own. With its outdated Holland submarines, Britain could do little except try to evade German submarines.[4]

The Hague peace conferences of 1899 and 1907 had defined rules for

2—First World War Fire Control Techniques

submarines in war. A submarine was constrained by those rules to signal a merchant ship of the submarine's intention to sink it. After giving clear warning, the ship's crew must be given ample time to abandon ship and move away to a safe distance. Neutrals could be stopped and searched if in the mind of the submarine's captain there was reason to suspect that the ship was carrying contraband material.[5]

By 1914 and the beginning of the First World War, the Germans had no intention of living up to these outdated and impractical rules. Even Admiral Lord Fisher realized that the submarine was a weapon that could not possibly provide for the welfare of merchant seamen. Such small boats had no facilities to take into consideration the welfare of a merchant crew. In fact, it would be impossible for the submarine to attack commerce if it were to take seriously the encumbrances of international law. If Germany, or any other nation, were to use the submarine's potential, it must be prepared to accept the role of the submarine as piratical.

Admiral Fisher stated publicly that the submarine was obliged to disregard the Hague Convention and international law and to simply sink ships.[6] This was a dismal view for a British admiral to take, since Britain depended on its commerce shipping for sustenance. By 1914 the British accepted the submarine, along with surface torpedo boats and mines, as one of the three most insidious menaces to surface warships and civilian commerce. Britain's effort must be to sink the submarines before they sank British ships. This was the beginning of anti-submarine warfare.

It did not take long for the fledgling German U-boat fleet to get into action. Otto Hersing in U-21 entered the Firth of Forth in a probing action to find anchored warships. Although finding none, he spotted a British light cruiser, HMS *Pathfinder*, together with her destroyer flotilla. On September 5, 1914, in seas so rough that the British thought a torpedo attack impossible, the U-21 fired a single torpedo which sent a cruiser to the bottom with a loss of 259 of her 296 crew members. This was the first victim of the German submarine effort in the First World War.[7]

Germany started the war with only twenty-nine U-boats in its fleet. Most of these were outdated and used only for training. Despite the few submarines at its disposal, the young German U-boat sailors were enthusiastic and their captains were well trained and eager to sink warships.[8]

On September 22, 1914, Kapitanleutnant Otto Weddigen in U-9 became the only submarine captain in naval history to sink three enemy

Submarine Torpedo Tactics

cruisers in a single hour. The British ships, *Aboukir*, *Hogue* and *Cressy*, were patrolling in the southeastern stretch of the North Sea known as the Broad Fourteens. Although the three British ships were within easy range of submarine activity, the British failed to take heed of the danger. Weddigen watched the three ships through his binoculars. The submarine was on the surface, but was too small to be seen by the British. At daybreak he submerged, came to periscope depth and brought his boat on a course to fire torpedoes with a zero gyro angle. In effect, he aimed his submarine at the target as if it were a gun. He set the depths of his torpedo at 12 feet to avoid the possibility of broaching in the heavy seas. The single torpedo struck HMS *Aboukir* amidships. She quickly flooded, rolled over and sank. The two accompanying cruisers, believing their sister ship had hit a mine, came alongside to render assistance to crew members in the water. The two ships stopped and lowered boats, presenting Weddigen with two perfectly positioned, stationary targets. He could not miss and by 7:30 in the morning all three ships had been sunk. An hour later Royal Navy destroyers came to the scene of the disaster where 1,459 officers and men had lost their lives. The German submarine returned to Germany, where its commanding officer Otto Weddigen was greeted as a hero.

Putting out to sea on October 15, 1914, U-9, still under command of Otto Weddigen, struck again. By this time England had established a blockade of Germany between Scotland and Norway. Weddigen attempted to move into position to repeat his previous performance in sinking three British cruisers.[9]

The following is an eyewitness account of U-9's attack of October 15, 1914:

> I gazed at the little picture of the upper ocean. The distant three cruisers were some wide space apart, but were converging, were steering for a point and that point apparently in the vicinity where we lay. No wonder our commander thought they must want a torpedo.
>
> We imagined they were bent on joining forces and steaming together, but it presently became apparent that they intended to exchange signals, drop a cutter in the water, and deliver mail or orders, and then go their respective ways. We steered at full speed for the point toward which they were heading, our periscope showing for only a few moments at a time. The cruisers, big armored fellows, came zigzagging. We picked one, which afterward turned out to be HMS *Hawke*, and maneuvered for a shot. It was tricky work. She nearly ran us down. We had to dive deeper and let her pass over us, else we should have been rammed. Now we were in position for a stern shot at an angle, but she turned. It was a fatal turning for it gave

us an opportunity to swing around for a clear bow shot at 400 meters. "Second bow tube, fire!" Weddigen snapped out the order, and soon there sounded that telltale detonation.

We dived beyond periscope depth, ran underwater for a short distance, and then came up for a look through our tall mast-like eye. The *Hawke* had already disappeared. She sank in 8 minutes. Only one boat was in the water. It was the mail dory that had been lowered before the torpedo explosion. At the rudder, the boat officer hoisted a distress signal on the boat's staff. That little dory with half a dozen men aboard was all that was left of the proud warship. Seldom has a ship sunk so quickly and carried so many men to the bottom of an icy sea. The two other cruisers were vanishing over the horizon. At the moment the torpedo explosion crashed they turned tail and ran as fast as they could. It may have been inhuman for our adversaries thus to abandon the survivors of the *Hawke*, scores of men struggling in the icy water, but by this time the British had learned not to repeat the mistake of September 22.[10]

The secret of Weddigen's success was attributable neither to complex mental arithmetic nor to elaborate fire control techniques. He had no plotting party that gave him accurate bearings and ranges. His success was simple. Get so close to the target ship that a torpedo could not fail to hit it. The C series torpedoes he carried in U-9 had an arming distance of 300 meters. A decent range for Weddigen was about 500 meters. "Fire when the target fills the periscope" was his motto. The range to HMS *Hawke* was only 400 meters. The target ship's proximity and U-9's quick maneuvering to bring its bow tubes into a zero gyro position provided Weddigen with a perfect firing point.

This is not to diminish his brilliance in visualizing the fast-changing situation as surface ships maneuvered above him. Although luck played an important part in providing the perfect set-up, his ability to conceptualize the tactical situation and act quickly to exploit an opportunity cannot be denied. It was a gifted commander who could keep a mental picture of what was happening on the surface, using only quick periscope observations to confirm his mental picture.

It must also be added that in the opening days of the First World War, most German commanding officers preferred to remain on the surface for an attack, when visibility and sea state allowed. It was much easier to maintain a continuing assessment of the tactical situation and to make rapid decisions in the fluidity of zigzagging ships.

As the First World War progressed, the German submarine service attempted to use an influence exploder as a revolutionary means of ensuring a sinking when using only one torpedo. The exploder was designed to detonate as the torpedo passed beneath the keel of the target ship. Since water is incompressible, the impact was directed upward with full force. The state of sophisticated engineering gave promise to this new concept, but it proved to be unreliable, as U-38 experienced. Its commander, Max Valentiner, carried the new influence exploder in his torpedoes. It was 1917, toward the end of the First World War, and the German Ordnance Office had confidence in its new design. It was sure the torpedo would break the keel of a surface ship. U-38's commanding officer was frustrated by the failure of the torpedo to explode. He returned to port and insisted that all torpedoes brought aboard his submarine would have contact exploders. The war ended before the failure of the influence exploder could be explained.[11] This same type exploder would be a far greater frustration to the commanding officers of American submarines during the first part of the Second World War.

In the years prior to the First World War, American shipyards specializing in submarine design produced a variety of boats, each of which had strengths and limitations. The early Holland designs were improved, and Electric Boat Company in Groton, Connecticut, produced a series of submarines, each one better than the last.[12] Meanwhile, Simon Lake's shipyard in Quincy, Massachusetts, produced submarines having qualities not found in the Electric Boat Company submarines. A feature of the early Lake boats was twin screws that provided for better maneuvering.[13] The Navy had provided general guidelines for the submarine's mission, which was confined to defense of American harbors. The submarine's role in defending harbors was left largely undefined, and as a result a variety of submarine designs marked a series of classes from both Electric Boat and Lake. Each competed with the other for the favor of those in the Navy Department responsible for awarding contracts.

The A Class, known as the Adder Class, gave way to the B Class, which was represented by the USS *Viper* with its two torpedo tubes and single screw. This class in turn was superseded by the C Class, which included the USS *Octopus*, a Lake boat reflecting his partiality for twin screw design.[14] Most submarines were built on the east coast at Quincy (Lake), Groton (Electric Boat), Newport News (Lake) and Philadelphia (the Cramp yards); however, submarines were also being built in San Francisco at the Mare Island Shipyard and in Puget Sound at Seattle and Bremerton yards.[15]

2—First World War Fire Control Techniques

The Board of Construction issued a request for design of a submarine with certain improvements. The E, F, and G classes followed in the series with the Bureau of Construction and Repair improving each design in the progression. Both Electric Boat Company and Portsmouth Naval Shipyard followed the bureau's specifications irrespective of improvement suggestions from submarine officers.

At the outbreak of the First World War the American submarine force consisted of a plethora of designs, all of which were meant for harbor defense, and as such could not seriously participate in a European conflict. As the war started, the Navy modified its submarine mission to "coastal defense," which broadened the concept, but did not modify the submarines assigned to the mission. The Bureau of Steam Engineering coordinated propulsion design in submarines, and those boats built during the First World War reflected significant improvements in propulsion, weapons, communication and habitability. While new American submarines could not be classed as oceangoing, they had the capacity to intercept any aggressor ships or submarines that might approach the eastern seaboard of the United States.

During the First World War, U.S. submarines attempted to assist Great Britain's struggle to contain the U-boat menace. In 1917 the Navy Department approved a British request for participation and assigned Captain Thomas Charles Hart to lead the expedition. Chester W. Nimitz was also assigned to help Hart in the effort. At the time, the U.S. had only 46 submarines in commission. The best of these were eight K Type boats and seven L Type boats. Four of the K boats were in Hawaii, and these were reassigned to Key West, Florida. The K1, K2, K5, and E1 got under way in October 1917, accompanied by the tender *Bushnell*. These boats were stationed in the Azores. They were followed up with L1, L2, L4, L9, L10 and L11, which sailed in December. Experiencing bad weather, the crossing was hazardous, but all managed to reach Bantry Bay, Ireland. The latter group made contact with U-boats and thereby contributed to the war effort. Those in the Azores made no contribution.[16]

In the Pacific, the submarine force was extended to the Hawaiian Islands. In 1917 the USS *Alert*, an early submarine tender, was stationed at Pearl Harbor. The Third Submarine Division, made up of four K Class boats, conducted exercises off Lahaina, Maui. As America entered the war, German submarines were soon sighted in the Gulf of Mexico and along the eastern seaboard. In response, the Third Division was ordered to Key West, Florida. The USS *Alert*, in company with USS *Gulfport* and USS *Cheyenne*, made the crossing with Submarine Division Three. K-4 remained in Key West while K-1, K-2, K-5, and K-6 were towed to the Azores Islands for possible action against Germany.[17] The K-boats had poor diving qualities, but were fast on the surface. After America's entrance into the war, a flotilla of K-boats were sent to Britain to operate under British control. Their only service was to act as ASW surface ships while protecting the British Grand Fleet.[18] Once the boats had established themselves in Key West, they commenced torpedo exercises. A record of these exercises was kept by the K-4 commanding officer, Lieutenant Junior Grade Thomas N. Vinson.

He described a unique method of making a torpedo attack when in rough seas. The K-boats' number 2 periscope's length was only 8 feet 11 inches.[19] This meant keeping a periscope depth so shallow that a running sea could cause an unintentional broach. In preparation for what he called a "porpoise," Vinson ensured that his XO's plot had a true bearing to the target. This was necessary because he had to adjust his course to purposely broach the boat into the waves. Since the boat's righting moment was minimal with full ballast tanks, a wave on the beam might dangerously roll the boat. He would order a sixty-foot depth and when at ordered depth he would ring up a full ahead bell. When sufficient speed had built, he would next order full rise on both planes. Meanwhile, the quartermaster converted the plot's true bearing to relative bearing and, as the scope reached observation height, he swung it to the proper relative bearing. The boat would take a firm up angle and its speed would drive it to the surface. With its ballast tanks still full, the boat maintained an approximate neutral buoyancy, but its inertia kept it on the surface long enough for the captain to observe the target and memorize its angle-on-the-bow and the number of telemeter divisions for an approximate range. As the quartermaster lowered the periscope he read the relative bearing from the periscope's ring and relayed it to the XO's plot. As the periscope went down, the captain ordered full dive on the places and the boat returned to its previous depth. As it descended, the captain repeated to his plotter the information on bearing, angle-on-the-bow and approximate range. This "porpoising" maneuver might be repeated until his geographical plot showed an acceptable range and favorable firing position.

Vinson recorded another approach that took place on April 18, 1918,

2—First World War Fire Control Techniques

as follows: "[T]he sea was choppy with enough white-caps to make it hard to pick up periscope wake. Attack was made with the wind so that periscope wake followed general direction of white-caps.... Plotting was discontinued when it was seen that USS *Chicago* (target ship) was heading on course nearly opposite to ours.... Attack could have been made by remaining at point of submergence, but sea was too rough to allow handling the boat with periscope out at anything under 8 knots."[20]

Submarines of that period had a normal underwater speed of two to four knots. Such a slow speed meant that if the target ship failed to enter the submarine's zone of weapon capability the submarine either had to surface, go to flank speed and try to get ahead of the target, or give up the chase. In the approach phase of a submerged torpedo attack, the submarine had to maneuver early to get within range. In doing so the captain kept a constant watch on the condition of his battery. If he had to remain submerged during the attack he would need to have a fully charged battery. Depending on sea condition and visibility, the submarine captain often elected to make an approach on the surface. Indeed, most attacks were made on the surface during both the First and Second World Wars. A state three or above sea with healthy wave action and whitecaps might render a submarine nearly invisible, particularly if it maintained a bow aspect to the target. Without electronic assistance such as radar, which was unknown in the First World War, the advantage went to the ship with the most alert lookouts. Submariners took pride in being expert lookouts. The submarine was usually able to maintain its stealth while maneuvering into position on the surface. Anticipating the target's movements, it could dive and make a periscope approach once within torpedo range.

Underwater communication used a Fessender oscillator with Morse code.[21] Internal communication between the control room, which housed the periscopes, and the torpedo room was by buzzer and speaking tube. The torpedo was normally the Bliss-Leavitt Mark 6 and later, the Mark 7.

The attack party was made up of the captain, who manned the periscope, or in the case of a surface attack, mounted binoculars with relative bearing ring. Assisting him was the plotter, who, with the help of a quartermaster, kept a geographical representation of submarine and target ship. A junior officer kept a range finder circular slide rule. A second quartermaster manned the periscope lever and read the target relative bearing ring at the top of the periscope.

The captain maintained a running verbal account of target bearing and angle-on-the-bow in short ten-second looks. Angle-on-the-bow was the target ship's aspect to the submarine port or starboard zero through one hundred eighty degrees. He also estimated the target speed by bow wake size and shape. He often used the "five knot rule," which was an estimate derivative of the distance equals time times speed equation. The rule states that a ship making five knots will advance five nautical miles in two hours. It was not difficult for the captain to make evenly timed observations and to apply the rule, interpolating for shorter time periods.

It took many hours of practice to be able to visualize the target after the periscope had come down and to order helm and speed changes resulting from the captain's mental picture of the situation. The plotter, normally the executive officer, confirmed the captain's observations or recommended corrections. Some captains relied on the executive officer's estimate of the situation.

Target bearing was accurate information and angle-on-the-bow was normally accurate, being a function of the captain's experience. These two factors gave the plotting party the target ship's course, and this combined with the captain's estimate of speed presented an initial set-up. As further observations were made, the geographical plot showed bearing change rate which corresponded with speed estimates.

Lieutenant Vinson's exercise attack on the cruiser USS *Chicago* was recorded on a geographical plot. The K-4 made ten observations as it tried to maneuver into firing position. Each periscope observation was noted as time and true bearing. The *Chicago* was on a zigzag course the last leg of which was 160 degrees. K-4 was on the surface and managed to close the range by initially heading due south. The initial observation put *Chicago* 090 from K-4. No initial target range, speed or course was recorded at 8:49. Staying on course 180, K-4 continued its observations every three minutes until at 9:07 Vinson changed course to his right, to 210. The target's bearings were drawing right, from 106 at the 9:00 observation to 114 at the 9:06 observation, at which time the target range was 6,000 yards with angle-on-the-bow of starboard 20. Unable to increase speed, Vinson's only hope of getting into a firing position was to turn right. Ranges continued to close and at 9:18 *Chicago*'s range was 2100 yards. At 9:13 Vinson came slightly left to 190. Ranges still closed and bearing rate had slowed to only one degree (from 105 at 9:18 to 106 at 9:20). At 9:20 Vinson came

2—First World War Fire Control Techniques

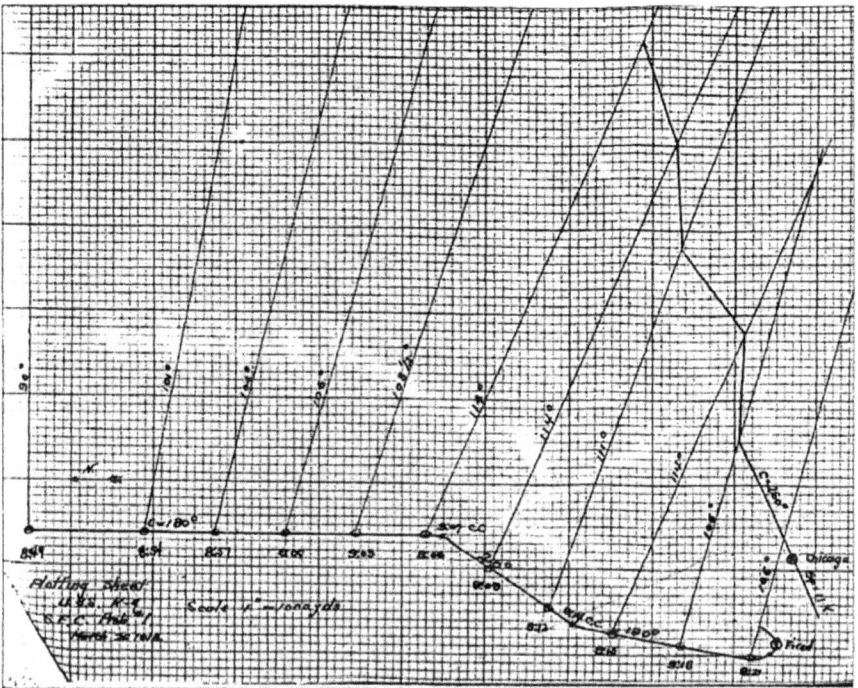

The First World War American submarine *K-4*'s exercise attack on the American cruiser *Chicago* is reproduced in its original form. Note the north orientation to the left. *K-4* spotted *Chicago* at 8:49 a.m. The cruiser's bearing drifted right, so *K-4* adjusted its course to a south direction to intercept the cruiser. Ten periscope observations were made until 9:20 a.m. at which time the range had closed to under 2000 yards, allowing *K-4* to shoot (courtesy Bill Lightfoot).

hard left, closing to about 950 yards. He fired on the swing with approximate zero gyros. At the time of firing, *Chicago* reversed course and managed to evade the torpedo. Nevertheless, Vinson's practice attack is a model of a good approach to an excellent firing position.

The most difficult piece of information to obtain was the distance (range) to the target. This was crucial in terms of accurately determining the impact point that would result in a hit. The early slide rule range finder was of some use in this respect, but the best range information came from the geographical plot, which used bearing change rate as its best clue to range. The captain also used the periscope telemeter reticules in conjunction with information on enemy ship lengths found in the enemy ship silhouette book. It was also necessary to take into consideration its angle-on-the-bow. Using the periscope telemeter scale demanded much practice, but with exercise on the submarine school training periscope, the prospective commanding officer could gain the necessary skill. The periscope telemeter scale of the First World War submarine was not appreciably different from that used in the Second World War. Although the use of this scale is later treated in more depth, a brief explanation will suffice to gain an understanding of its use in S class boats. The *Submarine Periscope Manual* of 1946 states, "The telemeter scale which appears superimposed on the field of the instrument enables the observer to make angular measurements of targets for range estimation purposes. Each major division of the telemeter scale subtends an angle of one degree with the periscope in high power and four degrees in low power. Each subdivision of the telemeter scale subtends an angle of fifteen minutes in high power and one degree in low power."[22]

Assuming that accurate information was obtained from the sources described, the captain continued to maneuver his boat into firing position. At the appropriate time he ordered the outer doors opened and ordered the torpedomen to set depth into the torpedo. Depending on the submarine type and its tube capability as well as torpedo type, speed selection and gyro course could also be set.

When the range was optimal in terms of his weapon capability, he ordered a single torpedo or spread of torpedoes to be fired. Often the captain would align the submarine to the target so that gyro settings would be as close to zero as possible. This minimized any errors in range.

As each submarine type was an improvement over the last, so too were succeeding torpedo designs reaching a high degree of excellence. The Mark 7 torpedo is defined by Wildenberg and Polmar as being 17 feet in length with a diameter of 17.7 inches. Its weight was 1,588 pounds and its normal explosive charge was 205 pounds of TNT. It was propelled by a steam turbine and could achieve a speed of 32 knots with a maximum range of 4000 yards at a slower speed.[23] Its guidance mechanism was the Navy Mark 7 gyro. The typical propulsion system's combustion chamber initially used Benzol as the fuel, but was replaced by alcohol. The fuel was sprayed into the combustion vessel, where it was ignited with air. Water from a specially designed water tank was turned to steam as it was injected into the vessel. The turbine was improved with added nozzles canted at 60 degrees to the blade face. This proved to be very efficient, making the Bliss-Leavitt Mark 7 torpedo a first-rate, reliable weapon.

Of critical importance to fire control procedures was the reliability of depth and course settings within the torpedo. The Mark 7 produced by the Bliss Company and Naval Torpedo Station, Newport, Rhode Island, was proven to be a reliable submarine torpedo. Manuals for the maintenance and lubrication of the torpedo were provided by the Navy. Those ratings responsible for the upkeep of the torpedoes were critical to the mission of early American submarines. The Mark 7 was provided both with exercise heads for training and with warheads during and after the First World War.

The American submarines of the First World War consisted mostly of the K, L and M class boats. These were launched from 1913 through 1916. As the war ended, R, O and S class boats, which had been authorized by Congress, were either still on the drawing boards or being built.

While the submarine was still a surface boat with the capability of submerging, the First World War had changed that image by changing its tactics. German submariner captains gained confidence that their boats could submerge ahead of a target and remain submerged for the entire approach. As torpedo tactics were improved, the submarine's capability was clarified. It was a weapon of stealth that was able to gain close access to a target. This meant that a faster torpedo was needed, even at the expense of range. The answer came in the form of the Mark 10, which had a range of only 3,500 yards but had a speed of 36 knots. This torpedo with its subsequent modifications became the standard American torpedo in service through the 1920s and well into the 1930s.

3

Between the Wars

Congress had allocated funds for the building of R and O class submarines with the assumption that the First World War would continue into the indefinite future. When an armistice was declared in 1918, the Navy pushed forward with the building program. As a result, several R class submarines were commissioned in the fall of 1918, through 1919 and 1920. The R and O class boats became the workhorses of the submarine force during the 1920s and 1930s. Some even saw training duty at New London during the Second World War.

Habitability was not high on the Navy's list of submarine priorities. Crewmembers slept in hammocks and ate their meals while standing. Tables in the crew's mess were drawn to the overhead when not in use. At serving times, they were lowered on chains, swinging in tune to the rolling of the boat. When Third Class Gunner's Mate Joseph Martin was assigned to R-14, the boat was only two weeks from being commissioned. It was winter 1919, the deck was slippery with ice, and he didn't look forward to wrestling with the deck gun in a running sea. He was happy to get submarine pay, but after having been on a battleship, he found the accommodations challenging. Never the less, the skipper, Lieutenant Vincent A. Clarke, Jr., impressed upon Martin the importance of his qualification in submarines. For the next seven months he studied the submarine's systems. His rate demanded that he become an expert on the R-14's torpedoes as well as deck gun.

Referral to his drawings and description of the submarine's sonar and Mark 7 torpedo is revealing as a first-hand source.

The boat's sonar hydrophones were mounted on deck and on the keel. They were called "rats" by the crew, because they looked like crouching rats mounted on stilts. The deck-mounted forward hydrophones were called Y-tubes because of the arrangement of the three small hydrophones,

3—Between the Wars

The R-14's Y-tube sonar hydrophones appear in upper right of photograph, as seaman works on bow plane tilting mechanism (Naval History and Heritage Command).

two of which were arranged athwartships on a pedestal resembling a Y. The S.C. tube was a trainable hydrophone aft of the Y-tube. It had a shaft running through the hull with a wheel in the after, port corner of the torpedo room. An approximate bearing of a noise source could be determined by sweeping the hand wheel across the bearing while searching for the loudest bearing.

A photograph taken of R-14's bow shows the arrangement of the transverse hydrophones mounted on a Y-shaped frame. While Martin's drawing shows only two hydrophones, the drawing's forward hydrophone is actually two with the second unit hidden behind the first. In 1920 synchronization of the multiple hydrophones was an art more than a science. In its infancy, sonar

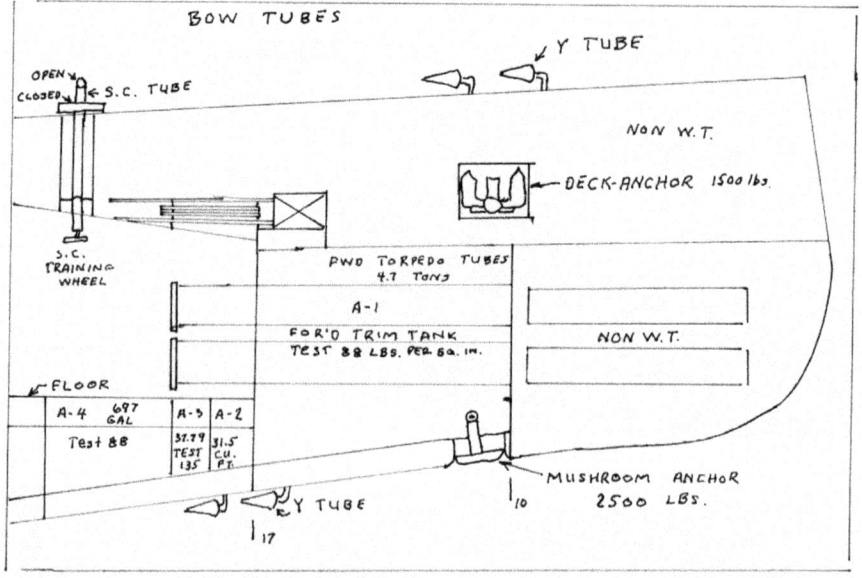

Joseph Martin's qualification notebook drawing of R-14 bow, showing both deck-mounted and keel-mounted hydrophones (Submarine Research Center).

information was valuable to the captain, but for reliable target information he relied upon the periscope. Martin's drawing of the R-14 bow is seen here.

In 1920 Joseph W. Martin completed his qualification notebook, and in it are to be found his detailed description and drawings of the Bliss-Leavitt torpedo, Mark 7. The description and drawings of the Navy's first production-line torpedo are unique in presenting an accurate picture of the Mark 7's mechanism. The following is that part of Martin's qualification notebook which pertains to the torpedo's mid and after sections. His description of the torpedo is as follows:

> The Mark 7 torpedo is made up of four sections. The nose is the explosive portion together with its detonator. Behind the warhead is the air flask. This is made of mild steel and is cylindrical in shape being 7 feet, 9 inches long. Its ends are domed to accommodate pressures approximating 2000 pounds per square inch. Behind the air flask is the water chamber. This chamber provides fresh water at about 500 pounds per square inch. Also within this section is the fuel flask which contains alcohol or similar fuel at 15 pounds per square inch. The mid section houses the filling valves for the air flask, water chamber and fuel chamber.

3—Between the Wars

Behind the mid-section is the after body and tail section. The tail section has six rear openings, two for the vertical rudders, two for the depth planes, and two exhaust valves. The top of the after body houses the starting valves connected to the tripping lever. With the muzzle door open and the breech door shut, the submarine's compressed air pushes the torpedo forward and in doing so actuates the tripping lever which starts the torpedo's engine.

Air pressure from the torpedo's air flask is reduced from 2000 pounds to 600 pounds through the first reducer and from 600 pounds to 440 pounds through the second reducer. This pressurized air is mixed with fuel and preheated water, then ignited in the combustion chamber. Check valves prevent return combustion.

Contra rotating screws at the extreme after end of the torpedo are driven by a turbine with its speed controlled by a governor. The high rate of spin is reduced by a pinion gear attached to the main drive spindle which turns two hollow, contra rotating shafts, one within the other. Thrust bearings and packing glands are at the after point of the tail cone.

The depth control mechanism consists of a spring-loaded hydrostatic piston and accompanying pendulum immersed in a chamber that is open to the sea. The spring tension acting on a diaphragm corresponds to a given depth setting. A depth index is set and the hydrostatic piston is thus positioned before firing.

The depth engine is secured to the gyro housing and consists of a cylinder and piston under reduced pressure from the air flask. The pendulum and hydrostatic piston actuates the engine piston, which, in turn, moves rods extending through the after body to the depth planes. The depth planes move up or down 7 degrees from centerline.[1]

The following drawing of the Mark 7 after body is a part of Martin's qualification notebook and offers a clear picture of the depth-keeping mechanism and gyro operation, notwithstanding his spelling errors:

A close examination of Martin's drawing clarifies the flow of compressed air, fuel and water to drive the propulsion turbine, gyro, depth mechanism, and starting valve. On the extreme left is the rear dome of the fuel flask and water check valves. Cold compressed air flows to reducers, start-up gear and gyro. Fuel, air and water flow through check valves to the combustion chamber (pot), where they are ignited. Low-pressure air flows back to water and fuel flasks, forcing the liquids to the combustion chamber. Hot steam-compressed air is discharged from the combustion pot to drive the propulsion turbine and steering engine.

The following, also quoted from Martin's qualification notebook,

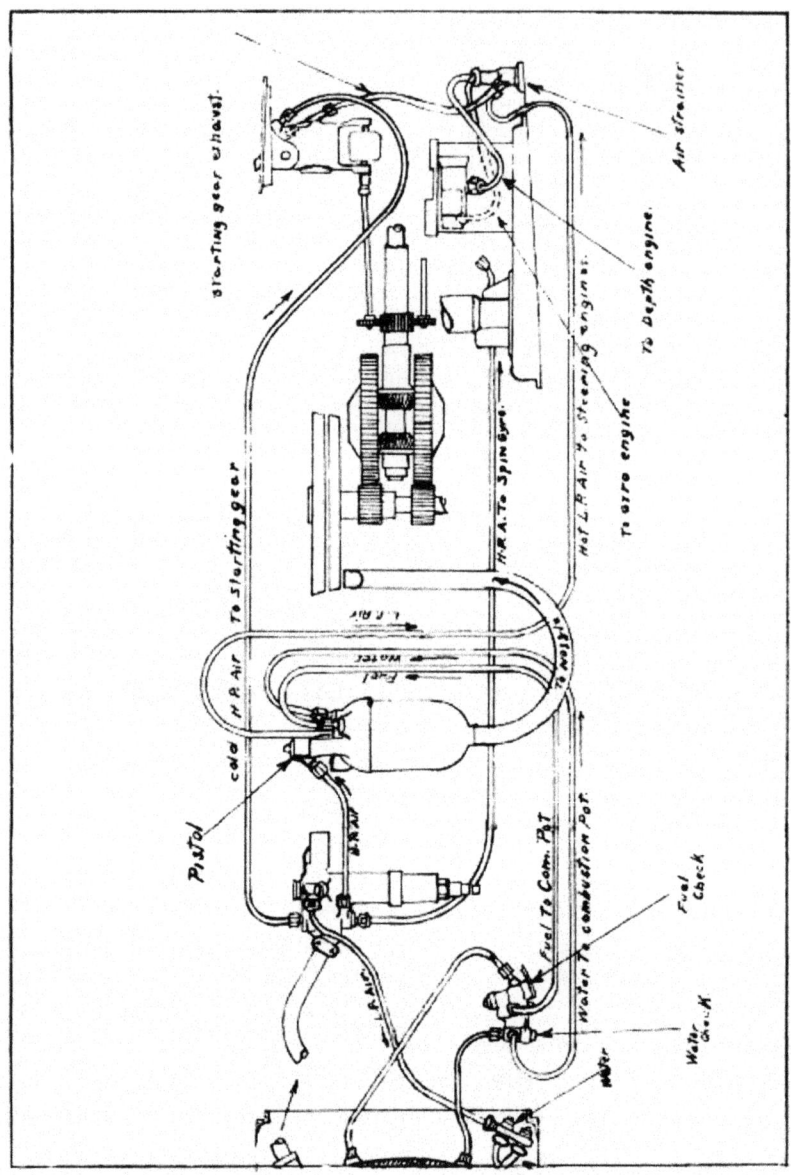

Martin's rendering of torpedo Mark 7 after body showing path of fuel and compressed air to combustion chamber and turbine drive train (Submarine Research Center).

describes the delicacy of the gyro: "The gyro is one of the most important parts of the torpedo and is perhaps the most sensitive. The gyro is a subject warranting all the care and study that can possibly be given it."[2]

In the years following the end of the First World War, naval planners came to grips with the definition of the submarine's mission. American naval architects, senior American naval officers and submariners butted heads on just what the role of the submarine should be. The opposing viewpoints stemmed from outdated planning and failure to view the Navy's mission in terms other than that of the First World War. Paderfield expressed this situation as follows:

> The strategic error which the U.S. shared with all major navies was, of course, an obsession with battleships and the great fleet battle for command of the sea. This was enshrined from before the first war in Plan Orange for war against Japan. After the decisive fleet battle, the U.S. Navy would blockade the Japanese islands much as the Royal Navy had blockaded its enemies during its centuries of supremacy. Had there been a proper analysis in light of the first war's U-boat campaign against the British merchant shipping, it would have been noted that Japan was even more dependent on imports by sea than Great Britain, that her merchant fleet was substantially smaller, that over 50 percent of the oil on which her armed forces moved was imported, and 40 percent of her foreign trade was carried in foreign ships, that she had no conceivable ally who could have made up the deficiencies. In short, she could be brought to her knees fairly quickly with comparatively little expense by an unrestricted submarine campaign.[3]

Submarine officers and those with experience in submarine design visualized the role of the future submarine as that of an independent marauder able to attack enemy merchant ships and combatants. Paderfield later analyzed correctly Japan's limitations during the 1930s, but the cruise submarine concept was an accurate response to the Pacific theater of contemporary operations. In such case the submarine would rely on its ability to remain hidden and to attack without warning. In large part this concept came from the bitter experience of Great Britain in contending with the German U-boat effort during the First World War. For the lack of a better term, the role of the submarine was defined as that of a "cruiser." Friedman suggests that American naval planners probably made the first formal proposal for a cruiser type submarine while in London in 1918.[4] This proposal called for a submarine with an operating radius of 10,000 miles and a surface speed of 10 knots. The cruiser type boat would carry a load of 24 torpedoes with four forward tubes and two stern tubes.

Most senior surface officers looked at the submarine from their perspective as commanding officers of heavy combatants. They saw only limited value in the torpedo and tended to visualize the submarine as a supporting scout that could radio any unseen hazards to the battleships. As such, they weren't much interested in the submarine's underwater problems. They wanted a fast surface speed and adequate radio communication so that a submarine could keep up with the fleet. In that role it was appropriate that they be referred to as "fleet" submarines.

The General Board's responsibility was to set general shipbuilding specifications and schedules. While favoring the fleet submarine concept, the General Board included in its deliberations many descriptions of future submarines that came from submariners who believed in the cruiser concept of independent submarine operations. It also was willing to profit from the German designs, which included large, oceangoing hulls of 1,500 tons and lengths up to 300 feet. The General Board had confirmed the 21-inch standard torpedo and tube, but saw no reason to go beyond four tubes forward, since four torpedoes were more than enough to sink a ship. That was the logic in the early 1920s.

Naval engineers and architects stood on the sidelines and for the most part waited until the dust had settled before getting down to the business of designing new submarines. In early 1920 most engineers and architects were in the Bureau of Construction and Repair. They saw little difference in the specifications of the fleet concept and cruiser concept submarines. They went to work on preliminary designs.

In the meantime, Congress had authorized the building of the V class submarine. OpNav planners and submariners agreed that only three of the V class boats should be built with pure fleet-type specifications. In doing so they were under pressure from the senior officers of the General Board. Immediately thereafter, specifications for a pure cruiser-type submarine were issued as having a length of 310 feet with a beam of 28 feet. It would be about 2,000 tons, would have 2 M.A.N. engines and would have a submerged speed of 9.5 knots.[5]

The remaining V class boats (six in number, totaling nine; SS-163 though SS-171), authorized by Congress in 1916, would be designed and built as cruiser-type submarines. The General Board's ultimate specifications drew heavily on the German U-142 design.[6] In the early 1920s a series of submarine disasters involving S class boats served to emphasize the need for greater safety in submarine training and design. These included crew training in damage control and procedures for overcoming other emergencies, automatic ballast tank blow valves if the submarine exceeded test depth, and the inclusion of diver-operated deck fittings for blowing compartments and ballast tanks with air from rescue ships.

While the role of the future submarine and consequent design were being questioned, torpedo improvements were progressing. Beginning in 1918 all submarines then under construction were fitted with 21-inch torpedo tubes. The upgrade applied to R class and subsequent classes of submarines. These tubes were compatible with the Mark 10, which carried a 500-pound warhead, the heaviest of the time. With a speed of 36 knots and a 3500-yard range, it marked the last design by the E.W. Bliss Company to be adopted by the Navy. Subsequent designs including exploder mechanisms would thereafter be the sole responsibility of the Naval Torpedo Station in Newport, Rhode Island.[7]

Aside from the "fleet" vs. "cruiser" controversy was the S-boat design. It was the Navy's mainstay submarine during the First World War. By 1921 the Navy had 51 S-boats either in commission or being built. But as the Navy began to look at the expanses of the Pacific Ocean, it realized it needed submarines with capabilities that outpaced the S design. They were high-maintenance boats with 6-cylinder Nelseco engines that produced 1000 horsepower at 375 rpm. The Navy sought to replace the Nelseco engine with German-designed M.A.Ns.[8] For every 24 days an S-boat spent at sea, 36 days in port were required to maintain the submarine.[9] Although the S-boat continued to be operational during the 1920s, 1930s and even into the Second World War, it was limited in range and therefore unable to fill the requirements of long Pacific Ocean transits.

The 1922 Washington Naval Treaty placed limitations on the number of capital ships allowed each nation. It had little affect on America's submarine building program since the treaty's only submarine limitation was the outlawing of submarine blockades. Japan was identified by the War Department as the most probable enemy should a war in the Pacific take place. In reviewing the role of the submarine in such a conflict, the smaller S-boats could play a significant role only if bases near Japan were retained by the United States. Still, the Navy's assessment of the Pacific strategic problem remained twofold: It must build fast (on the surface) submarines to keep pace with the fleet in a World War I–type battleship surface-gun engagement, and it also had to build long range, oceangoing submarines of great endurance, along the lines of the cruiser concept.

At the Naval War College in 1923, Captain Thomas C. Hart participated in a war game in which a submarine ran parallel to the fleet with the fleet on his beam. He fired all his tubes at the fleet with a 90-degree gyro angle on each torpedo. The game rules provided for poor torpedo behavior, but the exercise convinced Hart that shooting at maximum range with large gyro angles would still get good results. The concept was carefully considered by other submariners and subsequently discarded. Even though merchant ships might tend to mass into convoys and warships might bunch for mutual protection, a submarine shooting at a range of 6000 yards with a large gyro angle could not expect much success. It was referred to by some as the Browning shot, but the concept met with ardent rebuttal from submariners who had no taste for tactics that demanded so little of its fire control expertise.[10]

Improvements in hydrophone design during the 1920s were based on American research and British developments with First World War ASW operations. The acronym "sonar," for sound navigation and ranging, was of British origin and was quickly adopted by the American Navy. Active sonar is the term used to describe sending a sound impulse into the sea via a transducer. A return echo signals the presence of a metal target. While a surface ship has little to fear from a repeating sound impulse fired into the water, a submarine is unlikely to find such an instrument of much use since it broadcasts the submarine's exact position.[11] On the other hand, the hydrophone without a transducer is referred to as passive sonar. It is this type of sonar that is most central to torpedo fire control methodology.

Passive sonar had its beginnings in the First World War when underwater signaling was attempted by using the ringing of a bell as the transmitter and crystal oscillators that could resonate to the sound in the water. While this primitive experiment was not practical as a communication device, the receptor was improved at the Naval Undersea Systems Station in New London, Connecticut. The first successful receptor was the C or Coolidge tube, referred to by Martin as an S.C. Tube. This was a pair of small rubber spheres at the ends of a five-foot pipe. The T arrangement could be pivoted so that the spheres rotated about the axis. The minute difference in sound intensity from the nearest sphere to the sound source and the farthest sphere could be magnified and heard using headphones.

3—Between the Wars

The operator could swing the spheres and gain an estimate of sound source direction. It was accurate up to about 5 degrees over a range of up to 8,000 yards.

As old as S-boats might have been, they played an important role as the Navy's standard operational submarine and were updated with sonar as late as the latter 1930s. For example, the S-45 had a keel sonar, and others had both keel and deck hydrophones.[12]

By 1929 the Naval Research Laboratory had improved the hydrophone's ability using high frequency with a series of small receptors built on a trainable T-shaped bar. Later, sonar reception was further improved by the use of better hydrophone design using even higher frequencies. These were mounted on S-boats and the later V class submarines.

While basic research on the properties of sound in water were producing sonar equipment designs that would be of value to submarine fire control, the economic crash of the late 1920s resulted in sonar research stagnation.

In 1922 the U.S. Navy's inventory of torpedoes had consisted of the Mark 8 and 9 for surface ships and the Mark 10 for submarines. All earlier torpedoes were scrapped in the early 1920s. This would remain the status quo during the latter half of the 1920s until the early 1930s, when the Mark 14 torpedo was being developed, but it was undergoing basic tests under profound economic limitations. During the late 1920s the reduction in military expenditures meant that the torpedo station at Newport would receive only $30,000 per year. It also meant that the auxiliary torpedo manufacturing facilities at Alexandria, Virginia, and Washington Navy Yard were closed.[13]

In 1926 the chief of naval operations, Admiral Edward W. Eberle, had organized the Submarine Officer Conference. It was the first real attempt to integrate practical ideas coming from operational submariners with competent engineering expertise. The bureau listened and came up with sketches of equipment placement and compartment layout. It was a particularly fruitful give-and-take resulting in some innovative designs that attended to the concerns of submariners.

In 1928 the General Board under the direction of Rear Admiral Andrew T. Long recommended that the Mark 11 torpedo replace the Mark 10 as the fleet's standard torpedo. He said, "Submarines will in all probability make torpedo attacks when submerged to at least periscope depth. Under such conditions the limited range of visibility through the periscope and the inherently crude methods of tracking preclude the possibility of accurate torpedo fire at ranges in excess of the high speed torpedo range of 6,000 yards."[14] Submarine officers who thought of torpedo fire control in terms of less than 1500 yards were perplexed by the admiral's statement.

At another level, the first submarines to have partially welded hulls came off the ways. While this milestone might seem to have little relevance to torpedo fire control, it marked the beginning of pressure hull improvements that would greatly increase the test depths of coming submarines. Despite the obvious advantages of welding, Portsmouth Naval Shipyard continued to rely upon riveting as the best means of joining pressure and outer hull plates. Its resistance to changing its time-honored process was based not in science, but in the political ramifications of displacing a labor force of riveters, fitters and caulkers. The V-5 *Narwhal* (SS-167) and the V-6 *Nautilus* (SS-168) were both built at Portsmouth Naval Shipyard. They contained many ground-breaking innovations, but also retained many outdated construction methods. By 1930 the V-7 USS *Dolphin* (SS-169) was nearing completion. It had partial saddle ballast tanks, was 319 feet in length, and was about 1700 tons. With its riveted hull it had a test depth of only 250 feet.[15]

First in the next generation of American V class submarine were the *Cachelot* and *Cuttlefish*. They were the Bureau of Construction and Repair's initial attempts to incorporate the qualities demanded by both fleet and cruiser submarine concepts into a smaller hull of about 175 feet. While Electric Boat Company was encumbered by the Navy's requirement for a riveted hull, it used welded seams in the outer hull of the *Cuttlefish*, which solved the problem of leaking oil from poorly caulked saddle tanks. Portsmouth Naval Shipyard hung on to its completely riveted hull in the *Cachelot*. Both boats had elongated conning towers, complete saddle ballast tanks, and dedicated crew's mess, but they had only one engine room with M.A.N. engines and direct drive to the screws. They failed to live up to submarine officers' expectations, but they were crucial steps in the road to the World War II fleet-type submarine.

The officers of the General Board continued to see torpedo development within the limits of obsolescent submarine design. The senior officers reasoned that spending money on fancier torpedoes was a waste, since the status of the submarine that carried them had such severe limitations. This circular logic was pervasive in the higher echelons of the Navy, and it exacerbated the stringent economic conditions at the Newport Torpedo production facility.

As President Roosevelt swung into action after taking office in 1933, Congress, by way of the National Industrial Recovery Act of June 16, 1933, and the 1934 Vinson-Traummel Act, authorized 35,530 tons of new submarine construction. This meant that the General Board could respond more aggressively to the inadequacies of the smaller *Cachelot* class boat. The new designs embraced longer hulls that could accommodate crew habitability, four engines for greater reliability and conning towers that provided room for torpedo fire control. The M.A.N. engines were to be replaced by either General Motors or Fairbanks-Morse diesel engines.[16]

Despite the General Board's foot-dragging and economic constraints, modifications to the Mark 14 torpedo were progressing at almost the same rate as improvements to basic submarine design. By 1933 it included a two-speed spindle-setting mechanism that was compatible with modern electrical-set fire control systems. The high speed was 45 knots and the low speed was 36 knots.

As the torpedo improved to the point of what was considered a reliable weapon with predictable course, speeds and ranges, submarine officers at the Submarine School in New London developed a circular slide rule for assisting in quick solutions to the fire control problem. The instrument had been invented by Captain Nasmith of the Royal Navy in the late 1920s. It was actually two instruments in one, with concentric clear plastic discs that could be manipulated (usually by the executive officer, who acted as assistant to the captain in the fire control party) with the fingers to align inputs with the solution appearing on one of the discs. The instrument, approximately six inches in diameter, hung from the neck of the manipulating officer by a lanyard. It was officially the submarine attack course finder, and on the opposite side was a bearing rate computer or a form of speed omnimeter arranged to solve for target speed with data secured during the approach or for range if the speed was known.

The procedure involved some mathematics including trigonometry and was used to confirm or finalize initial ranges. The speed omnimeter was used only by the most competent submarine approach officers. Actually,

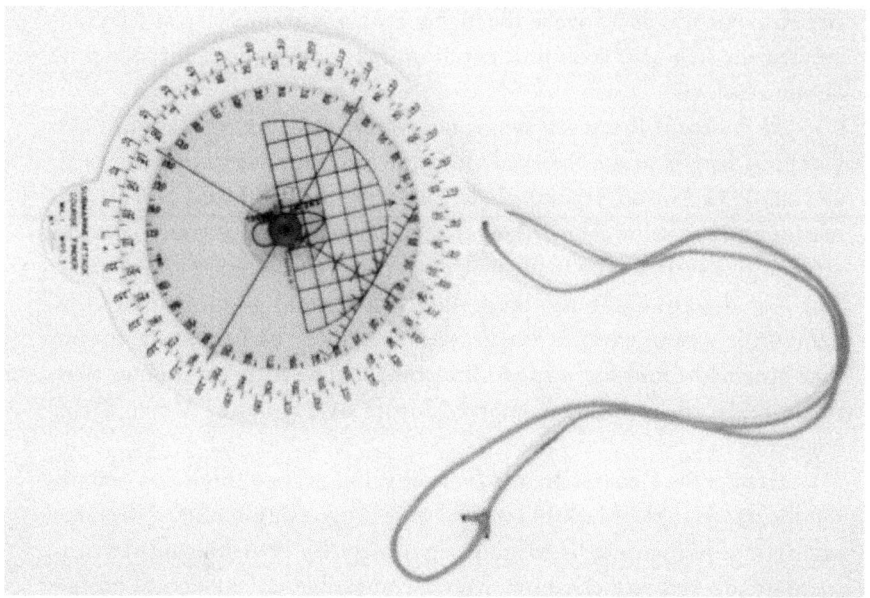

The course finder side of the Is-Was with lanyard (courtesy Naval Undersea Museum, Keyport, Washington).

there were several varieties, some more complex than others. The submarine attack course finder consisted of a base plate or "azimuth card" which was graduated to represent the periscope azimuth circle as bore-sighted with the torpedo tubes. The target's relative bearing was set on this scale. A second, clear plastic disc, slightly smaller in diameter, was a compass rose graduated clockwise in five-degree increments from 0 to 360 degrees. The disc smallest in diameter was the target disc. It was graduated in five-degree increments to represent the target's angle-on-the-bow. Sliding each of the discs, one on the other, produced the solution.

The little circular slide rule got its nickname of Is-Was from the fact that the fire control problem is always a problem of relative motion—that of the submarine and that of the target. Taking progressive periscope observations and plotting these, the fire control party often saw the tactical picture as, "There he was, but here he is." This was, of course, an expression of bearing change rate, the core of the fire control problem.

The submarine attack course finder could be used to determine the

3—Between the Wars

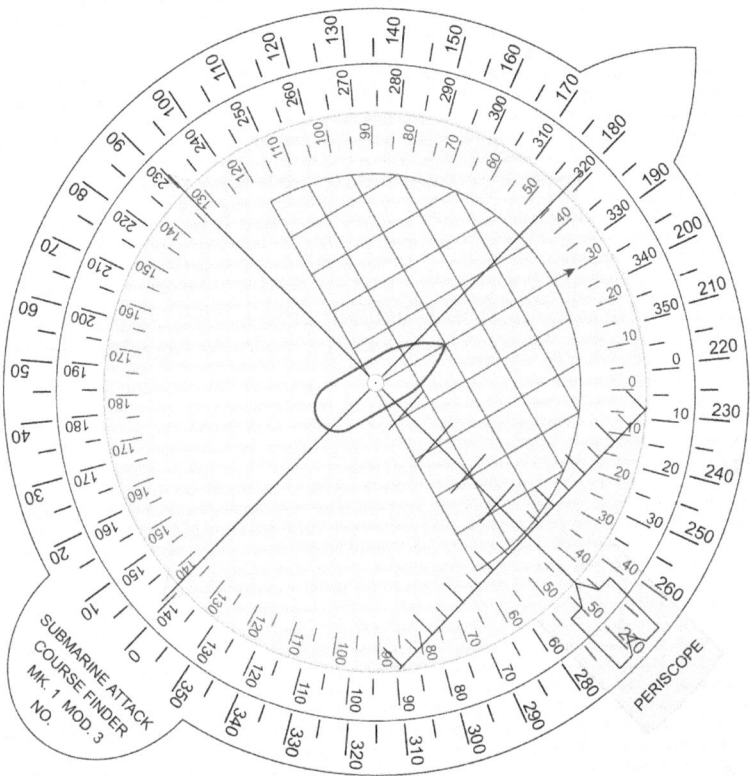

Submarine Attack Course Finder, showing three concentric discs and own ship's image with 90 degree presentation either side of bow (courtesy Naval Undersea Museum, Keyport, Washington).

best course for the submarine to take to bring the submarine into a good firing position. It could also be used to determine the submarine's best speed to get to that location.

The drawing below shows a typical fire control problem with the Is-Was providing the best course to a firing position. In this example, the assistant approach officer sets own course at 230 degrees, relative bearing of target at 315 degrees, target angle-on-the-bow port 25 degrees. These data give the target a true course of 030 degrees. The captain wishes to bring the target ship onto the submarine's starboard beam so that he can roughly parallel the target's course in his attempt to intercept it at the target's closest point of approach. To determine own course to bring the target onto the submarine's starboard beam, the operator sets the Is-Was to a 90-degree position on the submarine's starboard beam, while holding the other inputs. The desired approach course is shown as 095 degrees. The captain then orders the helm, "Left full rudder, all ahead full, come to course 095." He then waits for the next observation to see what his new course and speed has accomplished.

The latter half of the 1930s saw a series of submarine improvements incorporated into the accelerated building program. The *Tambor* class (SS-198–203) added two tubes forward for a total of six forward and two aft

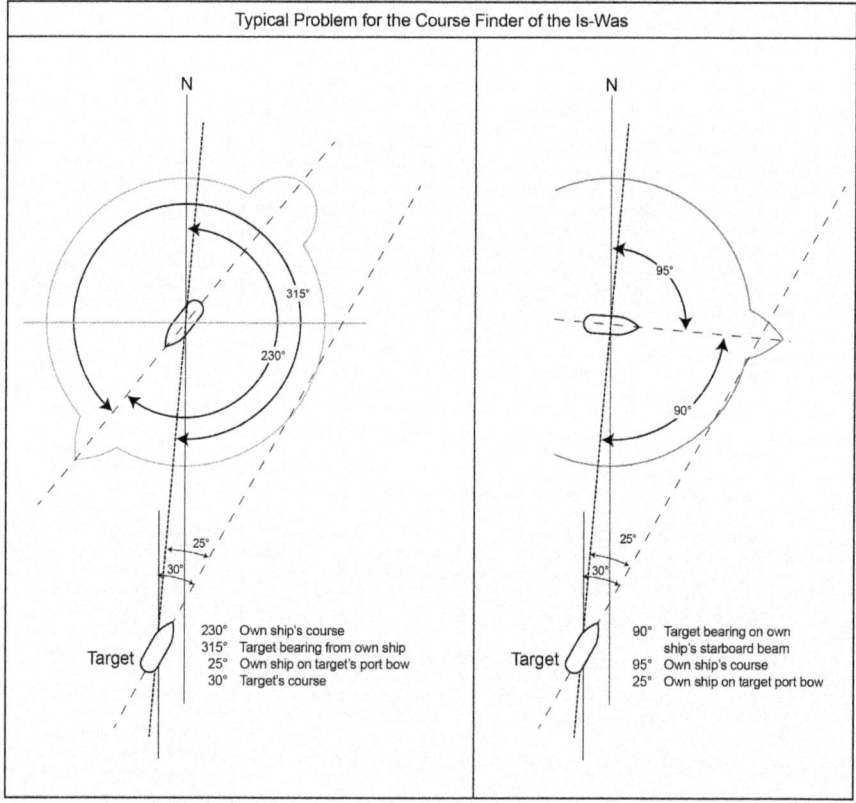

An illustration of Course Finder manipulation to solve for own ship's best course (Submarine Research Center).

with extended compartment size to accommodate a combined load of 24 torpedoes. Since the oil leak problem had been solved, the use of fuel ballast tanks provided for greater ranges.[17] A safety tank was included in the new design to be blown should the conning tower be flooded. A negative tank was added in response to submariners' request for cutting dive times and improving depth control. A submarine diving officer could then mathematically compensate the boat for weight changes prior to its trim dive, then, upon diving, adjust the water level in the negative tank to match the calculations and pump water between forward and after trim tanks to gain a fore and aft trim. This design improvement facilitated greater safety in the routine of the submarine.

The second submarine fire control instrument developed during the early 1930s was a device for computing the data needed to fire a torpedo or spread of torpedoes with given speeds and gyro angles. Because of its shape it was referred to as the banjo. It was a static computer that solved for torpedo speed and course. The custodian of the pictured banjo is the Naval Undersea Museum in Keyport, Washington. The top circular disc was graduated in degrees from 0 to 180 on port or starboard and was set knowing the target's angle-on-the-bow. This represented the target course. The lower disc was a compass rose which was set as own ship's course. The large base plate was the vertically oriented pseudo-torpedo run in yards, and the horizontally oriented torpedo gyro angle expressed as left and right angles from 0 to 180 degrees. The base plate was interchangeable for different torpedoes (e.g., Mark 14 steam-powered and Mark 18 electric-powered). The banjo was cumbersome and while being used in the 1930s was not popular in the crowded conditions of the conning tower during an approach.[18]

In 1938 the Washington Navy Yard started producing sonar T-bars for the first fleet-type submarines. It wouldn't be until later in the Second World War that JT sonar would become an effective, trainable, deck-mounted sonar that gave accurate bearings. Of greatest importance was the coupling of sonar inputs directly to the TDC and the imposition of a sonar repeater station in the conning tower. It should be noted, however, that although the JT sonar gave an accurate bearing it did little to indicate a range. During the latter part of the war, experiments were conducted to pair JT stacks at bow and stern and thereby create a triangle from which a rough range could be obtained. This refinement would wait until postwar developments brought huge improvements to the science of underwater sound reception.

Between the First and Second World War, torpedo fire control doctrine moved from the necessity to aim the submarine in the direction of

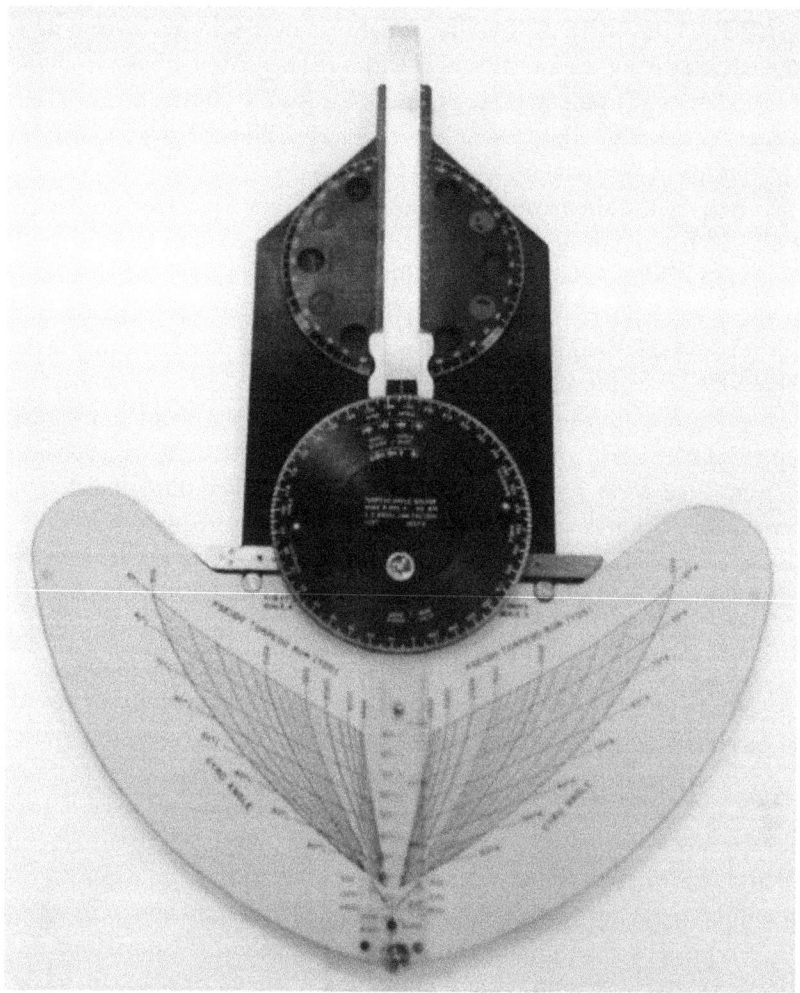

The banjo was the mechanical forerunner of the TDC's Angle Solver section. It measured nearly two feet across and three feet in length (courtesy Naval Undersea Museum, Keyport, Washington).

the torpedo run to using sonar as the primary source of target bearing information, which was then integrated with other sources in the torpedo data computer and automatically transmitted to the torpedo's gyro. While strides in fire control equipment were being made, the public's perception of weapons production suffered from antiwar propaganda. It was difficult for the Navy to overcome these perceptions and they placed the Torpedo Testing Station, Newport, Rhode Island, in the position of pressing forward with a minimum of resources. By 1940 the public's opinion changed and funds were dramatically increased, but it would take a gargantuan effort to make up for the lost years. The submarine building program accelerated and dramatically outpaced torpedo production at the Naval Torpedo Station in Newport. It quickly began building new production facilities, spending one and a quarter million dollars to increase production to about 650 torpedoes per year.

Despite the expansion, the production rate could not supply the surface ship, aircraft and submarine demands. It was predicted that by 1942, shortfall would be as much as 2,425 torpedoes. This realization caused the facility's testing measures to be limited to bench tests rather than actual shots that expended torpedoes. The necessity to forego real testing would result in enormous problems for submariners during the first year of the Second World War. The torpedo design engineers had almost no knowledge of how their designs might work in actual combat. Since only 11 torpedoes manufactured in the United States were actually used in the First World War, it was natural for them to assume that what they had on the bench would be exactly the same in combat conditions at various latitudes, with varying water temperature and salinities.[19]

It should be noted that the engineers at the Newport Torpedo Station who initially developed the magnetic exploder requested that extensive tests be conducted, including an actual warhead shot using one of the obsolete battleships destined for the scrap yard. The Bureau of Ordnance refused the request, saying that such tests had already been conducted at the Norfolk Navy Yard, that a projected test of a mine-housed influence exploder would be sufficient, and that the Newport magnetic exploder was not far enough developed to warrant such a test. During the early 1920s the Newport Torpedo Station under command of Captain Thomas Hart continued to badger the Bureau for live testing, but each request was refused. On May 8, 1926, the obsolescent submarine L-8 was approved as a target. The first warhead shot ran too deep and failed to explode, but the second one worked perfectly. Captain Hart was satisfied and the influence exploder was declared fit for the new Mark 14 torpedo.

Captain Ralph Christie was in charge of the Mark 14 project. It carried a 500-pound warhead, and had a high speed of 46 knots for 4500 yards or low speed of 31.5 knots for 9000 yards. The torpedo was designed to carry the Mark 6 exploder, which had both a contact and an influence igniter. Numerous tests were made using dummy warheads against the cruiser *Indianapolis*. Christie was satisfied with the tests. Other tests against the decommissioned destroyer *Ericsson* also used a dummy warhead. These tests and the previous ones convinced the bureau that the Mark 6 exploder and the Mark 14 torpedo should be put into production.

Unknown to each other, the navies of Britain, Germany and the United States independently developed magnetic influence exploders, most of which were faulty. In America, the confused but seemingly adequate testing hid another problem: the steel pistol pins of the contact exploder were too light and tended to bend in their sleeves. This meant that both systems of firing the warheads of Mark 14 torpedoes were prone to failure. And that was not the only problem. The engineers at the Torpedo Station regarded the magnetic exploder as totally reliable. This being the case, they weren't concerned about reports that the depth setting mechanism could be off by several feet. They tended to believe that a few feet of depth couldn't make much difference when the torpedo's impact would break the keel of the target ship from any reasonable depth. (Later tests showed that the torpedo ran approximately six feet deeper than what was set.) These oversights and misjudgments, along with sloppy engineering and questionable testing, might have been recognized, but the Navy was so concerned with secrecy that the faulty exploder and depth mechanisms went into production and then were immediately wrapped and stored for future use.

Paderfield defends those involved in the poor performance of the Mark 14 torpedo:

> The new exploder was developed in the utmost secrecy at the Newport, Rhode Island Torpedo Station of the Bureau of Ordnance, after which, trials were conducted with dummy warheads against a cruiser in equatorial latitudes off South America. The submarine officer overseeing the development, Lieutenant Commander Ralph Christie, tried to obtain an old hulk to use for trials with live warheads, but failed. Production of the exploders

was started on the strength of the dummy run results, which were judged a success, without a single live test taking place.[20]

The Mark 14 torpedo had problems that would take years to correct, but elsewhere in the arena of submarine weapons, huge strides were being made in equipment that would revolutionize fire control. In the mid–1930s the Arma Corporation produced the first submarine torpedo fire control computer. It took several years of modifications for this mechanical, electric-driven machine to gain a level of perfection worthy of becoming the central feature of torpedo attack doctrine. It not only replaced the banjo and Is-Was as mechanical aides, it revolutionized the whole torpedo fire control procedure. The torpedo data computer, or TDC, was specially designed to fit snugly into the fleet-type submarine's conning tower. Its revolutionary characteristic was its ability to continually generate and display the relative motions of target and submarine. It was the perfect match for submerged approaches using periscope observations spaced at intervals. As an approach was initiated and battle stations torpedo was sounded on the 1MC general announcing system, the TDC was turned on by the conning officer. The motors and gears within its interior spun up and the quartermaster set the initial inputs of bearing, angle-on-the-bow and estimated range of target. The captain took the conn, the TDC operator, usually a lieutenant, checked the initial input, and others in the tracking party took their places in the tight quarters of the conning tower. As the approach began, the captain took more precise observations and the TDC operator made appropriate corrections using the hand cranks at the bottom of the TDC's position keeper. As the approach developed (it might take up to eight hours to close to a favorable firing position), the captain would ask the TDC operator for information such as optimum approach course and distance to the track. Often the operator had to interpret what the TDC was indicating, quickly make mental calculations and provide the captain with specific courses and distances.

The TDC was actually two machines in one. On its left was the position keeper, which generated a graphic picture of submarine and target with range and target speed at the upper left and target course shown on a rotating compass dial at the top-center. The submarine's course was shown on the lower rotating compass rose. Both had small pointers that reflected the path that a torpedo should take to strike the target. This too was generated as the evolving submarine-to-target relationship changed.

Submarine Torpedo Tactics

The right half of the TDC was the angle solver, which was that part of the system that generated and transmitted to the torpedo rooms the settings for torpedo course, speed and depth. Of greater importance was its ability to compute the spread of multiple torpedoes shot at one target. Seldom was only one torpedo expended on a worthwhile target. The details of torpedo spreads are discussed later, but the TDC's angle solver had a red light that was marked "correct solution." When the captain was sure of the accuracy of his inputs from periscope and sonar, he announced to the plotting party, "Final bearing and shoot." The TDC operator was ready to make any last-second corrections, and the assistant TDC operator who manned the angle solver made sure his spread settings were made. At the confirming periscope observation the captain said, "Bearing mark!" The assistant approach officer read the relative bearing from the periscope's bearing ring and the TDC operator set the bearing into the TDC. He then said, "Set!" When the "correct solution" light blinked red, the assistant TDC operator said, "Fire." (To avoid confusion, the term "fire," to mean the impulse-air jettison of torpedoes, was changed to "shoot" during the Second World War.) The quartermaster pressed the electrical firing button as a torpedoman at the tube pressed a second firing button on the tube. The torpedo was ejected from the tube by impulse air and a tripping lever started the torpedo's engine. The submarine shuddered and the stopwatch began ticking off the seconds. This sequence of action took less than ten seconds.

The Arma Corporation described its remarkable torpedo data computer in the following terms:

> The Arma Corporation introduced the submarine torpedo data computer. It made several modifications in the succeeding years in response to submarine officers' comments. The resultant Mark III was paired with Arma's Gyro Setting Indicator Regulator (GSIR). About two out of every three Japanese merchant vessels sunk were credited to the TDC and its operators in the fire control party. One out of every five Japanese warships sunk were at the hands of U.S. submarines. The Mark III TDCs were installed beginning in 1938. The GSIR coupled to the TDC was installed on U.S. submarines beginning in 1941. The system provided for a variety of torpedo ballistics, including extremely long ranges with long periods of travel, operation from intermittent inputs of information, generated and instant gyro angle settings to torpedoes while in the tube and offsets in spreading torpedoes into one target. By war's end the TDC Mark IV handled the Mark 18 electric torpedo and the Mark 16 Navol torpedo.[21]

3—Between the Wars

On September 1, 1939, Nazi Germany invaded Poland without warning. After occupying the Rhineland, Sudetenland, Austria and Czechoslovakia with timid response from France and England, Hitler was surprised when Britain declared war on Germany two days later. Although Karl Doenitz, who commanded Germany's U-boat arm of the Kriegsmarien, was alarmed at the turn of events, he pressed into action his meager number of U-boats.[22] His pitiful U-boat fleet consisted of a total of 38 submarines,

The Arma Corporation Torpedo Data Computer Mark 4 showing the position keeper and the angle solver sections (Submarine Research Center).

but only about one-third of these Type VII and IX boats could be on station at any one time.²³

In contrast, the U.S. Navy, President Roosevelt, Congress and the majority of the American people were convinced that it was only a matter of time before America would be involved in the Second World War. Congress acted to allocate funding for the building of submarines, and the traditional yards at Portsmouth and Groton were augmented by the Cramp yard in Philadelphia, the Manitowoc yard in Wisconsin, and the Mare Island yard in California.

While Americans were enthralled with Clark Gable and Vivien Leigh surviving the South's Civil War demise, shipyards on both coasts as well as Manitowoc, Wisconsin, were furiously constructing submarines. The Arma Corporation was employing young technicians to assemble the torpedo data computers, and the Torpedo Station in Rhode Island was desperately trying to speed up its production of the Mark 14 torpedoes. While the American government kept its eye on Europe falling into the hands of Nazi Germany, the Navy kept an eye on the Pacific and the Far East, where Japan had occupied Manchuria and invaded China. As the decade of the thirties came to an end, it was clear to the Navy Department that the vast Pacific Ocean might well be a future battleground between America and Japan. In such a conflict the submarine would be called upon to help stem the tide of Japanese aggression.

In the late 1930s, aircraft were having success in finding submarines running at periscope depth by simply seeing them in clear water. Accordingly, skippers tried using sonar-only approaches at 100 feet. The depth created many problems for the firing of torpedo tubes and the integrity of the Mark 14 torpedo. Such approaches were deemed unworkable, but the exercises revealed shortcomings of the fleet-type boat and the *Tambor* Class submarine resulted. This class boat not only had six torpedo tubes forward and four astern, it was equipped with the new Mark III torpedo data computer.

In December of 1939 the USS *Tambor* (SS-198) was launched. It was followed by *Tautog*, *Thresher*, *Triton*, *Trout*, and *Tuna*. These were the first in a series of fleet-type submarines that would be the backbone of the American submarine effort in World War II. Only the name remained from the longstanding dispute of "fleet" versus "cruiser" submarine concepts. These 312-foot boats had been refined and modified through a decade of "cruiser"

3—Between the Wars

design improvements. The birth of the fleet-type submarine ran in parallel with the birth of the Mark 14 steam torpedo and the torpedo data computer, Mark III.

Just prior to America's entry into the Second World War, problems with the Mark 14 torpedo remained hidden. A more difficult problem also lay hidden in the Navy's assumption that it was prepared to fight both Germany and, if need be, Japan. There was no test that could be given to submarine commanding officers that might reveal those who had the character to be aggressive and competent commanding officers in combat. Inversely, there was no test that might reveal the lack of these qualities. Promotion to submarine command was in the hands of the Bureau of Personnel, which relied upon a system of seniority that was bound in tradition, and therefore unshakable.

Clay Blaire Jr. described the submarine commanding officer progression as follows:

> During peacetime, selection to command of submarines (and other vessels) was usually made by "class year"; at a certain period, all members of a certain Naval Academy class would, in the ordinary course of events, become eligible for command of an S boat or a fleet boat, depending on seniority, and those qualified (for command) would move up to command more or less as a group. Of course, there were overlaps. It was not possible to work it as smoothly as the Bureau of Personnel might have wanted. In the year or so before the war, the classes of 1925, 1926, and 1927 had become eligible for command of fleet boats and moved up accordingly.[24]

Paderfield saw the problem as one of faulty expectations of senior submarine officers:

> The second failure lay in the training of submarine commanding officers.... In exercises, submarines attacked high-speed targets screened by both aircraft and sonar-equipped destroyers. Commanding officers who were detected in their approach and assumed to have been caught and sunk, were reprimanded. In the Asiatic Submarine Squadron, Commanding officers were threatened with instant dismissal from command if their periscopes were sighted during an exercise. This led to habits of extreme caution.

He continued his explanation, "Commanding officers were judged in peacetime more by their regard for the regulations, paperwork, good discipline and bright ships than by the less measurable qualities needed in war, especially in submarines. Thus, too many U.S. COs when faced with the real test were found wanting in aggression and confidence."[25]

Submarine Torpedo Tactics

To summarize the readiness of the American submarine force to enter a war with Germany and Japan, the following may be noted:

1. Alerted to the probability of a war with Germany and Japan, American shipyards were responding to sweeping government contracts calling for increased submarine production.
2. The *Tambor* class submarine possessed the design and equipment to make it a first-rate oceangoing submarine.
3. The continuing development of sonar and radar coupled with the excellent performance of the torpedo data computer made the torpedo fire control system one of great accuracy when in the hands of aggressive skippers.
4. The Mark 14 torpedo may have had undiscovered flaws, but its gyro and propulsion systems were generally reliable.
5. While submarine commanding officer performance had as yet to be well defined, there were those already in command and those qualified for command who would prove to be brilliant combat commanders.

4

An Analysis of the Fire Control Problem

Commander Submarines Atlantic published a basic fleet-type submarine training manual used at the New London Submarine School during the Second World War. It provided a check-off list for the approach officer as follows: "Make tubes ready early; give the classification officer all necessary information early; slow sufficiently for safe periscope observations; make sufficient all-around observations for air patrol and other surface patrol craft; make observations frequently; as range decreases, run at deeper depth; keep the ship informed of progress of approach as consistent with circumstances and rig the ship for depth charge attack."[1]

While the description of the approach officer's duties is accurate for the purpose of introducing submarine school students to the procedures of fire control, it only scratches the surface of the rather complex concepts of shooting a torpedo at a moving target. Accurate interpretation of ever-changing relative motion was needed during the Second World War to bring a slow-moving submarine into firing position and to send a torpedo or salvo of torpedoes toward a target with expectation of sinking it. The *Submarine Fire Control Manual*, which was first published by Commander, Submarine Force, U.S. Atlantic Fleet during the Second World War, provides a much more comprehensive analysis of the era's submarine torpedo fire control methodology. That publication and its successors were important resources for the conceptual presentations of this chapter.

Review of the fire control vocabulary presented in the introduction to this work may be helpful when examining the fundamentals of torpedo fire control.

While each member of the fire control party played a critical role in a successful approach, in nearly all cases during the Second World War it was the captain, in his role as approach officer, who was responsible for decision-making. As early in the approach as possible, he informed his fire control party of the target or targets to be attacked, whether the attack was to be made upon a single target or multiple targets, whether it was to be from a single tube or nest of tubes, and whether he intended to fire the bow tubes, the stern tubes or both. He also informed the fire control party of the number of torpedoes to be fired at the target or targets, the depth and speed setting he anticipated, and the type and amount of spread that would be necessary. When this information was provided to the fire control party well in advance of firing, each member could then plan his own actions accordingly and be ready at the firing point to commence shooting with a minimum of confusion. The approach officer also informed the tor-

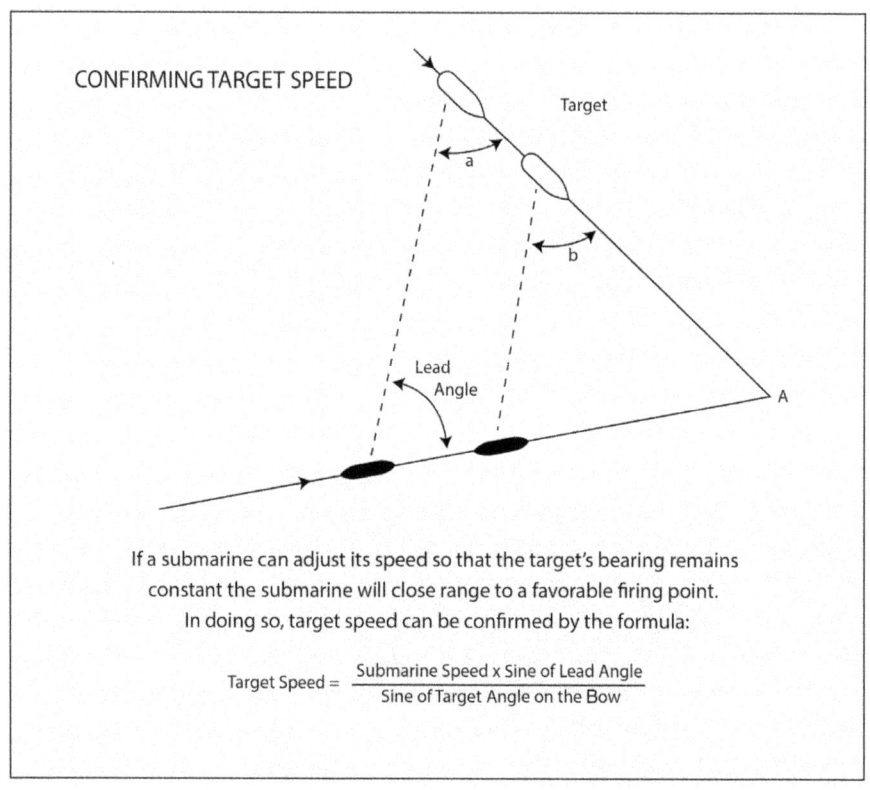

If a submarine can adjust its speed so that the target's bearing remains constant the submarine will close range to a favorable firing point. In doing so, target speed can be confirmed by the formula:

$$\text{Target Speed} = \frac{\text{Submarine Speed} \times \text{Sine of Lead Angle}}{\text{Sine of Target Angle on the Bow}}$$

To close a target, the submarine adjusts course and speed to keep the target on the same relative bearing (Submarine Research Center).

4—An Analysis of the Fire Control Problem

pedo rooms early in the approach as to the probable firing order of the torpedoes. When a full load of one type torpedo was being carried, the order in which the tubes were to be fired was not of great importance.

A well-coordinated fire control party consisted of individual members who knew what would be expected of them at any given time and under any given conditions. This level of competency was not arrived at overnight or by any quick and easy method. It depended upon practice in which the approach officer devoted much thought and time to self-training and the establishment of set phraseology and procedures with each member of the fire control party.

The navigation plot was one of the most important stations in the submarine fire control party. It was the only source from which a geographical picture of the entire approach could be obtained. The navigational plot furnished valuable information on target speed, target course, past times of target zigs, average length of zig legs, and predicted target range when the submarine was below periscope depth. In order to furnish the fire control party with this valuable information, the navigational plotter exercised accuracy, neatness, and speed. This was only accomplished with knowledge of the plotting instruments and continuous practice.

As early as possible in an approach, the target's speed had to be refined and firmly established. The TDC operator acted as the primary coordinator in determining target speed, through his own analysis and analysis of plot. After the angle-on-the-bow had been set on each observation, the TDC operator mentally calculated target speed using generated changes in angle-on-the-bow, confirmed by periscope observations. This he did through his own mental calculations using mathematical shortcuts and thumb rules.

If the submarine was able to close the target while keeping the target's angle-on-the-bow constant, the TDC operator could get an accurate target speed using the sine of the lead angle.

Since the approach officer often did not have satisfactory access to the position keeper, the TDC operator provided him verbally with generated range, generated angle-on-the-bow, generated true and relative target bearing, torpedo course and torpedo gyro angles as requested by the approach officer.

It was the job of the assistant TDC operator to cut in both the forward and after GSIR early in the approach phase. Assuming the gyros were less than 150 degrees at the firing point, he turned the switch to the indicate-regulate position, which electrically set the proper gyro angle into the torpedo. When the gyros matched, he reported to the approach officer that the TDC gyros were matched in automatic. At the firing point, and upon hearing the TDC operator announce "set" for the first torpedo, the assistant TDC operator watched for the "correct solution" light to appear. When the solution light glowed red, he ordered, "Shoot."[2] The firing button was then pushed and the respective torpedo was fired electrically using impulse air.

A submerged approach and attack demanded the utmost skill on the part of the approach officer and the fire control party to maneuver the submarine into the optimum firing position. The low speed and poor maneuverability of the submarine and the limited opportunities for observing the target required prompt and correct action by every member of the fire control party based on the information available. The term "approach" was a general term for the spotting of a potential target, identifying it as enemy, determining its direction, maneuvering the submarine to a position from which it could fire its torpedoes, and solving the problem of relative motion to obtain a hit. Within that general term were three distinct phases of an attack: the contact phase, the approach phase, and the attack phase.

The contact phase demanded some quick, preliminary decisions, the first of which was the determination of target relative movement. When contact was made with only the masts or smoke of a target on the horizon, no angle-on-the-bow could be visually obtained. The conning officer (and commanding officer, when he was summoned to the bridge) had first to determine the approximate course of the target. The surfaced submarine changed course toward the target and increased speed to bring more of the target into view. When the target was in sight, the quickest and simplest way to determine the direction of target motion was by visual observation of angle-on-the-bow. Using the TBT, the captain could also observe the direction of the target's true bearing change. In order to obtain the maximum affect of change of true bearing due to the target's movement, the submarine kept heading directly toward the target, or when visibility demanded, the submarine stopped dead in the water or submerged. In doing so, any change in the target's true bearing indicated the target's general course. Having a rough estimate of the target's course, the submarine could then change course to a normal approach course, gain maximum speed on the surface and begin to close the target.

4—An Analysis of the Fire Control Problem

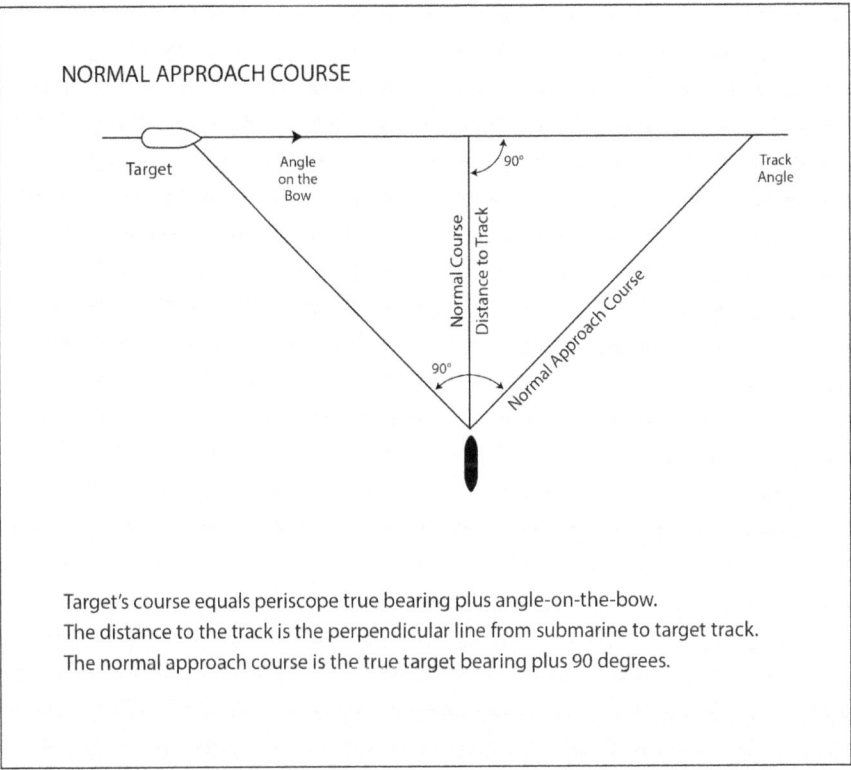

Target's course equals periscope true bearing plus angle-on-the-bow.
The distance to the track is the perpendicular line from submarine to target track.
The normal approach course is the true target bearing plus 90 degrees.

The normal approach course is the bearing of the target plus 90 degrees. It is used as a preliminary set-up once target motion is known (Submarine Research Center).

Once the target ship came into clear view and its angle-on-the-bow was established, the submarine assumed that the target was using high speed. The submarine might then take an optimum approach course which lagged the normal approach course by 10 degrees. When either a normal approach course or optimum approach course had been set and the submarine closed the target at high speed, the contact phase ended and the approach phase was begun.

The approach phase was intended to close the target in order to bring the submarine within torpedo range and to attain the best possible position from which to commence the attack. The low speed and poor maneuverability of the submerged submarine made it mandatory that prompt and correct action be taken as early as possible while the submarine remained on the surface. If the target was to be brought within torpedo range, intelligent tactics had to be employed from the first contact and continued throughout the approach phase. Nothing was so discouraging to a submarine captain than to see his quarry escape because of a mistake in the early stages of an approach. The submarine had to race ahead of the target's bearing change so that the target's rate of bearing change slowed and changed direction to lag behind the surfaced submarine running at high speed. The best position for the submarine to reach was directly ahead of the target at a range which would allow time for the submarine to maneuver to a favorable firing position. When the submarine reached such a position, the approach phase ended and the attack phase began. At this point the submarine submerged, and in doing so, lost most of its ability to maneuver.

Even at this late stage in an approach, the captain had to contend with the possibility that the target might radically change course and move beyond torpedo range. This possibility was a product of the submarine's slow submerged speed.[3]

The submarine had to stay at a slow submerged speed in order to raise the periscope and gain an accurate visual estimate of angle-on-the-bow and target range.

The attack phase centered on the fire control problem so that an accurate target speed, course and range were set in the torpedo data computer. It would be from this machine that inputs to torpedoes would be inserted immediately before firing. A description of the processes involved in ascertaining accurate target information, setting this information into the TDC, and making the many pertinent decisions is presented herein in their historical context.

Blaire presented a prewar picture of torpedo attack training:

> In peacetime they [commanding officers] had trained with high speed fleet units, such as destroyers with known masthead heights. Setting up on slow moving, shallow draft merchant ships whose masthead heights could only be guessed at, was a wholly different ball game. Where there were two or more ships involved, or ships were zigzagging, it was even more difficult. The skipper had to keep in his head at all times a picture of what was happening on the surface. The approach party, centering on the plot officer, had to guess the zigzag pattern, estimating when the zigs and zags would occur so the submarine did not set up in one place and then find itself far out in left field.
>
> Then there was the question of torpedo spreads—how to space the firing

4—An Analysis of the Fire Control Problem

of torpedoes to obtain hits. Under ideal circumstances, peacetime exercises had shown, it was best to fire three torpedoes; one forward of the bow, one at the middle of the target (MOT), and one astern.[4]

Attacks by the fleet-type submarine of the Second World War used optical, acoustic and mechanical-electrical instruments for it to see, hear and assist in thinking.

The eyes of the submarine were its periscopes. The conning tower of a fleet-type submarine had two periscopes, one designated as the search periscope and the other as the attack periscope. Both periscopes had a low power magnification of 1.5 and a high power magnification of 6.0. The neck of the search periscope was 3.75 inches in diameter. The neck of the attack periscope was 1.4 inches in diameter, making it difficult to detect by surface craft. The optical length of the search periscope was 36 feet from the conning tower, making the normal periscope depth to keel at 58 feet. The attack periscope had a 40-foot length, making the normal depth for an attack about 60 feet.

There were three methods of estimating range using the periscope. Range could be estimated by using the telemeter reticules in the periscope. The true field of the periscopes in low power was 32 degrees and in high power, 8 degrees. The periscope had inscribed on its optical image a series of vertical and horizontal lines. In low power each small division represented one degree, while in high power each division represented .25 degrees. If the approach officer knew or could estimate the masthead height of the target in feet, the number of horizontal divisions covered by the ship between its waterline and masthead height would be a measure of the range to the target.

A target's range was a function of horizontal reticules from bow to stern modified by its angle-on-the-bow.

The second method of obtaining ranges was by means of the stadimeter installed in the periscope. The stadimeter relied for its operation upon the formation of two identical images which could, by means of a hand wheel on the periscope, be vertically displaced with relation to each other. Normally, the hand wheel was at the limit of its counterclockwise travel. To obtain a range, the hand wheel was turned clockwise until the target masthead in one image coincided with the target waterline in the other image. The range was then read by the periscope assistant from the stadime-

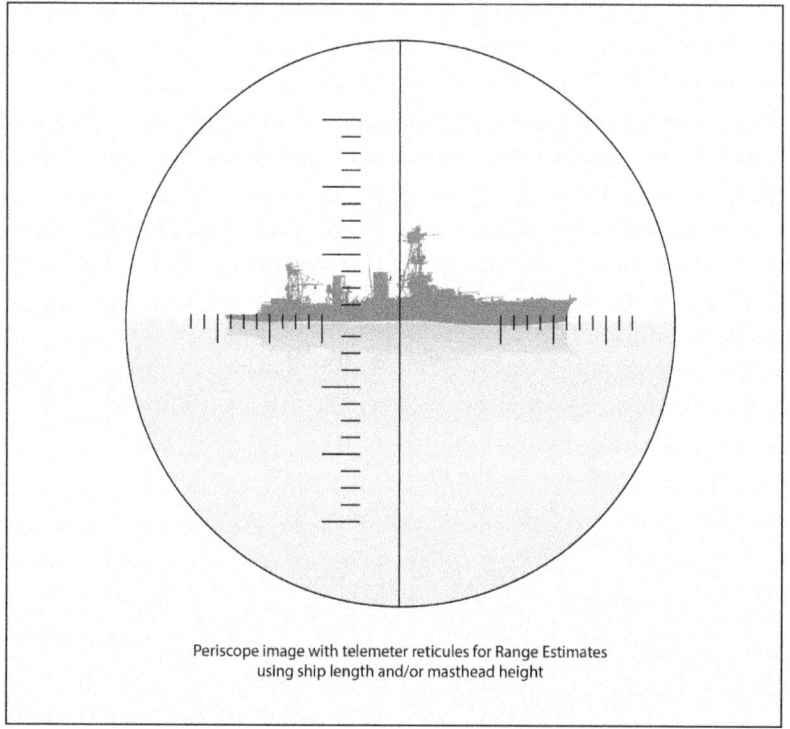

Periscope image with telemeter reticules for Range Estimates using ship length and/or masthead height

Using the telemeter scale and knowing the target masthead height can give the approach officer an approximate range (Submarine Research Center).

ter scale on the opposite side of the periscope eyepiece. The periscope assistant read the range matching the appropriate masthead height. The key to the use of the stadimeter was to gain an accurate measure of the target's masthead height. One method was to use the height of the target's bridge structure above the visible waterline as a yardstick, then to approximate the masthead height by simply doubling the bridge height.

Getting a quick target range using the stadimeter could be simplified. It was only necessary to remember that a ship of about 400 feet would have a masthead height of about 110 feet. Starting with this relation and refining it as the problem generated, provided the captain with an initial, tentative range. The conning tower periscopes were constantly being used when in transit to exercise skill in using the stadimeter and telemeter reticules. Clay Blaire, Jr. described the use of the periscope: "It had long been clear to Joe

4—An Analysis of the Fire Control Problem

Grenfell and Dusty Dornin that even with the help of the TDC, the firing of torpedoes at an enemy ship would be a complex and difficult business. To obtain a fairly accurate range estimate, it was necessary to guess accurately the masthead height of the mast of the target vessel, then extrapolate from the horizontal lines in the periscope cross hairs, using a slide rule (Is-Was) or a device built in the periscope called a stadimeter."[5]

The third method of obtaining a range was by use of the ST stub radar installed in one of the periscopes. In this method the range of the selected target was measured directly by the ST radar operator when the periscope was raised and trained on the target. Of course, this range was accurate and much superior to the telemeter or stadimeter, but the ST radar was not installed on American submarines until the last years of the war.

The ears of the submarine were its sonar, which in the fleet-type boat was the SJ and JT sonars. While these instruments were a vital part of the submarine's sensors, sonar is not discussed in the context of Second World War torpedo fire control, since its fire control role during this time period was as confirmation of information produced from other sensors.

The approach officer relied heavily on the torpedo data computer to digest, integrate and generate target information coming from periscope, navigational plot, sonar and the approach officer's assessment of the tactical situation. The TDC was an amazing machine for its time, but it could not outpace the human brain. Quick-witted fire control team members played mind games in the wardroom during off-duty hours. They challenged each other in seeing how quickly fire control problems could be solved by using a few simple shortcuts or thumb rules. Some of the following thumb rules may even be useful for seamen of today.

To obtain the reciprocal of any point on the compass from 000 degrees to 180 degrees, add 200 and subtract 20. To obtain the reciprocal of any point on the compass from 180 degrees to 360 degrees subtract 200 and add 20. For example, the reciprocal of 103 is 303 − 20 or 283. The reciprocal of 279 is 079 +20 or 099.[6]

When plotting periscope observations, a good thumb rule to remember was one knot at one mile equals one degree in one minute. For example, if a captain observes a ship bearing 270 with a 90-degree angle-on-the-bow, making 8 knots at a range of 4 miles (8,000 yards), he notes the time. One minute later, he again raises the periscope and takes a bearing. If his range estimate is reasonably accurate the target should bear 272. For the purpose of the thumb rule, the submarine is assumed to be stationary. It is reasonably accurate, between angles-on-the-bow of 50 to 130 degrees, to assume that a target with a beam aspect will have a one degree change of bearing per knot of target speed at 2000 yards. This thumb rule is based on the fact that one degree subtends 35 yards at a 2000-yard range, while one knot equals 33 yards of advance per minute.

The torpedo fire control problem unavoidably hangs on trigonometric functions, namely the sine values of angles. An applicable thumb rule was that every six degrees was a tenth and every 10 degrees was a sixth.[7]

No device in the submarine could match the human mind for quick analysis of complex situations; however, the TDC was an excellent device for presenting a picture of the tactical situation at any given moment during an approach.

The TDC was a system which electrically transmitted continuously changing gyro, speed and depth inputs to torpedoes in tubes ready to be fired at any time. The changes in submarine and target relative motion were continuously adjusted to accurately represent inputs from periscope, TBT, sonar and radar or any combination of these sources of target information. The component of the TDC that performed this function was the position keeper, and it was the duty of the TDC operator, normally the torpedo officer, to coordinate the inputs as directed by the captain.

The relative bearing of a target and target angle-on-the-bow were set into the TDC by manipulating cranks at the base of the position keeper. These inputs were formulated into true bearing and true target course by auto inputs from the submarine's master compass. Through successive periscope observations, sonar turn count information and geographical plot interpretation, a target speed could be obtained. This was entered and adjusted by another crank manipulation of the TDC operator. Target range, always the most difficult and most vital of the total target picture, was continuously adjusted by the TDC operator as information from periscope or radar clarified the set-up. As each aspect of relative motion was refined, the TDC computed the correct gyro input to give an accurate torpedo course to the target. This information was then transmitted to the angle solver, which was the TDC component that determined the order of fire and the spread of multi-torpedo salvos. The angle solver display was divided between the aft and forward torpedo tubes. The assistant TDC operator, who entered the number of torpedoes to be fired, the

4—An Analysis of the Fire Control Problem

sequence of the torpedoes and the percentage of spread, received such information from the captain, who made his decisions in response to a mix of data including target size, range, and estimate of number of torpedoes needed to sink the target. When the inputs from position keeper and angle solver were confirmed and the torpedoes had received the proper inputs, a red light appeared on the angle solver. At that point in the attack, the torpedoes could be launched with expectation that they would leave the submarine, come to the preset depth, and course at the preset speed.

Not all the brass thought the TDC was such an invaluable machine. Blaire painted a discrepant view as follows: "While Admiral Thomas Hart still believed that the Fleet Type submarine was too large and the TDC was simply a gadget, admirals Wilkes and Fife were not in agreement. Indeed, Admiral Wilkes, then Commander Submarines Pacific said, 'The present day action against well screened forces such as the vessels of this command have encountered in the majority of their attacks makes the use of the TDC or similar instrument almost mandatory.'"[8]

Hart's opinion was his alone, and as history has proven, the TDC was not only a remarkable achievement in design, it was the forerunner of modern computers, which are indispensible to modern technology. Not only did the TDC master the problem of target course, speed and range, it produced, in its angle solver section, the problem of using multiple torpedoes to sink a single target.

The term used for multiple torpedo separation was "spread." A spread was a salvo of torpedoes fired to hit different points along the length of the target or its length extended. The approach officer determined early on how many torpedoes to use and the type of spread to be used. The quality and size of target were the primary factors in determining the number of torpedoes to be used in a spread; however, the purpose of using more than one torpedo on a single target was also to compensate for possible errors in the estimates of target course, speed, and range. These errors might also be caused by faulty fire control estimates or TDC inaccuracies, particularly if the target maneuvers at the firing point. The unit of spread can be defined as the linear distance between adjacent points that torpedoes hit along the length of the target or expressed in seconds between each torpedo launch. The unit of spread can also be expressed as the number of degrees that separate each torpedo of the salvo. Basically, an approach offi-

Submarine Torpedo Tactics

cer could use a divergent spread or a longitudinal spread. This choice was made at the beginning of the attack phase.

The divergent spread was changes in target bearing applied to the gyro angle order of each torpedo of a salvo to cause successive torpedoes to hit at different points along the target length or extended track.

The divergent spread was used for slower-moving targets. It was accomplished by adjusting the torpedoes' gyro angles in successive shots. The divergent spread was most typically used in a three-torpedo salvo to hit the middle of target (M.O.T.), then aft, then forward of the middle of target. The additional gyro angle, over that required for hitting the same point of a moving target, applied to successive torpedoes was solved by the angle solver of the TDC.[9]

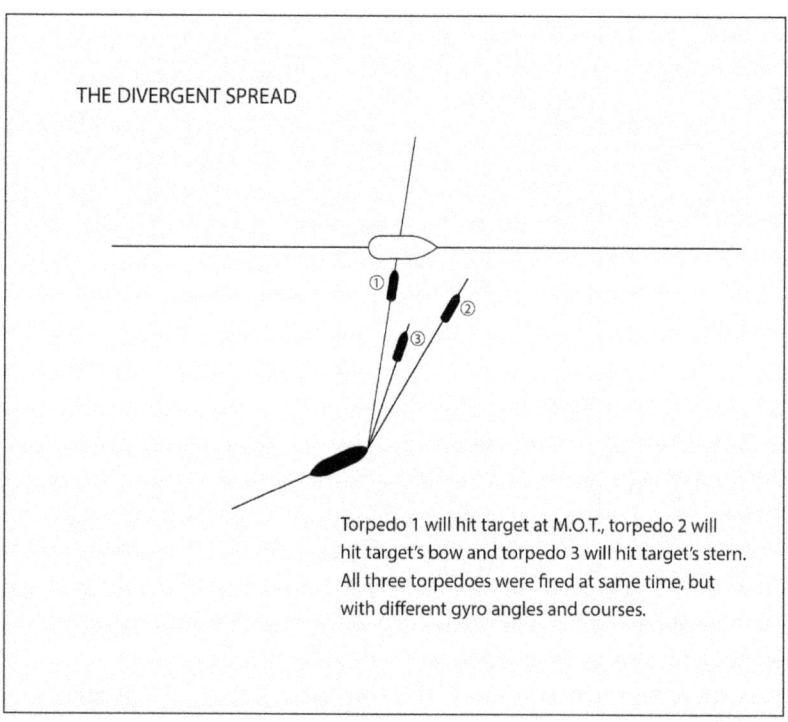

Torpedo 1 will hit target at M.O.T., torpedo 2 will hit target's bow and torpedo 3 will hit target's stern. All three torpedoes were fired at same time, but with different gyro angles and courses.

The divergent spread adjusts torpedo gyro angle, keeping time intervals as short as possible (Submarine Research Center).

4—An Analysis of the Fire Control Problem

When firing a salvo to hit the same point of aim of a moving target, the difference in gyro angles between successive torpedoes was the target advance angle. When firing a salvo, which was spread to hit at different points along the target's length, the difference in gyro angles was equal to the sum of the target advance angle with the addition of the spread angle. Once again, it was the angle solver that produced these complex mathematical operations in a matter of seconds.

The approach officer often elected to use a longitudinal spread. A longitudinal spread was one in which the torpedoes of a salvo intersected the target's track at different points along the target's length, but at the same point on the target's track, and at the same torpedo track angle.

This type of torpedo spread was most effective against high-speed targets. While the divergent spread was used for slower-moving targets,

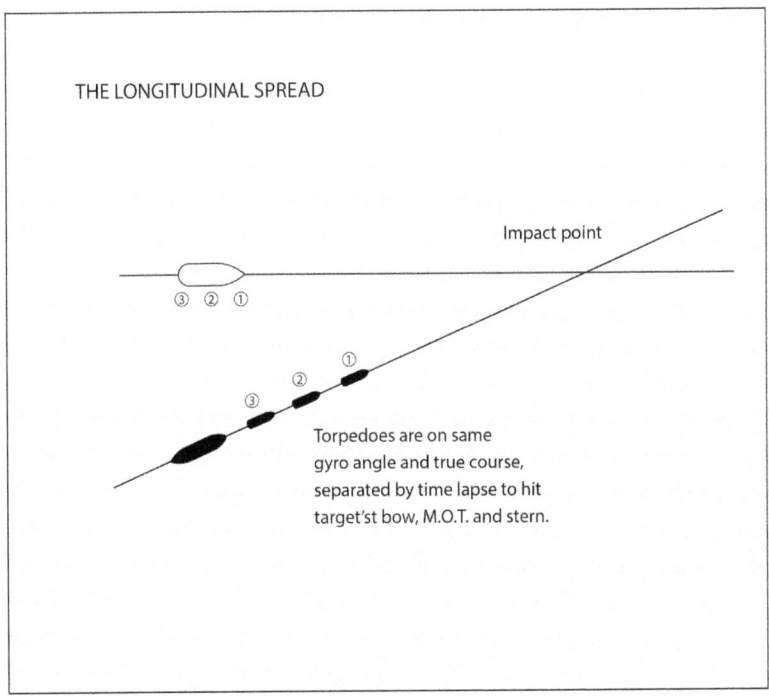

The longitudinal spread adjusts the time intervals while keeping the torpedo gyro angle constant (Submarine Research Center).

this type of torpedo spread did not rely on a mathematical definition of gyro angles. All that was needed for a quick salvo was an initial torpedo gyro angle. It was only necessary to time-sequence each torpedo along the same track. In so doing, the first torpedo would strike the target at its bow, the second at the midpoint, and the third at the stern.

The approach officer had to estimate the significance of possible errors caused by routine or target evasive maneuvers prior to firing or at the instant of firing. These errors would influence torpedo run, torpedo track angle, tactical characteristics of the target, and ratio of target speed to torpedo speed. For this reason, the approach officer often spread his salvo over a distance along the target's track that was longer than the target's length. This compensation was expressed in percentage, such as a 140 percent spread, which in the case of the divergent spread increased the separation of gyro angles, and in the case of the longitudinal spread increased the time lag between each torpedo.

In Otto Preminger's motion picture *In Harm's Way*, the captain of a cruiser, at sea off Oahu Island on December 7, 1941, was notified of the Japanese attack on Pearl Harbor. Because he was concerned about his low fuel, but was determined to seek out the enemy force, he elected to hold a straight course to where he had determined the enemy might be. A Japanese submarine sent a salvo of torpedoes into his cruiser, sinking it. The captain lost his command and was assigned to a desk job as punishment for not zigzagging. While the film was a fictional story, a similar event on July 30, 1945, was the sinking of the cruiser USS *Indianapolis* in the Philippine Sea. After having carried a nuclear device to Tinian Island, the cruiser, under the command of Captain Charles V. McVay III, failed to keep a zigzag course as it maneuvered from east to west. A Japanese submarine shot a salvo of torpedoes into the cruiser, which sank in a matter of minutes, taking over 300 lives with it.[10] The tragedy was exacerbated by a lack of communication combined with an apathetic command structure that assumed *Indianapolis* was steaming independently and in no danger. The story didn't end with the sinking. Sharks attacked and killed over half of the survivors before a Catalina flying boat discovered the few remaining crew members, who were drained of life after enduring the nightmare for over a week. The captain of the cruiser was court-martialed, the only American commanding officer to be so prosecuted during the war. The court held that the captain had "hazarded his ship by failing to adhere to a zigzag

4—An Analysis of the Fire Control Problem

evasive procedure." Investigations after the war found that the Navy's higher command was culpable in the loss of *Indianapolis*.[11]

Zigzagging was employed by surfaced American submarines as well as surface vessels, and during the latter years of the Second World War a sinuous course clock was installed at the conning tower helm station. This instrument gradually adjusted the submarine's course to be steered so that its angle-on-the-bow would never act as an indicator of its true course. The sinuous course clock was mathematically programmed to maintain the submarine's true course. Prior to this invention, simple zigzag patterns could be designed to accomplish the same deviations from a basic course. The purpose of these was to confuse a submarine's fire control effort by changing the angle-on-the-bow at intervals. It was the job of the geographical plot in a fire control party to determine the time periods of each leg and the

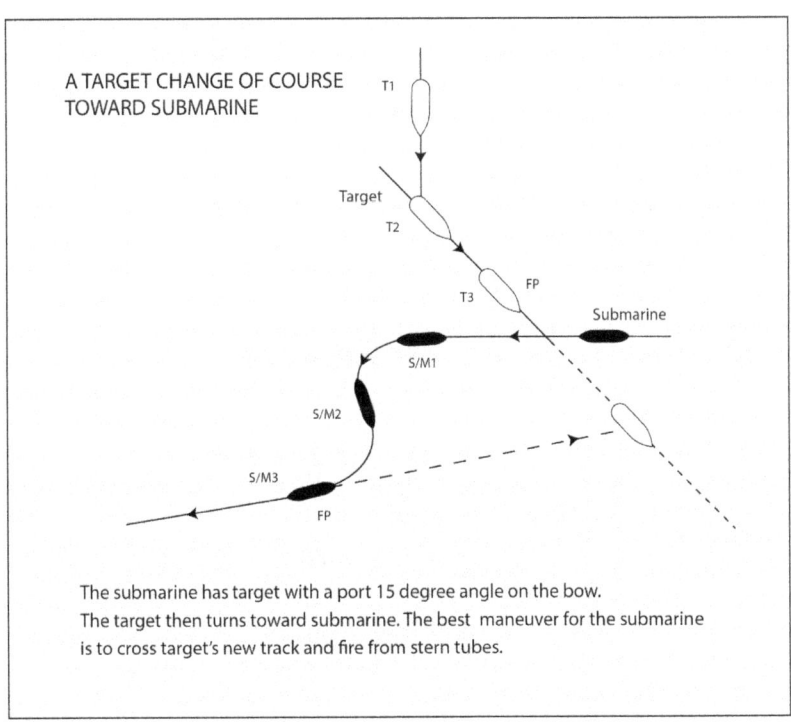

The submarine has target with a port 15 degree angle on the bow.
The target then turns toward submarine. The best maneuver for the submarine is to cross target's new track and fire from stern tubes.

When target turns toward, the submarine crosses the target's track to obtain a favorable attack position (Submarine Research Center).

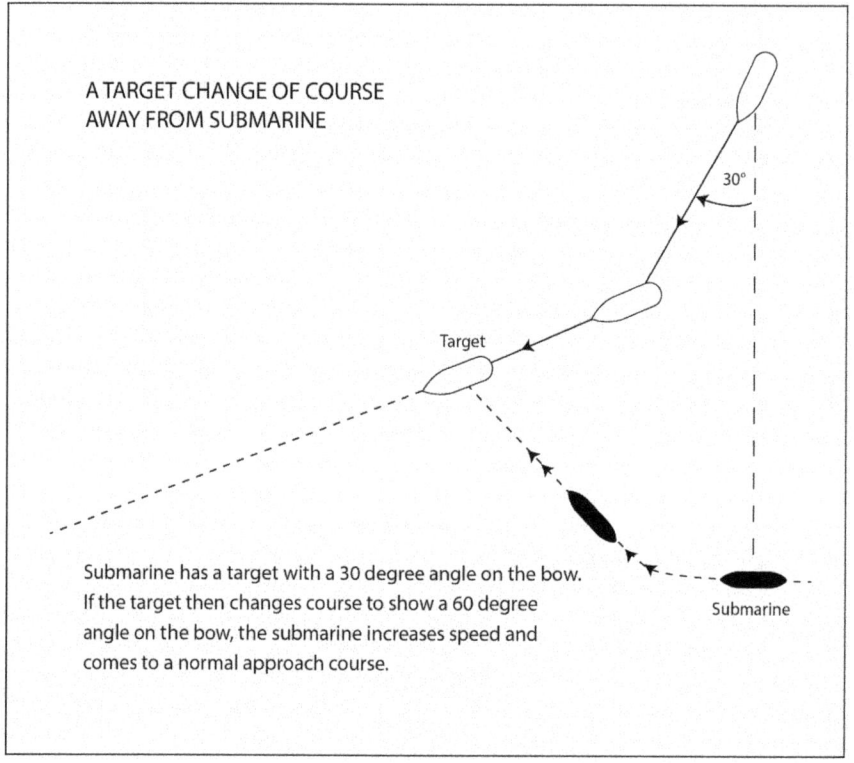

A target turns away from submarine, the submarine increases speed and changes course to quickly engage target (Submarine Research Center).

course changes employed on each leg. This was a level of sophistication that added a difficult dimension to torpedo fire control. The experienced submarine approach officer could quickly change his course and speed to accommodate a target's zig. If the target changed course to pass too close to the submarine's track, the submarine could cross the target's track and switch to stern tubes.

On the other hand, if the target changed course away from the submarine, the submarine could speed up and change course to engage the target at its closest point of approach.

Both maneuvers depended on the navigational plot of the fire control party to predict the next target zig. This gave the approach officer time to prepare for the anticipated zig.

4—An Analysis of the Fire Control Problem

Without doubt the solving of the fire control problem was manifold and complex at several levels. With an understanding of what a complicated problem faced an approach officer in trying to hit an evasive target, it is appropriate that a few of the more remarkable approaches of the Second World War be recorded.

5

The Second World War

On Sunday, December 7, 1941, beginning at 8:00 a.m. aircraft of the Imperial Japanese Navy attacked ships in Pearl Harbor, parked aircraft on Ford Island, at Hickam Field, Wheeler Field and Kaneoe Marine Air Station. They failed to hit the auxiliary fields at Bellows, close to Waimanalo and Haleiva, from which a few American fighters managed to engage the Japanese fighters. The American battleships moored on the east side of Ford Island were either sunk or severely damaged. There were actually two raids, which included high level bombers, dive bombers, torpedo planes and fighters. Admiral Nagumo, commanding the carrier strike force from which the planes were launched, declared the mission of the strike force completed when his carrier pilots returned and reported that the battleships of the U.S. Navy had been destroyed.

The primary target of the strike force had been the American aircraft carriers, but they were at sea, having delivered planes to Wake Island. Both Nagumo and the commander of the Japanese Combined Fleet, Admiral Yamamoto, were aware of the importance of a navy's air strength, but they were under the same historical misconception as the American admirals. The senior officers of both navies imagined that the Second World War on the seas would be decided by a single, massive battleship gun engagement similar to the First World War Battle of Jutland. With the destruction of the American battleships, Japanese admirals believed it would be possible to contain the few remaining American aircraft carriers.

The Japanese tactical victory at Pearl Harbor was, in the broader, strategic sense, a catastrophic failure. Among the targets at Pearl Harbor overlooked by the Japanese planners were the fuel depots, most of which were above ground, and the submarines tied up at the submarine base finger piers. This oversight would play a large role in America's immediate response to the attack.

5—The Second World War

On December 8, 1941, President Roosevelt addressed an emergency joint session of Congress and delivered a rousing request for a declaration of war against Japan. Only one vote was against the declaration. As an indignant public demanded retribution, the Navy had only its submarines to throw against Japan, and Commander Submarines Pacific lost little time in pushing his boats westward. The S-boats at Tsingtao got underway, but those at Cavite, on the south side of Manila Bay, were caught by Japanese bombers as they were taking aboard torpedoes and stores. *Lionfish* was lost and *Dragonfish* was damaged. The submarine base took a pounding.

American submarines based in the Philippines and elsewhere in the western Pacific made their way south, drawing fuel and stores from Dutch bases in Indochina as they continued to Darwin, Freemantle, Brisbane and other Australian ports.

In 1940 American military strategists and legislators had been convinced that it was only a matter of time before American forces would be committed to the conflict. Congress therefore authorized adequate funding for the National Defense Research Committee. Submarines were recipients of much of the resulting basic sonar research from Columbia University and the University of California.

In that same year Congress had also approved the Two-Ocean Navy concept with a four-billion-dollar authorization. By February 1941 the first six *Tambor*-class boats had been put in commission. U.S. submarine design efforts had accomplished their goals with propulsion, habitability and weapons integrated with the boat's diving, trimming, and fire control systems. It could make 21 knots on the surface and 10 knots at the half-hour rate submerged. With all-welded pressure hull and external framing (except in torpedo rooms), the boat could descend to 300 feet without pressure hull damage. This compared to the *Narwhal*, with its riveted outer hull leaking oil despite the Navy's best efforts to make the boat combat-ready. The combination of improved periscopes, sonar, TDC, fire control circuitry to torpedo rooms, and sound-powered phones for instant internal communication made the *Tambor*-class boat worthy of combat against the Navy's perceived opponent, Japan.[1] As a weapon platform for torpedo attack, the United States Navy at last had a submarine that was tested, proven and combat-ready. Within this submarine were well-trained officers and men who strove to improve their fire control techniques through endless practice.

Submarine Torpedo Tactics

Captains had freedom to modify their respective fire control party organization to suit their particular taste. Lcdr. Dudley "Mush" Morton, captain of USS *Wahoo* (SS-238), preferred to turn over the periscope to his executive officer, Richard O'Kane, when making submerged approaches on Japanese shipping. This left Morton free to reflect on the tactical situation and observe the attack procedure without becoming involved in the detail of periscope observations. Morton moved from his geographical plot to the TDC, conferred with O'Kane and issued speed and helm orders, and determined the spread for specific targets.[2]

For America, December 1941 was the beginning of the Second World War, but Britain had been fighting the Germans since September 1939. For Great Britain, this earlier conflict was centered on Germany's attempt to cut off the island fortress from American and Canadian supplies by sinking as many merchant ships as possible. An understanding of German fire control techniques serves as a basis for comparison in the later effort by America to cut off Japan from its Southeast Asia supply source.

American submarines had not shot a single warhead torpedo since World War I, and during that war fired only eleven warhead torpedoes. On the other hand, German submariners gained valuable experience during the first year of the Second World War, even though their numbers were small. The limited number of U-boats was, in part, due to Hitler's interest in large fighting machines, and for the navy, this translated to battleships. While the German yards built the battleships *Deutschland*, *Admiral Scheer* and *Admiral Graf Spee*, little was done to build a submarine force.[3] With only 57 U-boats, most of which were obsolete and used only for training, Karl Doenitz went to war against the English merchant fleet. The torpedo at hand was the old G-7 with unreliable exploders, but with only six boats at sea during the early months of the war, Doenitz's submarines sank over 650,000 tons and several important warships.[4]

On September 14, 1939, *Ark Royal*'s hunting group blundered across U-39, which fired four torpedoes at the carrier. Only the fact that the torpedoes' magnetic exploders detonated prematurely saved *Ark Royal* and betrayed U-39's presence to the destroyers, which closed in amid a flurry of depth-charge attacks. Too damaged to escape, U-39 surfaced and her crew surrendered—the first U-boat lost in the war.[5]

German fire control practices improved rapidly. While Britain struggled with ASW measures not much improved from the First World War,

5—The Second World War

German submarines honed their fire control skills. The Type VIIC was small and cramped. It had no conning tower, so the fire control party was crammed into the control room along with two periscopes and the diving station. The typical arrangement was the captain at the periscope, the torpedo officer, and petty officer as plotters, and another petty officer who manned the torpedo computer. Target bearings were electrically transmitted from the periscope to the computer, and the plotters had a small table with a dead reckoning tracer, which also had electric inputs to the computer. All other target inputs were made by the computer petty officer on voice commands from the captain.

Heinz Schaeffer was a crew member on U-977, a Type VII boat. He describes two attacks, the first submerged, the second on the surface, using G-7 torpedoes with influence exploders. His description illustrates the mutual responsibilities of the captain at the periscope, and the torpedo officer keeping a geographical plot. The description includes the German torpedo data computer operated by a torpedo petty officer who was also in the control room.

> "Fire," repeats the torpedo petty officer, and the torpedo gunner's mate at the fore tubes hears the order through the loudspeaker system. He has a hand on the two firing levers and a leg across the third, in case of a failure of the remote-controlled firing gear [referring to the computer]. The boat shivers three times in succession and three short, heavy hissing sounds are heard. The noise is the compressed air by which the torpedoes are discharged. Firing is staggered at 2-second intervals to prevent mutual interference between the discharges. At the order, "Fire," the Chief floods to the prescribed amount in order to compensate for the weight of the three torpedoes—for the boat must be ready for an instantaneous crash dive if necessary. The Commander looks at his wristwatch—fifteen seconds running time yet.
>
> Boom! ... The magnetic pistol has worked well, it appears. In a submarine attack the Commander controls the ship, gives the target information and fires the torpedoes himself. The torpedo officer only sees that the proper settings are put on the attack-table. This time we are going to fire the stern tubes, which we don't often get the chance to use.[6]
>
> "Range, 400 meters ... fire!"
>
> The roar is terrific. We've fired from much closer this time. Underwater the noise is frightful. The tanker has broken in two.[7]

The German torpedo had hardly run its arming distance before hitting the target. This narrative bears witness to the German emphasis on close-range attacks as a means of ensuring hits. First World War German submarine tactics called for close-in attacks, and that protocol continued into the Second World War.

The captain swung his submarine to engage his next target. Schaeffer continues:

> Target Red 90 [port 90 degree angle-on-the-bow], speed 16 knots, range 7,000 meters [this time, a very long range], torpedo speed 30 knots, running depth 7 meters. Our torpedoes are set to run at a depth of 7 meters below the surface, to pass about 2 meters beneath the target. A magnetic pistol fires the charge, which blows in the keel plates and causes the ship to break up.... The torpedo officer at the attack-table reports, "Lined up," and the switch is made by which the attack-table is connected with the gyro compass and the attack sight [periscope]. The mechanism churns round and two red lamps indicate that the process of calculating the information which has been fed into it is not yet completed. The lights go out after a few moments, and the petty officer reports the resulting settings to the torpedo officer. From this point onward our own alterations of course are of little importance, being allowed for automatically. The target must simply be held in the cross wires of the attack sight in order that the apparatus can do its job.... Meanwhile, the constantly changing firing settings are being transmitted automatically to the torpedoes and set on their angling [spread] mechanism. With this system we can fire at any moment and on any course, provided that the 90 degree limiting angle is not exceeded. The torpedoes will run to a pattern that spreads over roughly a ship's length by the time they reach the range of the target. We turn to our attacking course.[8]

What Schaeffer refers to as an angling mechanism is the German version of the angle solver in the American torpedo data computer. It is a much simpler computer than the TDC, and lacks the ability to generate the movements of own ship and target ship.

Generally speaking, the German T Vorhalt Rechner G-3 torpedo computer used in both Type VII and Type IX submarines lacked the sophistication of the American TDC. Without the generated functions of the TDC's position keeper, it really amounted only to a means of calculating multiple torpedo spread patterns and adjusting gyro inputs to compensate for course alterations of the submarine. While later models of the TDC also had the capacity to integrate sonar inputs with those from the periscope, the T Vorhalt Rechner G-3 only transmitted to the G-7 torpedoes in the tubes, gyro and depth spindle inputs based on static target information. The only way instant target information could be transmitted through the Vorhalt was by the captain making sequential observations with less than one-minute intervals. This limitation was crucial because

British ASW methodology relied heavily on lookouts spotting the exposed periscope. It was necessary for the German captain to have his periscope raised at the instant of firing. Furthermore, it was necessary either to track a target continuously or to fire when the target passed the Vorhalt pre-set bearing. The Vorhalt provided no means of analyzing the errors in quantities such as target speed, angle-on-the-bow and range. It did have the capacity to continuously calculate the spread angle of a three-torpedo salvo taking into account own ship's movements.[9]

The Vorhalt had to be fitted into a control room already stacked with equipment. It was therefore compact, light and sturdy. It was built by skilled hands with typical German precision. It was mechanical, as was the American TDC, but its functions were a product of polished cams rather than motor-driven gears as in the TDC. Since it was assembled by hand, its parts were not interchangeable. When the Vorhalt failed, torpedo inputs were made by the men at the tubes hearing shouted commands via the voice tube.[10]

The analysis of the T Vorhalt Rechner S-3 was conducted by Edgar O'Niel of the Bureau of Ordnance in cooperation with Arma Corporation, manufacturer of the American TDC.

The German U-boat service contended with G-7 influence exploder problems, but limitations in the Vorhalt rendered the machine incapable of compensating for such failures. On the other hand, while American submarines also suffered from torpedo reliability problems, the TDC and superlative fire control techniques were important factors in compensating for the Mark 14's shortcomings. The ability of a submarine to achieve success was a direct function of the competency of its captain.

Some submarine commanding officers of the Second World War became legends of the submarine service, emerging from the rank and file of commanders considered at the outset of war to be equally competent. The factors that enhanced competency in submarine commanding officers is of interest to this study.

Tactical competency was influenced by a combination of characteristics including aggressiveness, defined as persistence in the face of danger or the ability to weigh the chance of success against the hazards of pursuing an attack; spatial perception, defined as the ability to visualize complex relationships of relative motion; respect of colleagues, defined as a willing-

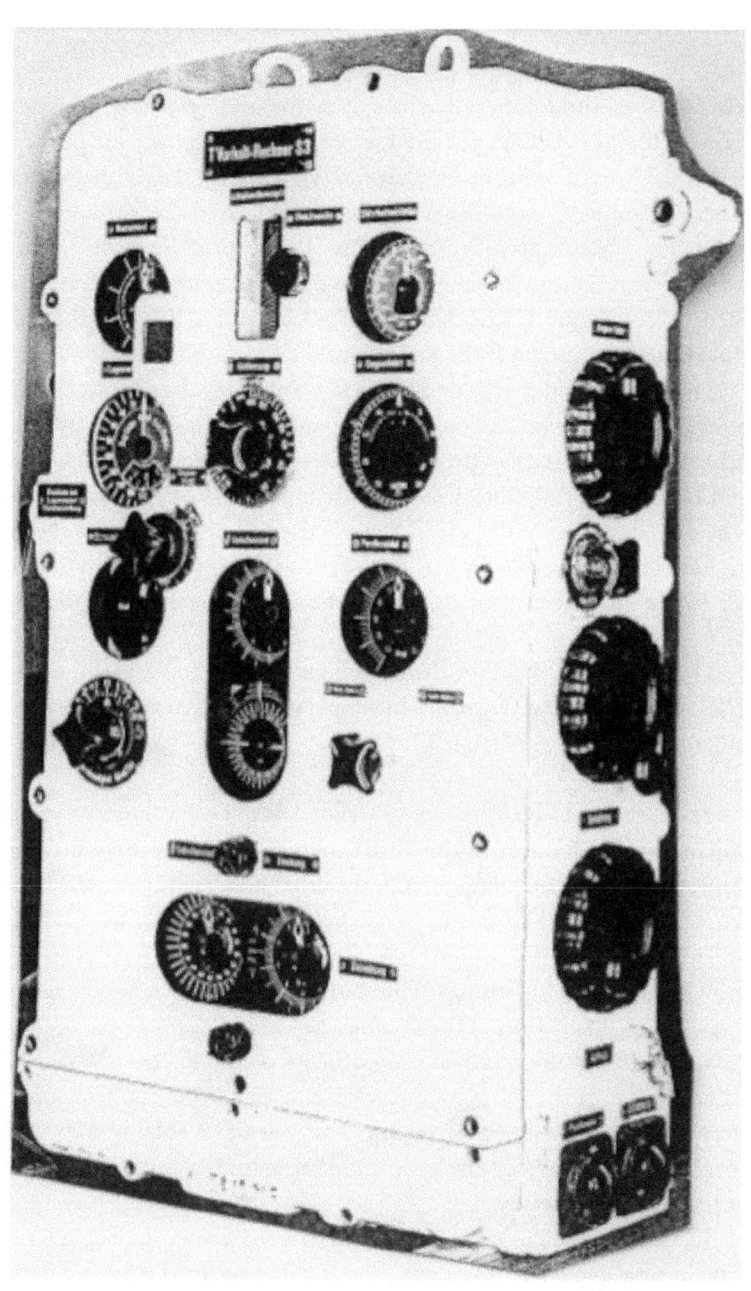

An oblique view of the T-Vorhalt Rechner torpedo fire control computer used on German U-boats during the Second World War (Submarine Research Center).

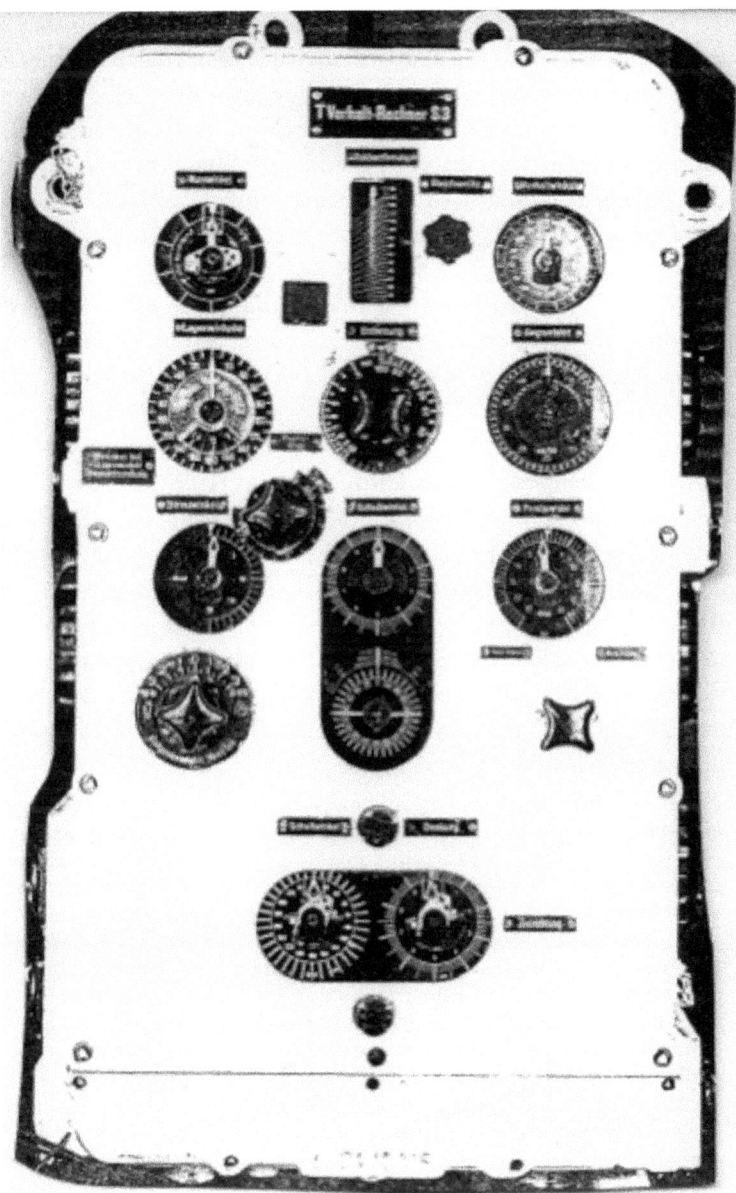

The T-Vorhalt Rechner G-3 was a static display that produced spread angles, but required the periscope to be on target at time of firing (Submarine Research Center).

ness to listen to the ideas of others and to assimilate them when they are of merit; trust, defined as the ability to demand competence in other fire control team members and to trust their abilities thereafter; self-confidence, defined as a trust in one's ability to conquer the obstacles presented when conducting an attack; patience, defined as a willingness to accept the tedium of lengthy end-around pursuits; and finally, a sense of humor, defined as a tendency to lighten the worst situation by seeing in it a bit of humor.

No one of these attributes was to be found alone in the successful commanding officer. Rather, the make-up of the successful commander was the contribution of several, or perhaps all, of these qualities that, in combination, were to produce the tactical competence of the successful commanding officer.

One such exemplary commanding officer was Slade Cutter, who commanded *Pompano* (SS-181), *Seahorse* (SS-304) and *Requin* (SS-481) during the Second World War. The story, as told by him, of his simultaneous qualification in submarines and qualification to command a submarine not only reveals his exceptional intelligence, but his freewheeling spirit as well.

Slade Cutter, a lieutenant junior grade in 1941, described one of his practice approaches under the instruction of then Lcdr. Lewis S. Parks, commanding officer of USS *Pompano* (SS-181). It was his qualifying exam and he described it in the following words:

> Parks made some arrangements to impress the division commander. He got an old destroyer, *Litchfield*, to act as target. It made 25 knots, zigzagging. And we were going to fire exercise torpedoes. Now, he also taught us how to—and not too many people could do this—solve problems in our heads. We never used what was called the "Is-Was," which was an instrument to get distance to the track, gyro angles, and things like that. It was like a slide rule, a circular slide rule. And then you also had the torpedo data computer. Also, you had the Banjo, which was the angle solver, which told you what angle to put on the torpedoes and so forth. We couldn't use that either. We could use nothing. We couldn't even use the stadimeter in the periscope. There were about eight horizontal lines etched in the lens of the periscope, about one-eighth inch apart. You knew that when a target with a masthead height of 100 feet subtended one of those spaces between the notches, the range was 8,000 yards, and if it subtended four of those spaces the range was 2,000 yards. You would have to extrapolate if it was more than 125 feet or less. We could use a plot to determine target course and speed. So we took our division commander (ComSubDiv 13), Commander Merrill Comstock, along to observe. He was familiar with modern fire control equipment. So we went out for a day of firing.

5—The Second World War

> There is a lot more I could tell you about it. For instance, we would not say, "Come to a certain course." See, a torpedo problem is all relative. You don't need true bearings, all you want to know is your bearing in relation to the target, the range, and the angle between the target axis and line of bearing. The plot will give you target course and speed. Parks said, "I don't want you to do anything except say, Make the tubes ready, and then, fire. You can say, Come right or left so many degrees by compass, but don't give a course."

Cutter and two other junior officers then fired several torpedoes, all getting hits.

He continued:

> And the division commander was sitting there, and he didn't know what the hell was going on. All he knew was that they [the destroyer] kept signaling hits every time we fired, but he didn't know how it happened.... Normally, you'd get qualified in submarines, and then a year later or so, you'd get qualified for command. But Parks was a showman, you see. He turned to the division commander while we're all right there and said, "Commodore, I think these officers are ready to be qualified for command, too, don't you?" And the division commander had to agree after our show. We were qualified for command the same day we qualified for submarines.[11]

Captain Cutter went on to become one of America's submarine legends of the Second World War.

A successful torpedo attack was a matter of getting the submarine to the right place at the right time. This was the approach phase of a torpedo attack and it could be long, tedious and draining of stamina. Those in the torpedo fire control party had to have great patience under conditions of stress. The following is taken from William J. Ruhe's account of *Crevalle*'s frustrating 1943 patrol:

> The USS *Crevalle* (SS-291) had conducted an exercise off the shore of Brisbane, Australia. She was under the command of Lcdr. H.G. Munson. Riding in *Crevalle* was Cdr. Chester Bruton, ComSubDiv 81, who didn't like what he saw in Munson's imitation of Mush Morton's style of fire control organization. Munson paced the conning tower as his executive officer, Frank Walker, manned the periscope. Walker hummed and sang softly as he did his job. The exercise torpedo passed under the practice target ship and the commander was forced to grant Munson the OK for *Crevalle*'s first war patrol.
> In October 1943 while operating in the South China Sea, *Crevalle* attacked a large merchant target. Munson fired all six forward torpedoes. Each one exploded prematurely. The captain turned and fired the four after tubes. They too detonated before hitting the target. The torpedo officer asked for permission to remove the influence exploder from all remain-

ing torpedoes. Munson refused, saying that he'd report the event to Admiral Christie. After all, it was Christie who had been responsible for the development of the exploder.[12]

Also in 1943 another U.S. submarine fired eleven Mark 14 torpedoes at *Tonan Maru*, a 19,000-ton whale factory ship. All were duds. When the skipper returned to Pearl Harbor and reported his experience to Rear Admiral Charles Lockwood, Commander, Submarines Pacific, there could be no mistake. The Mark 6 exploders didn't work. Prior to this time in the war, the Bureau of Ordnance rejected all claims of exploder failures, claiming poor marksmanship by submarine commanding officers. But competent submariners reported that only the contact exploder worked when the target angle-on-the-bow was off the beam. It seemed that glancing blows allowed the pistols to travel without bending. Of course, most skippers had long since instructed their torpedomen to disconnect the influence part of the exploder. They had also learned to correct the depth mechanism error by setting the running depth about six feet less than the index. By October of 1943 American submarines were sinking ships by taking things into their own hands. With on-board fixes and careful off-the-beam shots, the scores were improving.

Admiral Charles Lockwood then approved test firing of Mark 14 torpedoes against a cliff on the island of Maui. With absolute confirmation of the torpedo's poor design, the Bureau of Ordnance conducted its own tests and at that late date in the war declared the problems rested solely with the Bureau. Bureau Chief Admiral Blandy wrote, "Even with the relatively meager funds available in time of peace, much of the work now being done after more than a year and a half of war, could and should have been accomplished years ago.... I therefore direct that as a matter of permanent policy no service torpedo device ever be adopted as standard until it has been tested under conditions simulating as nearly as possible those which will be encountered in battle."[13]

On another patrol *Crevalle* was running on two engines while the other two were devoted to the battery charge. It was the night of November 18, 1943. Every ten minutes its surface search SJ radar made one sweep on the 20,000-yard scale. At 2005, just after the evening meal had been served to the relieving watch, the oncoming officer of the deck was informed that radar had a contact at 16,000 yards off the port beam. The captain was called to the bridge, where he peered into the blackness on the bearing

5—The Second World War

indicated. He could see nothing, so he descended to the conning tower. Radar made another single bearing five-second sweep of ten degrees and again picked up the target. The captain saw that he had two targets, one large and one small, probably the escort. Bearing of the target was 262, drawing right. The captain increased speed to flank on four main engines, dropping the charge. *Crevalle*'s speed increased to 20.5 knots. Battle stations torpedo was called on the 1MC and the quartermaster at the DRT plot in control began a geographical presentation by lining in the course of the submarine. The initial TDC set-up was own ship's course at 350 and target ship's course also at 350, range 16,000 yards by radar. After ten minutes the captain ordered another radar five-second, on-bearing sweep. The bearing drift had stopped and had begun to slowly drift left, but it was hardly detectable. Calculation showed a speed deference of only 1.5 knots. It was apparent to all in the conning tower and in control that this was going to be a long night. The captain ordered the helm to come left to course 340 to approximate the best course to intercept.

A submarine captain in such a situation examined several conflicting options. If he continued the chase he would subject his engines to a prolonged ordeal at maximum power. At the least, their reliability would be harmed. If a bearing overheated it might reduce his boat's fighting ability to three engines. Crew fatigue could not be ignored. Submariners were eager to perform at their best, but long hours at battle stations eroded their judgment. On the other hand, if the target were of significance, such considerations might be worth it. The situation pivoted on the value of the target. With an escort, it was a probability that the Japanese ship was carrying needed supplies to the home islands. The captain elected to press on.

At 2200 the range had closed to 10,000 yards and the target still had a bearing on *Crevalle*'s port beam. At this range sonar confirmed by turn count the target speed of 19 knots. A fleet type submarine's maximum speed was slightly less than 19 knots. Both radar and sonar thought the target was a very large ship with a single escort.

At 0200 the range had dropped to 4,000 yards with the Japanese ships still on the port beam. Another two hours went by. In the conning tower the men stretched their legs and worked their shoulder muscles. In control, whispers of a few at the DRT could be heard. On the bridge the captain told the port lookout to keep a good horizon sweep and not to concentrate too much on the target bearing. At 0041 the first glimmer of daylight began to appear in the eastern sky. Radar made a quick "squirt" and reported the target at 1500 yards. It was time to set up for firing. The captain altered course slightly to the left, gave the order to the torpedo room to open the outer doors and ordered the periscope raised. He could just see the ships' hulls and so reported the final bearing of the target. The bearing was entered into the TDC and the quartermaster pressed the firing button.

The torpedoes left the submarine running hot, straight and normal. Then the sky lit up, flames and debris shot into the air and the target's whistle blew in short blasts. The destroyer escort swung toward the submarine and the captain dove the *Crevalle* to avoid depth charges.[14]

It had taken just over eight hours to close the target.

Another example of how an aggressive captain with an expert tracking team can deftly manipulate his submarine was provided by USS *Trigger*'s Dusty Dornin.

On January 31, 1944, Cdr. Dornin, commanding officer of USS *Trigger* (SS-237), spotted a convoy. On the surface, Dornin remained on the bridge while his executive officer, Ned Beach, was in the conning tower, coordinating plot and TDC inputs from radar and the TBT on the bridge. Dornin intended to fire six torpedoes, three at an escorting destroyer and three at a merchant ship beyond. He would use the TBT for inputs on the destroyer and radar inputs on the merchant vessel. The three Mark 14 torpedoes shot at the destroyer spun off wildly, giving away *Trigger*'s position. The destroyer veered toward to attack *Trigger*. Dornin dove the boat while turning to bring his stern tubes to bear. He fired all four stern tubes shortly thereafter. While missing the destroyer, one torpedo from the first salvo hit another escort, which blew up and sank in minutes. Upon returning to Pearl Harbor he discovered that he had also sunk the 12,000-ton *Yasukuni Maru*, a submarine tender. This action illustrated what could be done by aggressive and competent fire control teams in the face of undependable torpedoes.[15]

The foregoing two examples of how tactical competency resulted in high-tonnage sinkings must be viewed from the perspective of the few who rose to greatness from a peacetime standard of punctual paperwork. In December of 1941, the test of battle had yet to weed out the many mediocre peacetime officers.

America entered the Second World War with submarine commanding officers judged to be of approximately equal merit. These officers who took their boats to sea during 1942 and early 1943 were responsible to their respective division commanders, squadron commanders and eventually to Commander Submarines Pacific. Admirals Fife and Christie, based in Australia, reviewed the recommendations of squadron commanders. Some submarines returned to their bases in Freemantle and Brisbane without having scored a single sinking. Others came home with Japanese ships claimed to have been sunk or damaged. A few returned to Pearl Harbor and Midway with brooms hanging from their periscopes, signifying a clean sweep. Those captains that were scoreless blamed faulty torpedoes and bad luck. There was a certain truth to these claims, and unsuccessful captains were given second chances when judged by their superiors to have been victims of circumstances. In many cases, however, it became clear that certain boats had poor morale brought about from commanding officers who failed to press home attacks in the face of obvious danger. Most of all, fear and timidity were the hallmarks of the commanding officers heading for a quiet desk in Washington, D.C.

On the other hand, commanding officers began to emerge from the rank and file as having qualities of leadership and brilliance that placed them above the average. There were Dudley "Mush" Morton in *Wahoo* (SS-238), Richard O'Kane in *Tang* (SS-306), Slade Cutter in *Seahorse* (SS-304), Eugene B. Fluckey in *Barb* (SS-220), Sam Dealey in *Harder* (SS-257), George Grider in *Flasher* (SS-249), William B. "Barney" Sieglaff in *Tautog* (SS-199), Lucien Chappell in *Sculpin* (SS-191), Roy Benson and Robert "Dusty" Dornin in *Trigger* (SS-237), to name only a few.

It is appropriate to reiterate the qualities that propelled these captains from the rank and file to the status of legends in the American submarine force. The more prominent qualities were those of patience, willingness to admit mistakes, eagerness to learn from mistakes, listening to the criticism of others, learning from those who had experimented with innovative fire control techniques, an ability to visualize a complex problem involving spatial relationships, a trust in subordinate officers and petty officers to provide reliable information, an aggressive spirit that balanced probability of success against the hazards involved, and strangely enough, a sense of humor that broke the monotony of long pursuits and the tedium of standing at battle stations for prolonged periods. The strength of American submarine torpedo attack success lay not in its weapons, but in its officers and men. Fire control teams took every opportunity to sharpen their skills, and these skills were soon to be enhanced by dramatic advances in radar and sonar applications to submarines. Electronic research prior to the Second World War had made significant progress in the development of sonar, radar and the detection of radar impulses (ECM). In the first two war years, research and production of electronic equipment for submarines was accelerated.

The development of submarine radar (acronym for radio detection and ranging) lagged behind that of sonar, but by the start of the Second World War, radar was projected to be installed in new-construction submarines as an integral part of the submarine fire control system. Both radar and sonar equipment were to be directly linked to the TDC, giving the American submarine a huge advantage over Japanese information acquisition and control.

The United States Navy had a longstanding interest in the potential of radar. In the 1930s the U.S. Naval Research Laboratory in Washington, D.C., conducted studies of high-frequency radio wave propagation, and while it could produce a return echo, it was of little value since bearing and range of the echo remained a mystery. By emitting radio waves in pulsed sequence and encoding the return waves to be seen on an oscilloscope, an operator could adjust the antenna's direction and thereby obtain a bearing. Approximate range could be determined by the height of the spike on the oscilloscope. This was a remarkable achievement in itself, and was the status of radar at the beginning of the Second World War.

The Massachusetts Institute of Technology's Radiation Laboratory spearheaded advances in radar and maximized its effort by tapping the cooperative spirit of British scientists who were in the van of innovation. The British supplied the scientists at MIT with their magnetron, which was the principle high-frequency method of focusing radio waves. Immediately after the bombing of Pearl Harbor, MIT sent recruiting scientists to American commercial broadcast stations and privately owned electronic firms. Those radio engineers identified as innovatively gifted were given contracts to join the laboratory. These men quickly moved to Cambridge and went to work to develop radar systems for surface ships, submarines and aircraft.[16]

The first production submarine radar useful to fire control was the SJ surface search equipment, which became an integral part of the conning tower arrangement starting in 1944. A few submarines prior to that date had SJ radar and its use allowed night surface attacks. For example, *Haddock*

(SS-231) detected a target at 13,000 yards on her SJ radar, set its bearing and range inputs into the TDC and fired at 1,300 yards with a perfect approach. On this moonless night the target was never seen, but the torpedo ran true and the merchant ship was sunk.

During the summer of 1942 the SJ radar was dramatically improved by the addition of a plan position indicator, or PPI scope.[17] By war's end the fleet type submarine had a PPI in the conning tower. This gave a relative geographic picture of the submarine at the center of the scope with the target appearing as a flare when the turning antenna scanned across it. The difficulty of obtaining range information was overcome by mounting a stub antenna on the search periscope. A single ping while remaining at periscope depth was transmitted directly to the TDC. With this presentation, the operator could adjust the appropriate range scale up to 20,000 yards, track the target's bearing and bearing drift, holding the submarine as the center of the 360-degree sweeping impulse. Accurate information for both bearing and range was fed into the TDC and the solution was generated and sent to the angle solver. It only remained for the captain to bring his boat into firing position, determine the spread, open the outer doors and fire the torpedoes electrically from the conning tower.

SJ radar inputs were directly transmitted into the TDC, Mark 4, Mod 3. While the limited height of a submarine prevented acquisition of targets farther than five nautical miles, it could pick up an aircraft at similar ranges.[18] In 1942 submarine radar included an SS improvement which superseded the SJ model. The SS radar had the capability of SJ fire control, but could detect aircraft at up to twelve miles. The PPI scope was improved to include an expanded section which gave greater resolution of an area of particular interest. With periscope-mounted radar, a single bearing radiation in a spurt could be aligned to the bearing of the periscope image. The problem of quickly gaining an accurate range was solved, without the submarine having to surface.

The Japanese found a way to detect the radar emissions and use their bearings to send ASW craft along its beam, but the short burst emission on a single bearing of the ST periscope radar evaded the electronic search of the Japanese.[19] Radar became such an integral part of fire control that captains often preferred to make night attacks on the surface when total darkness prevented a visual contact. Many successful attacks were made using only information from sonar and radar inputs to the TDC. The

Crevalle patrol of November 1943 described above was an example of a radar-only surface attack.

At the same time, American submarines were often provided with electronic information gathering equipment in the form of the APR-1 receiver and APR-6 analyzer. This first-of-a-kind electronic surveillance was applied, for the most part, to Japanese shore installations, but was destined to form the backbone of the basic submarine mission of the Cold War.

The status of submarine sonar equipment at the beginning of the Second World War was the WCA, which operated on 18 to 24 kHz. This sonar was a combination passive hydrophone listening array and an active transducer. Since submariners were disinclined to use active sonar, research centered on improving the listening acuity of hydrophones. The JP sonar, which covered 70 Hz to 12 kHz, replaced the WCA and became the standard submarine sonar during the bulk of the war years. JP sonar information proved to be so valuable to target acquisition and torpedo fire control that captains relied on their sonar operators for accurate target bearing change rates and target speed estimates through turn-count frequency. Late in the war the JP stacks were augmented by JT sonar, which was a horizontal series of small hydrophones mounted on a trainable "T" pivot mounted on deck. When each of the hydrophones signaled the same amplitude by training the array, an accurate bearing of a target could be transmitted to the TDC. The JT sonar was used on American submarines well after the close of the Second World War.[20]

A distant relative of active sonar, the fathometer, was used for detecting the sea's bottom. The depth beneath the submarine's keel could be found by a low-powered beam pointed downward.

Another critical instrument that was not related to sonar was the bathythermograph, which registered temperature and salinity of the water as the boat passed through it. This instrument was the product of the Woods Hole experimental station on Cape Cod, Massachusetts, as an adjunct of MIT's Radiation Laboratory. Water temperature tends to be higher at shallow depths, and as the intensity of the sun's rays decreases with depth, the BT's graph shows this change. If the decrease is constant the water is referred to as isothermal, and inversion layers, or positive gradients (a sandwich of higher temperature water within colder ambient water), offered an opportunity for evasion. Active sonar beams directed downward from a surface craft tend to bounce off these layers, and a sub-

5—The Second World War

marine could hide from the probing pings of ASW surface craft by finding a layer on the BT and descending beneath it. The BT was located in the control room at the diving officer's station. The instrument's value lies in a graphic presentation which, during the Second World War, was a needle that etched temperatures and salinities on a depth-indicating, turning drum. The BT was of critical importance to a captain making an approach, because once a torpedo had been fired, the submarine typically took evasive action on the assumption that it would miss, but would give the target escort a good idea of the submarine's position.[21]

The fleet-type submarine underwent several modifications to its conning tower, both before the war and during the war. During approaches it was always a crowded and often stifling compartment crammed with equipment and fire control personnel. In the compartment's middle were the search periscope and the attack periscope, both of which swung in a three-foot arc so that the two periscopes, both of which would normally be used sequentially in an attack, occupied a great deal of space. At the forward end of the conning tower was the helm with compass repeater, motor order telegraphs and a compass course clock for sinuous zigzagging. On the starboard side immediately behind the helm was the access hatch to the bridge, and on the port side, about the same size, was the hatch leading to the control room. This hatch had a guardrail to prevent personnel from falling down the ladder. At the opposite end was a small table which housed the DRT. This was the geographical plot that was manned by a quartermaster under the direction of an officer. The TDC was on the aft port side of the compartment, and forward of that was the torpedo tube switching and indicator panel, above which was the red firing button. Opposite the TDC on the starboard side was the radar equipment with PPI scope, and forward of that was the SJ or JT sonar equipment, just aft of the bridge access hatch. Into this equipment-crowded space during an approach went the captain, the executive officer, the TDC operator, the plot officer, the assistant TDC operator, the quartermaster and the helmsman. It was a rather silent space with only the humming of equipment cooling motors and air conditioning, and the hydraulic squishing sound of periscopes going up and down. Voices were not whispers, but they were soft, both in response to the lack of need for any greater modulation and to maintain an atmosphere of calm. In this tiny space the fire control problem was solved, the success of the mission was determined, and the destinies of many Japanese sailors was defined.

Submarine Torpedo Tactics

In December 1944, George W. Grider commanded the USS *Flasher* (SS-249) in the South China Sea. This was a singularly successful patrol when Japanese merchant shipping was scarce, always in convoy and well protected. Grider had a smooth operating approach team and was typical of fire control organization of the day. It was described by then Lt. Tom McCants. He listed the various functions of the tracking party as follows:

> Phil Gleason, the executive officer, acted as safety officer in the conning tower's fire control party. I was the torpedo data computer operator with Ensign Eddie Atkinson acting as assistant TDC operator. Lt. Kiko Harrison stood behind me at the TDC, observing the solution. Lt. Snap Coffin was the engineer and diving officer during battle stations torpedo. Lt. Jim Hamlin headed the fire control plotting party which ran a geographical plot of submarine and target course and speed. The quartermaster kept a log of unfolding events. He tended the periscope's stadimeter and bearing ring when Glennon was otherwise occupied. At the opposite end of the conning tower was the battle stations helmsman who minded course and transmitted speed changes to maneuvering. The radar/sonar operator tried to take up as little space as possible in the Gato class conning tower. Of course, the captain was at the periscope during submerged approaches and the TBT (target bearing transmitter) on the bridge when making a surface approach.[22]

To gain a real understanding of what it was like to witness heroism in the making, it is necessary to read the actual patrol reports of commanding officers who were awarded the nation's highest medals including the Medal of Honor. Each of these men personally wrote his respective patrol report using the quartermaster's log and their memory of the events. Since each report was written shortly after each action, such reports in their original form represent the most reliable, firsthand account available to historians. Presented here are the patrol reports of Dudley "Mush" Morton of *Wahoo* (SS-238) and Eugene B. Fluckey of *Barb* (SS-220) as they were written shortly after the events described. The two patrol reports are different in that one describes an action that was undertaken with almost no prior information of the harbor to be reconnoitered, and the other details the required careful analysis of the hazards involved in entering a heavily protected harbor.

Wahoo was preparing to enter Wewak Harbor, a deep harbor on the north shore of New Guinea. Morton's problem lay in the lack of information and charts about the area to be examined. Machinist Mate Dalton Keeter had purchased a tour book of the Southwest Pacific when he had been on leave in Brisbane. It served to provide only the most meager basis for navigation into a harbor of which nothing was known to American intelligence. The excerpted portion of the after action patrol report describes *Wahoo* after it had negotiated its way deep into Wewak Harbor. The boat was running submerged, using its periscope to identify the ships at anchor.

January 25, 1943

1429—It was our intention to fire high-speed shots from about 3000 yards which would permit us to remain in deep water and facilitate an exit. However, on the next observation, when the generated range was 3,750, our target, a Fubuki class destroyer was underway. Angle-on-the-bow, 10 port, range 3,100 yards. Nothing else was in sight. Maneuvered for a stern tube shot, but on next observation target had zigged left giving us a bow set-up.

1441—Fired spread of three torpedoes on 110° starboard track, range 1800 yards, using a target speed of 15 knots since there had been insufficient time to determine speed by tracking. Observed torpedoes going aft as sound indicated a target speed of 18 knots, so fired another fish with enemy's speed 20 knots. Destroyer avoided by turning away, then circled to the right and headed for us. Watched him come with our bow pointed at him. Delayed firing our fifth torpedo until the destroyer had closed to about 1,200 yards, angle-on-the-bow, 10° starboard. Then, to insure maximum likelihood of hitting with our last torpedo in the foreword tubes, withheld fire until range was about 800 yards.

1449—This last one, fired at 1449, clipped him amidships in 25 seconds and broke his back. The explosion was terrific! The top side was covered with Japs on turret tops and in the rigging. Over 100 members of the crew must have been acting as lookouts. We took several pictures, and as her bow was settling fast, we went to 150 feet and commenced the 9 mile trip out of Wewak. Heard her boilers go in between the noise of continuous shelling from somewhere plus a couple of serial bombs. They were evidently trying to make us lie on the bottom until their patrol boats could return. No difficulty was experienced in piloting without observation out of Wewak using sound bearings of beach noises on reefs and beaches. With the aid of a one knot set we surfaced at 1930 well clear of Kairiru and Valif Islands.

Cleared area on four engines for 30 minutes on course 000° true. Huge fires were visible in Wewak harbor. We wondered if they had purposely created these fires to silhouette us in case we tried to escape out of the harbor. Slowed to one engine speed at 2000 to cross the enemy convoy route from Palau to Wewak.

January 26, 1943

0757—Sighted smoke on the horizon, swung ship toward and commenced surface tracking. Adjusted course and speed to get ahead of the enemy. After three quarters of an hour and when we had obtained a favorable position with masts of two ships just coming over the horizon, dived and commenced submerged approach. Two freighters were tracked at 10 knots on a steady course of 095° true, which was somewhat puzzling as it led neither to nor from a known port. Determined that the best firing position would be 1,300 yards on the beam of the lead ship. This would permit firing with about 15° right gyro angle on approximately a 105° track on the lead ship, and with about 30° left gyro angle and 60° track on the second ship, 1,000 yards astern in column.

1030—However, found we were too close to the track for this two ship shot so reversed course to the right and obtained an identical set-up for a stern tube shot.

1041—Fired two torpedoes at the lead ship and 17 seconds later, two at the second freighter. The first two torpedoes hit their points of aim in bow and stern. There was insufficient time allowed for the gyro setting angle indicator and regulator to catch up with the new set-up cranked into the TDC for the third shot. This torpedo passed ahead of the second target. The fourth torpedo hit him. Swung left to bring bow tubes to bear in case these ships did not sink.

1045—Took sweep around to keep the set-up at hand and observed three ships close about us. Our first target had listed badly to starboard and was sinking by the stern, our second was heading directly for us, but at slow speed and the third was a huge transport, which had evidently been beyond and behind our second target.

1047—When the transport presented a 90° starboard angle-on-the-bow at 1,800 yards range, fired spread of three torpedoes from the forward tubes. The second and third torpedoes hit and stopped him. We then turned our attention to the second target, which was last observed heading for us. He was still coming, yawing somewhat, and quite close. Fired two torpedoes down his throat to stop him. The second torpedo hit, but he kept coming and forced us to turn hard left, duck and go ahead at full speed to avoid. There followed so many explosions that it was impossible to tell just what was taking place. Eight minutes later came back to periscope depth, after reaching 80 feet, to observe that our first target had sunk, our second target still going, but slowly and with evident steering trouble, and the transport stopped. Headed for transport and then maneuvered for a killer shot.

1133—Fired a bow torpedo at 1,000 yards range, 85° port track, target stopped. The transport was firing continuously at the periscope and torpedo wake with deck guns and rifles.

1135—Fired a second torpedo with the same set-up except that the transport had moved ahead a little and turned towards us, presenting a 65° angle-on-the-bow. The torpedo wake headed right for his stack. The explosion blew her amidships section higher than a kite. Troops commenced jumping over the side like ants off a hot plate. Her stern went up and she headed for the bottom.[23]

Unlike *Wahoo*'s entry into Wewak's deep harbor, which gave the boat a submerged exit riding the ebb tide, and Morton's subsequent attack against Japanese shipping, *Barb*'s commanding officer, Eugene B. Fluckey,

5—The Second World War

faced a difficult decision of entering a shallow harbor that would necessitate remaining on the surface for the entire attack. Fluckey's analysis of the hazards involved was exceptional. The *Barb* was running on the surface at night in the midst of numerous Chinese junks. It was the night of January 21, 1945.

> 2200—There are many junks in our area as we seek a convoy heading north but keeping close to the China coast. Seas are continually state 5 to 7. Our prospects appear poor, unless we can find a suitable opportunity at night so we can resort to torpedo boat tactics. Basing the remainder of our patrol on the latter assumption, made a complete study of the China coast from Wenchow south to Lam Yit. Recent unknown mining has taken place north of Wenchow. If our assumptions are correct, the present convoy, for which we are searching is anchored at Foochow tonight and will be en route to Wenchow tomorrow. To substantiate our conclusions, plan to mingle with the junk fleet to the east of Wenchow tomorrow afternoon at a point 10 miles inside the 20 fathom curve and 15 miles from the coast where we can observe the passage of our convoy.
>
> January 22, 1945
> 0656—Surface patrolling, searching for convoy in accordance with plan. Seas have abated to state three. Skies are overcast. Have decided not to sink the drifting mines for they may possibly damage Jap traffic.
> 1203—Maneuvering among junk fleet. Passed 20 fathom curve.
> 1421—Ship contact. Sighted smoke of 3 to 6 ships moving in column along the coast. Closed to 18,000 yards for accurate tracking and to determine types. Two ships are large cargo ships. Lost sight of others shortly. Their course is 225, speed 10 knots, their position, in 3 fathoms, several miles inside the 10 fathom curve. At 10 knots they could not make Samsa Inlet before 2100. If the overcast remains heavy enough to hide the moon, we can tackle them in Siaoan Channel just north of Samsa Inlet. Sent contact report to *Picuda*.
> 1512—Secured tracking. SJ radar lost target at 28,000 yards. Still within junk fleet, outside of island visibility range.
> 1820—It is now dark. Commenced approach to coast.
> 1900—Past edge of junk fleet. Approaching 10 fathom curve. Sorry to clear the junks even though they provide an obstacle race, for we depend upon their routes to keep us clear of minefields.
> 1915—Quartermaster tugged at my sleeve and confidentially said, "Don't look now, but we just passed a floating mine 10 yards off our beam to port."
> 1926—Picked up a junk, 6,000 yards ahead. Joined him in 9 fathoms and commenced patrolling to seaward on his quarter, using him as a minesweeper.
> 2100—Still no coast lights burning and no ships. Requested *Picuda* to patrol off island in event ships had departed coast. Also informed her that convoy had not passed our position.

2120—Have now covered route of convoy, but no contacts. Estimate its speed at 13 knots, so it must have turned west into a harbor. Ships must have anchored. Decided to search coast. Lack of junks between coast and Piseang Islands may indicate a mine field. Instead of going directly up coast we will ease out around Piseang Islands and close coast north of them.

2326—Closing coast escorted by junk fleet, all constant helming. Visibility is lowering. Cannot see junks outside of 1,000 yards. Conning by a PPI.

January 23, 1945

0015—Conducting inshore surface search for convoy anchorage. Maneuvering constantly to avoid collision with junks. Present entourage consists of several hundred darkened junks.

0030—Commenced taking PPI coast contour plots, for plexiglass matching with large scale chart of coast, to search for ships.

0112—Chart plot matching showed an uncharted smear northwest of Incog Light. Checked this on A-scope which showed saturation pips at 29,800 yards. Radar officer and operator said they were definite ships. Doubt existed, however, for our radar as never before had saturation pips on so many ships at such a range. Continuing search up coast toward Incog Light.

0137—Moon set.

0240—Cleared junks. None ahead. Much prefer to have them, or know the reason for their absence.

0300—Rounded Incog Islands and had radar contact on a very large group of anchored ships in the lower reaches of Namkwan Harbor. Slowed to take stock of the situation. Fully realize our critical position and the potential dangers involved. Estimate the situation as follows:

Recent unknown mining in this vicinity is a known fact. Mines could be laid, however, a more effective minefield would be farther to the south at the eastern entrance to the harbor, which would provide a protected anchorage behind it. Since the position of the anchored convoys is too close to this line, assume the latter minefield does not exist. The former though doubtful, must remain a possibility, particularly in view of the absence of junks.

Jap radar interference is showing up on the A-scope and PPI sweeping. One escort appears to be patrolling several thousand yards north east and a second escort to the east of the anchored ships covering the most logical position for entry and attack. A third escort is working close to Incog Light apparently more concerned with using his radar to keep himself off the rocks. Visibility is very poor.

Assume the closely anchored columns would be heading about 050° true heading into the wind and seas with a current of one knot. Plotted the navigational position from which we would attack, making our approach from the southeast. The attack would be made on approximately a 60° track so that our stern tubes would be fired with zero gyros on our selected retirement course.

Elected to retire through an area marked "unexplored" and "rocks," position doubtful to make any overly-ambitious escorts think twice before risking a chase. This course would also cross the mass of junks, which would be a definite and final barrier to our pursuit. While retiring. radar will only be used sweeping quickly from broad on our port bow to broad on the other.

Counter-measures expected will be searchlights, gunfire, and hot pursuit. Against this we will have a stern tube salvo, 40 mm and automatic weapons.

In as much as our attack position will be 6 miles inside the 10 fathom curve and 19 miles inside the 20 fathom curve, we will require an hour run before being forced down. Consequently our attack must be a complete surprise and the force of our attack must be sufficient to completely throw the enemy off balance. We have four torpedoes forward and eight aft. No time will be available for a reload, but a speedy, darting, knife-thrust attack will increase the probability of success.

0320—Figure the odds are 10 to 1 in our favor. Manned battle stations torpedo.

0325—Fortunately we have a flexible fire control party and at this point we flexed it. Commanding officer secured the bridge and took over the conning tower; target plot was secured and the assistant approach officer was shifted to navigational plot; plotting officer was shifted to PPI; and another officer was shifted to the bridge. Seriously considering placing crew in lifejackets, but the atmosphere throughout the boat is electric. The men are more tense than I've ever seen them. Save for an occasional report of "Single ping sounding, 6 fathoms," the control room is so quiet the proverbial pin would have sounded like a depth charge. Discarded the idea of lifejackets as definitely alarmist, with so many hearts doing flip-flops. Do not consider it advisable in our present precarious position to send a contact report to the *Picuda*. She could not possibly attack before dawn and get out. Will send one after the attack when our presence is known.

0352—Range 6,000 yards. Made ready all tubes. Ships are anchored in three columns about 500 yards apart with a few scattered ships farther inshore. This, frankly, must be the most beautiful target of the war. Actual measurement of target column length is about 4,200 yards. Ships are banked three deep. Even an erratic torpedo can't mess. Radar officer counts 12 ships on one bearing. Estimate at least 30 ships present. Our biggest job will be to prevent too many torpedoes from hitting one ship. For purposes of set-up, chose one of the large ships to left of center of the nearest column as target. Using TBT bearings.

0402—Fired tubes one, two, three, and four with 150 percent spread, track 65 starboard, gyros 30 left, torpedo run 3,225 yards, depth set at 6 feet, target speed 1½ knots to counter current, target course 040° true. Right full rudder, all ahead standard. Sounding 5 fathoms. Shifted target to right for ships ahead in near column.

0404—Fired tubes 7,8, 9 and 10 with 300 percent spread, track 65 starboard, gyros 3 right, range 3,020 yards, depth set 6 feet. All ahead flank! Commanding Officer manning the bridge.

0409—All torpedoes fired hit targets. Main target was a large cargo ship in first column hit by torpedoes numbers two and three. Target observed to settle and to sink. Unidentified ship in second column was hit by torpedo number one. This was not observed since the ship was shielded by main target after turning to right and other large cargo ship in third column was hit by torpedo number four, then shortly thereafter caught fire. Fire later flared up, then flickered out similar to a sinking ship. Torpedo number six hit in the first column, believed to have hit in main target or ship in second column. Ship in second column hit by torpedo number five. The whole side of this ship blew out in our direction in a manner similar of an oiler or the magazine of a large warship. This ship sank. A large auxiliary ship in the third column was hit by torpedo number seven. Ship blew up with a tremendous explosion and sank. Tracers of all descriptions flew out from the two ships which exploded. At the same time several large caliber projectiles, estimated 6 to 12 inch, with tracers hurtled through the air. A moment after this, searchlights were soon sweeping about for a short while.

0413—Smoke from the ships hit, on fire, and exploding completely obscured all ships and prevented any further observation of other damage. The *Barb* is now high-balling it for the 20 fathom curve at 21.6 knots. Broken field running through the junk fleet, with the radar sweeping rapidly 30° either side of the bow, wildly maneuvering when some of the junks are inside radar's sea return. Expect to see a junk piled up on the bow at any second.

0436—Gunfire from well astern. Some poor junks getting it.

0438—Some form of navigational light on Tae island. Probably to aid the escorts navigation.

0511—The Galloping Ghost of the China Coast crossed the 20 fathom curve with a sigh. Never realized how much water that was before. However life begins at 40 fathoms! Kept going.

0512—Slowed to 19 knots.

0550—Dawn. Assume the Japs will expect us to submerge, so we will stay on the surface.

1220—Retiring to the east.

The above described action was one of the most remarkable of the Second World War, and Fluckey was awarded the Medal of Honor with *Barb*'s crew getting a Presidential Unit Citation.[24]

Not all of the action resulted in submarine captains attaining fame and postwar recognition. Mush Morton went down with *Wahoo*'s crew near La Perouse Strait, and Richard O'Kane spent three years in a Japanese prison camp when *Tang* was the victim of an erratic torpedo.

Although by 1944 the exploder problems of the Mark 14 torpedo had been corrected, the gyro-driven course-keeping mechanism was less than one hundred percent reliable. Stuck rudders and linkages occasionally caused a torpedo to leave the tube and to continue turning while seeking its course. One such instance was the tragic loss of the USS *Tang* (SS-306).

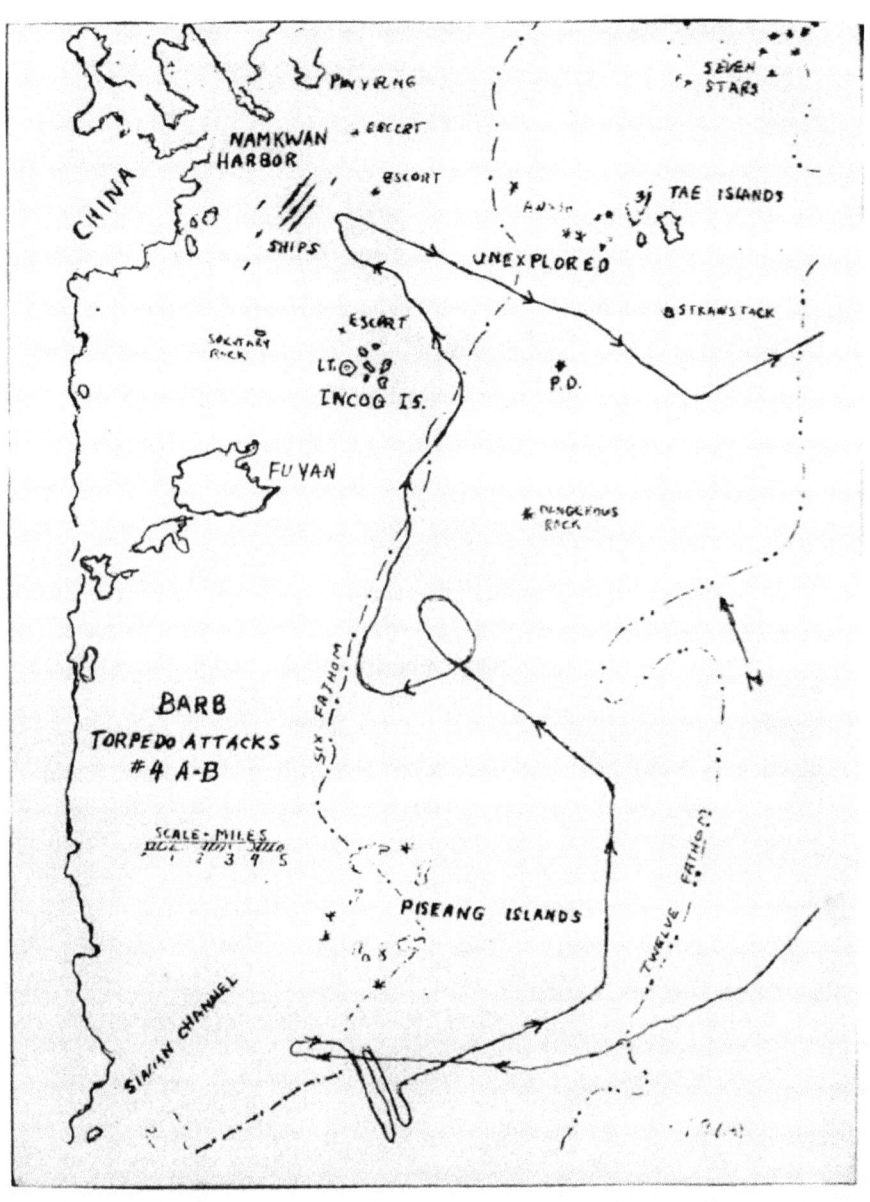

Gene Fluckey drew a sketch of his daring attack on Japanese shipping anchored in a seemingly impenetrable harbor (National Archives).

Submarine Torpedo Tactics

Alex Kershaw described the October 25, 1944, sinking of USS *Tang*. Lieutenant Commander Richard O'Kane was in command during its last attack on the surface in broad daylight:

> There was a massive explosion as number 23 torpedo hit its target, sending flames and debris shooting into the sky and quickly sinking the 6,957 ton *Ebaru Maru*, officially the twenty-fourth victim during O'Kane's eighteen months in command of *Tang*. On the bridge, Bill Leibold scanned the waters with his binoculars. He stood next to O'Kane. Suddenly, he saw the first torpedo, number 24, broach and then begin to porpoise, phosphorescence trailing behind it. A few seconds later, it made a sharp turn to port and then, unbelievably, began to come about.
> "There goes that one! Erratic!" shouted O'Kane.
> The last torpedo was now heading like a boomerang back to its firing point ... back toward the *Tang*. Something had gone terribly wrong. Perhaps its rudder had jammed or the gyroscope in the steering engine had malfunctioned.[25]

Tang was hit in the port side of the maneuvering room. The boat sank by the stern. All but a few perished, but Richard O'Kane and a few of those on the bridge and in the conning tower managed to be rescued by the Japanese destroyer. The story of their incarceration is one of extreme cruelty.

The memory of great American submarine skippers of the Second World War is kept alive by the geographical landmarks found on each submarine base. There are Dealey Center and Gilmore Hall, now an administration building, in the submarine school at New London. Streets on the submarine base at Bangor, Washington, are named after the famous boats of the Second World War and Cold War. The south gate is approached from Trigger Avenue.

The critical nature of the TDC during the Second World War can be appreciated from the following 1944 testimony of George Grider, captain of USS *Flasher* (SS-249):

> When two days later the TDC failed, Firecontrolman Joe Webb pronounced it dead on arrival. Chief Cypheard held the little follow-up motor in his hand when he told *Flasher*'s commanding officer that the boat had no replacement. Not giving up, *Flasher*'s captain sent a message through ComSubRon 18 riding on *Hawkbill* asking any boat heading for the barn to lend *Flasher* the crucial follow-up motor. In four hours the boat rendezvoused with *Hardhead* (SS-365) which high-lined a replacement part to *Flasher*. George Grider said he couldn't get that kind of service tied up alongside the tender.[26]

The question arises as to whether the United States Submarine Force could have accomplished what it did without its remarkable torpedo data computer. As important as the instrument was to the fire control problem, it was probably not as critical to success as one might think. Referring once again to the German success in the early years of the Second World War, it is reasonable to assume that a simpler device such as the T Vorhalt might have served to solve the spread problem and the brilliance of American submarine fire control personnel could have solved the problem of relative motion. The TDC was certainly a huge factor in what American submarines accomplished, but it was only one of the many superlatives that gave the American submarine its dominance over Japanese efforts to stop the attrition of its merchant fleet.

The facts are undeniable. About one-third of all Japanese merchant ships contacted were attacked and about three-fourths of these were hit. Two-thirds of all ships hit were sunk. Japanese warships evaded American submarines by maintaining high speeds on zigzag courses. Despite this, seventeen percent of those sighted were attacked, sixty-six percent of these were hit and thirty-five percent of those hit were sunk.[27]

Fifty-two American submarines were sunk in the Second World War with a loss of over 3,131 crewmen and 375 officers. But the submarine force played a major role in the interdiction of supplies flowing to Japan. Of the 122,000 Japanese merchant sailors who began the war, about 116,000 were lost. Of these, about 16,200 killed and 53,400 wounded were the victims of American submarines. The U.S. submarine force during the Second World War consisted of about 50,000 officers and men or 1.6 percent of the total navy complement. So it was that a force of 2 percent of the total U.S. naval strength accounted for 55 percent of Japan's maritime losses. The Second World War was a war of attrition and Japan's isolation put it into the hands of aggressive American submarine personnel.[28]

6

The Era of the GUPPY

The Second World War had ended, and on the following March 6, 1946, Winston Churchill, the retired British prime minister, delivered a speech at Westminster College in Fulton, Missouri. In it he said, "An iron curtain has descended across the continent."[1] In so doing he not only described the state of hostility between America and Britain on the one hand and the Soviet Union on the other, he defined in one statement the future, four-decades-long power contest that was to embrace the military establishment of the United States.

During the war the mission of the American Pacific Submarine Force had been clear: sink Japanese ships. Having accomplished that formidable task, American submarines fell into a morass of uncertainty after the war ended. The later hulls were "mothballed" to spend their retirement years up the Sacramento River. Others were used as targets and met their fate in ignominious plunges to the bottom. Some friendly nations were rewarded with submarines, most of which were overhauled and brought up to near-perfect condition. In those years the submarine force struggled to find a new identity.

In the years immediately following the close of the Second World War, the submarine force continued to think in terms of attacking enemy surface ships. Friedman's description of the era might be paraphrased as, "Submarine planners first denied that any change had to be made in submarine force doctrine. Then it entertained the possibility of change, but had no idea as what the future of submarines might be. Finally, it recognized its obligation to redefine the submarine's mission in terms of Cold War realities."[2]

At the same time, American engineers were dissecting advanced German technology incorporated in the German Type XXI submarine. High-capacity batteries, hull design for great underwater speed, and the snorkel

6—The Era of the GUPPY

were only some of the Type XXI characteristics. The Germans had not conquered the difficulties of building a watertight telescoping snorkel, but this seemed to be the boat's only shortfall. It was apparent to American engineers that the fleet-type submarine had to be modernized while a successor submarine was designed and built along the lines of the Type XXI. Any open conflict with Russia would be preceded by Soviet submarine incursions into American waters and in all probability in advanced submarines of the Type XXI quality.

The immediate postwar period was also marked by the formation of the Bureau of Ships, or BuShips. The Bureau of Construction and Repair had been staffed by naval architects, while the Bureau of Engineering had housed most of the Navy's engineers. There had been a natural competition between these two aspects of submarine design since they tended to approach submarine innovation from the opposite direction. Architects centered their work on the theoretical factors of hull volume and weight to give the best possible submerged vehicle. Engineers were more practical. They added up all the equipment that would be needed to meet the demands of a reconstructed Cold War mission, then designed a platform to carry the underwater load. Engineers looked on the problem from the view of its many component parts. They saw the problem from the inside out and naval architects worked from the outside in.

While competition stimulated some vigorous work, such duplication could no longer be accepted in view of budgetary constraints. BuShips was confronted simultaneously with several design projects. The advent of the nuclear age was evident as civilian contractors visualized nuclear power plants as a means of cheap energy. The concept of nuclear propulsion for ships was a concept that could not be ignored by BuShips. If the Navy were to seriously engage in a long-range nuclear ship building program it would draw funds from the Type XXI postwar fast attack project. The many fleet-type boats resting in America's rivers could be modernized to incorporate the innovations of the Type XXI design. BuShips then pushed ahead with three concepts: the nuclear ship; the Type XXI boat, to be called the *Tang*-class submarine; and the stopgap conversion of fleet-type hulls into Cold War–capability submarines.

It was clear to many in BuShips that if America was to build a nuclear reactor that could be a source of propulsion for Navy ships, the natural platform for such a reactor would be the submarine. A reactor that could provide heat for propulsion would not need oxygen as a constituent of fuel. It was obvious to Captain Hyman G. Rickover that the real future of American submarines lay in the development of a reactor that would be the foundation of a new class of true submersibles. Gaining the support of Congress to allocate significant funds for so radical an idea would take painstaking patience and determination. Rickover was single-minded as he assumed the lead in this effort. He was a naturally competitive naval officer and was willing to do whatever it would take to win. Captain Cutter described a fleet exercise in which fuel oil conservation was one of the competitive factors:

> Take Rickover, Admiral Rickover. He was on the *New Mexico* as a lieutenant. Well, Rickover was doing his job. I mean it was dishonest. For the fuel situation he bribed the oiler who came alongside, gave him a bottle of booze or something so he would give the *New Mexico* 100 extra gallons and take them away from the next ship or something. Turned off all the lights and turned down the ventilators so people would be miserable, but it would save oil—anything to win that efficiency pennant for engineering. I don't think Rickover did it for his career so much as the fact that he was a competitor, a great man. I have always admired that fellow. I don't think we would be where we are today if it weren't for him, in the nuclear power business.[3]

For the United States Navy to embark on an experiment of such extravagant technical dimensions and at such huge cost required it to have a steadfast faith in the outcome. It would take a person of Rickover's drive to stay at the helm through the manifold problems and to never let obstacles get in the way of the final goal—a submarine nuclear power plant for a breakthrough type of submarine.

But the transformation of the nuclear power concept into reality would take many years, and the Navy had to fill these years with a counter to the Soviet submarine threat. Thus, as work began on the nuclear power plant and the *Tang*-class boats were moving from the drawing board to shipyard construction, it was necessary to fill the gap with what the Navy had in its pocket: the fleet boats quietly resting in mothballs in the fresh water rivers of the United States. BuShips started with de-mothballing a series of *Tench*-class fleet-type boats. The superstructures were modified and streamlined by sloping the vertical plates to minimize deck width. The prow was rounded and an aluminum sail covered the conning tower and periscope shears. All guns and other deck equipment were removed or made flush with the deck. For example, the cleats were pivoted to fold into the deck. The battery was doubled in size from 126 cells to 252 cells, and a telescoping snorkel was inserted into the aft area of the sail. Twenty-seven tons of air conditioning and the elimination of the battery exhaust system helped in habitability. These features and others made up the GUPPY, acronym for Greater Underwater Propulsive Power.

During the 1950s, GUPPY submarines were stationed in Groton, Norfolk, Charleston, Key West, San Diego and Pearl Harbor. Each station had a designated submarine operating area. Some lucky boats had operating areas close enough to allow daily operations. The resulting overnight liberty was good for morale and these boats had brows bouncing as their crew members ran to 0800 quarters after overnight liberty. The ritual morning quarters lined the enlisted men on one side of the after deck and the officers on the other. A few short words from the captain and executive officer ended in, "Set the maneuvering watch, make preparations for getting underway."

Norfolk submarines were not so fortunate since the distance through Hampton Roads to the operating area meant weekly operations: out on Monday mornings and in on Friday afternoons. On these Fridays competitive captains drove their boats on an all-ahead-full bell, the quicker to get home and the better to beat out rivals for coveted pierside berthing. Those in maneuvering added turns of their own as each boat raced from sea up the channel entrances to their respective tenders and piers. When close to the berth assignment, the captain entered the next phase of self-made competition. The number of maneuvering bells (changes in twin screw manipulation) was the subject of crew pride stemming from admiration of the captain. The "three-bell landing" was the best. It was forbidden to change from an ahead bell directly to a back bell. Such a command placed a hardship on the maneuvering watch while straining the main motors. This mistake marked the conning officer as an amateur and invited ridicule from other officers. Certainly, the captain was bound to order an "all-stop" bell before going to "all-back-full." The boat would shudder as the propellers dug into the sea at full power. If the landing was perfect, the boat would come to rest alongside the pier with the final order, "All-stop. Secure main engines. Get over all lines."

Pride in one's submarine was built on such competence. Each crew member of each boat knew that his submarine was the best and that his responsibility was do his job to keep it that way. GUPPIES spent much time at sea diving, surfacing, snorkeling and conducting each exercise as expertly as possible.

The relationship of pride in one's submarine and one's job directly affected the proficiency of the fire control party. The GUPPY was the Navy's workhorse during the decades following the Second World War, when the fire control problem shifted from periscope information to sonar-only information. The difficulty of submarine vs. submarine tactics demanded mathematically based analysis and innovative methods. Dedicated minds worked to improve the quality of undersea tactics.

The GUPPY assumed several roles in the 1950s and '60s. It played the hostile submarine when providing services to ASW surface units, it performed sonar picket duties when operating as a part of a hunter-killer group, and it trained its crew in practice periscope and sonar attacks. It departed its home base to render services to Navy and Allied units in the Western Pacific, Mediterranean Sea, North Sea and other locations. Finally, of greatest importance, it conducted special operations, which involved surveillance of Soviet forces and installations. About every other year, the GUPPY had an overhaul at one of the Navy's shipyards in addition to upkeep periods alongside its tender. This period was usually about six months in length and was intended to make major repairs and alterations in response to the ever-changing demands of the Cold War.

There were a series of improvements starting in the latter part of the 1940s and continuing into the 1970s. The GUPPYs continued as the workhorse of the submarine fleet even as nuclear powered submarines were entering service. The first of the series was the *Odax* (SS-484), a GUPPY I. Thereafter, modified fleet-type boats were put in commission as fleet snorkels, and GUPPY IIs. Special conversions included special BQR-4 bow-mounted sonars. These were to be used as listening posts at the ocean's choke points.

The most prevalent modification was the GUPPY IIb with a step sail, chin-mounted BQR-2 passive sonar array, and deck-mounted transducer. In the mid–1950s fiberglass full sails called northern sails replaced the aluminum step sails. The GUPPY III offered improved bridge visibility, at the expense of increased underwater drag.

Sonar improvements concentrated on detection of modern Soviet submarines that were anticipated to represent improvements in the best

6—The Era of the GUPPY

German designs. Detection of hostile submarines would rely upon sonar as its primary source of target information. The periscope would become a secondary tool of torpedo fire control as the submarine's primary mission was redefined as a member of an ASW group that included surface, air and undersea components.

The GUPPY JT sonar was a passive listening device not significantly different from its first installation in 1942. It was retained for a number of years as an additional passive sonar to the postwar BQR-2. The sonar head or hydrophone was approximately 5 feet in horizontal length and was located forward of the conning tower. It had a shaft that could be trained to locate the bearing of a sound source such as a ship's propeller or submarine internal noises. American submarines would continue to use JT sonar with improved bearing deviation indicators which could detect surface ships at ranges approximating 4000 yards.[4]

The Germans had used a passive array sonar called "Gruppenhorchgeraete," which was a horseshoe-shaped array equivalent to a straight-line array.[5] The GHG was installed on the converted American submarine *Cochino* (SS-345) in 1949. It formed the basis for further American sonar improvements during the 1950s, including a bearing deviation indicator with a radar-style plan position indicator. This improved sonar was mounted on the USS *Clamagore* (SS-343) in 1948. Further improvements in the array-type sonar resulted in the BQR-2. This version of the original German GHG had 48 vertical staves, each 3 feet long, in a 6-foot circular width housed in a 5-foot-high dome. The array operated at 150 Hz to 15 kHz. A later, improved model, the BQR-2b, had an improved display that included a bearing time recorder (BTR). A paper rolled down past the BTR stylus that moved horizontally, reflecting a full commutator scan. The BTR provided a record of the target's motion as well as its bearing. This innovation was to have enormous benefit as a source of bearing change rate necessary for plot analysis.

In the early 1950s the Naval Underwater Sound Laboratory at New London worked on further improvements to the BQR-2b. By the end of the 1950s the renamed Naval Undersea Systems Center produced the BQR-5 and 6. These advanced passive sonar systems incorporated both detection and automatic target tracking.

The wardrooms of the GUPPY II type boats were modified in the 1950s to provide a makeshift attack center. Geographical plot and Ekelund ranging techniques were performed on the wardroom table while the opaque panel separating the wardroom from the passageway was replaced with a transparent plexiglass relative-bearing compass rose display. A quartermaster in the passageway kept a relative-bearing plot on the display and fire control communication linked sonar, the attack center and the conning tower. This system, as crude as it may sound by today's standards, worked well, and each person in the fire control party performed specialized functions in relative comfort.

The wardroom navigational plot consisted of a dead reckoning tracer or DRT mounted into the eating table. It had a glass top through which could be seen a light point driven from the master gyro compass and pit log. A sheet of graph paper overlaying the glass top represented a geographical plot with automatic own ship inputs represented by the moving point of light. Above the dead reckoning tracer was a small repeater for target bearing and course information from the TDC.

The GUPPY II fire control organization was divided between the conning tower, wardroom and sonar space. With the TDC in the conning tower and the various bearings-only plots in the wardroom, communication and coordination were critical to smoothly functioning fire control. The system included a direct sound-powered telephone link between the plot coordinator in the wardroom and the assistant approach officer in the conning tower who monitored the set-up in the TDC and advised the approach officer of the best solution for target course, speed and range. The plot coordinator had another link with the sonar supervisor so that the wardroom acting as attack center became the crucial analysis station in submarine-versus-submarine sonar-bearings-only approaches. The role of the TDC became one of receptor of information coming from plot.

The GUPPY III conversion included a modification to accommodate the ever-more-complex demands of expanded fire control equipment and organization. One of the four engines was removed to make room for the pumping equipment that was formerly located in the pump room below the control room. The vacated space below the control room became the attack center where various plots were managed in the bearings-only fire control analysis. Because the periscope wells occupied the center of the pump room, the location was far from ideal as a dedicated fire control space. The dimensions of the Mark 101 fire control console made it imprac-

6—The Era of the GUPPY

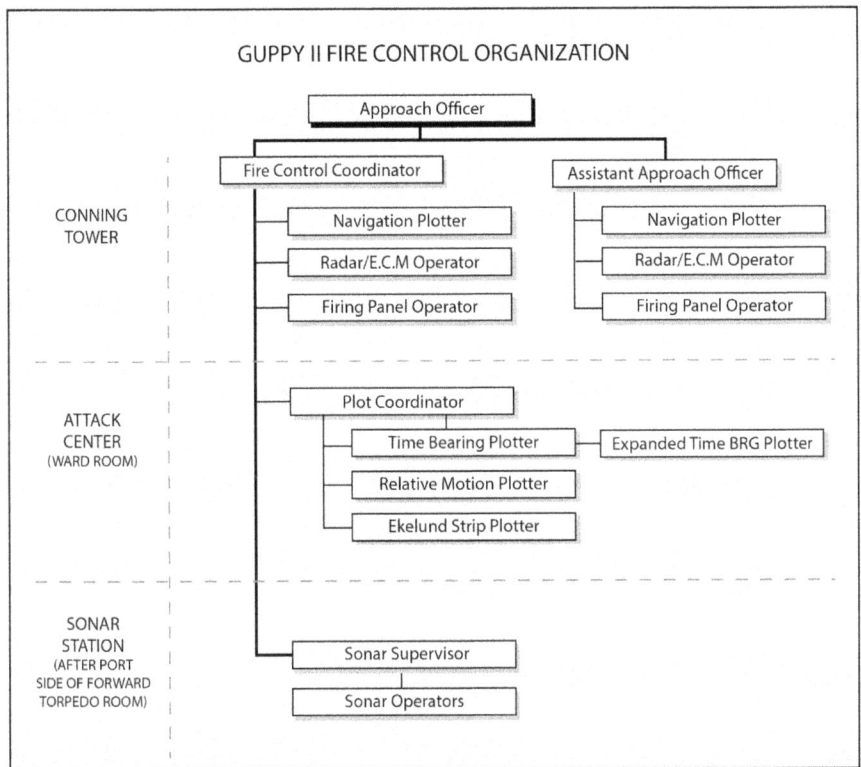

Most GUPPY IIs used the wardroom as an attack center with the eating table converted to accommodate a DRT from the master gyro (Submarine Research Center).

tical to place it in the pump room. Additionally, the captain, acting as approach officer, was committed to the conning tower. As a result, the ultimate GUPPY III conversion lengthened the conning tower to accommodate the Mark 101 fire control console as well as its associated sonar display. The final version of the modification included an outsized fiberglass sail that reduced underwater speed.

Any sound can be analyzed into components by centering on different frequencies. A truly random signal carries all frequencies at about the same level of amplitude, but screw and equipment noise displayed a distinctive spectrum or signature on sonar screens. For example, a snorkeling subma-

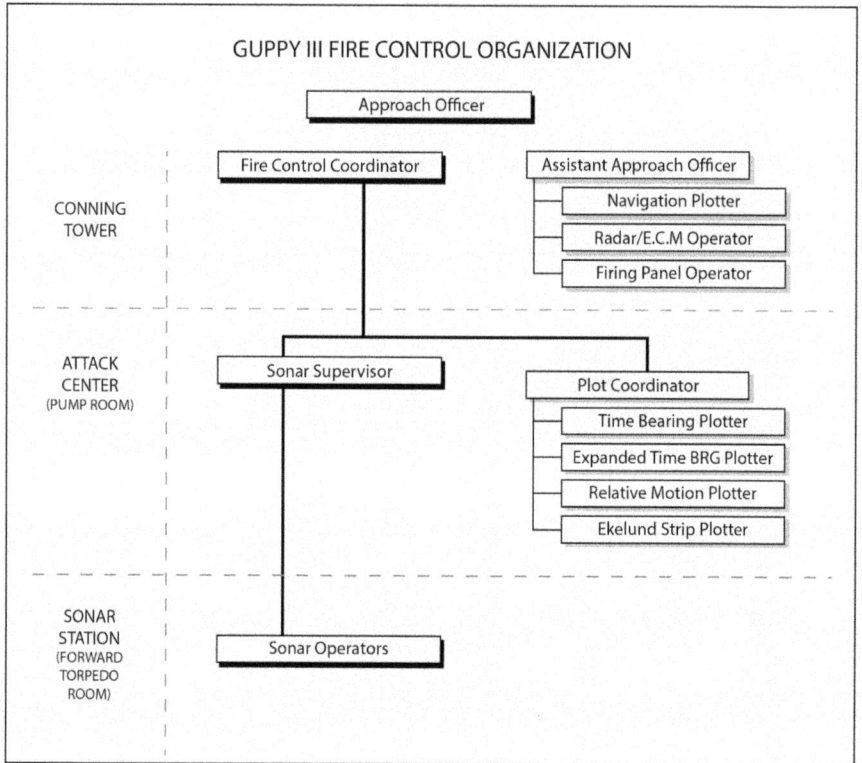

GUPPY III conversions initially used the pump room as an attack center by removing an engine and placing the pump equipment in the vacated space. Some conversions removed both engines in the after engine room and placed the fire control plots in the vacated space (Submarine Research Center).

rine produced a strong signal at a discrete frequency from emitted noise of combined engine vibration and screw cavitation. If the pattern of a noise source was traced by stylus on a uniformly moving roll of graph paper, the sonar operator could examine the narrow spikes and determine the nature of the noise source. The pattern was referred to as a signature because it was consistently distinctive. Even a submerged submarine running on the battery would emit a signature noise, although much less apparent. This noise would be represented by a mix of flow noise over the submarine's hull, noises from inboard piping, screw cavitation and pumps.

Low-frequency components of sound can travel great distances through the sea without serious distortion. The sea produces a variety of ambient noises and the sonarman had to know these sounds in order to eliminate them as potential contacts. Shrimp make a clacking noise like fans at a football game and whales sing songs of long-distance romance. In addition, one's own submarine makes abundant noise that had to be filtered out in the receptors and minds of the sonarmen. Bow plane noise was the most egregious and its placement in future submarine design would become a subject of concern. Sonar operators prided themselves on being able to identify the noise pattern of a specific submarine, even through all the background interference. Soon, the Navy's sonar schools were training sonarmen to recognize the noise patterns of the various Soviet submarines.

Sonar could provide a reasonably accurate estimate of target speed. The sonar operator counted the rhythmic beat of a target ship's screw, which indicated the speed of the propeller, the probable size of ship being driven by it, and the most probable speed of the ship through the water. Operators became proficient at this analysis and comparison sound tables were at hand to match target sound with known profiles.[6]

The time-bearing plot furnished valuable information for other plots requiring accurate estimates of bearing change rates. The plot was a board upon which bearings were marked against their corresponding times. When sonar reported an initial bearing drift, bearings along the abscissa were noted at specific bearing intervals. The times of sonar-reported bearings (normally at four-minute intervals) were noted along the ordinate of the plot board. A mark was placed where the two intersected. As multiple contact reports from sonar were plotted, they emanated from the lower portion of the plot, starting with the time of the first reported sonar bearing. Since sonar bearings were not without error, it was necessary to reduce the bearing errors to as close to zero as possible. This was accomplished graphically to obtain the best indication of target bearing change rate. Straight-line fairings indicated a constant bearing change rate from which other plots could estimate target range, knowing target speed. The time-bearing plot could also signal possible changes in target speed or course or both when the array of time-bearings bent downward or upward.

One of three true bearing indications told the approach officer the relative movement caused by own ship's course and speed and those of the target:

Submarine Torpedo Tactics

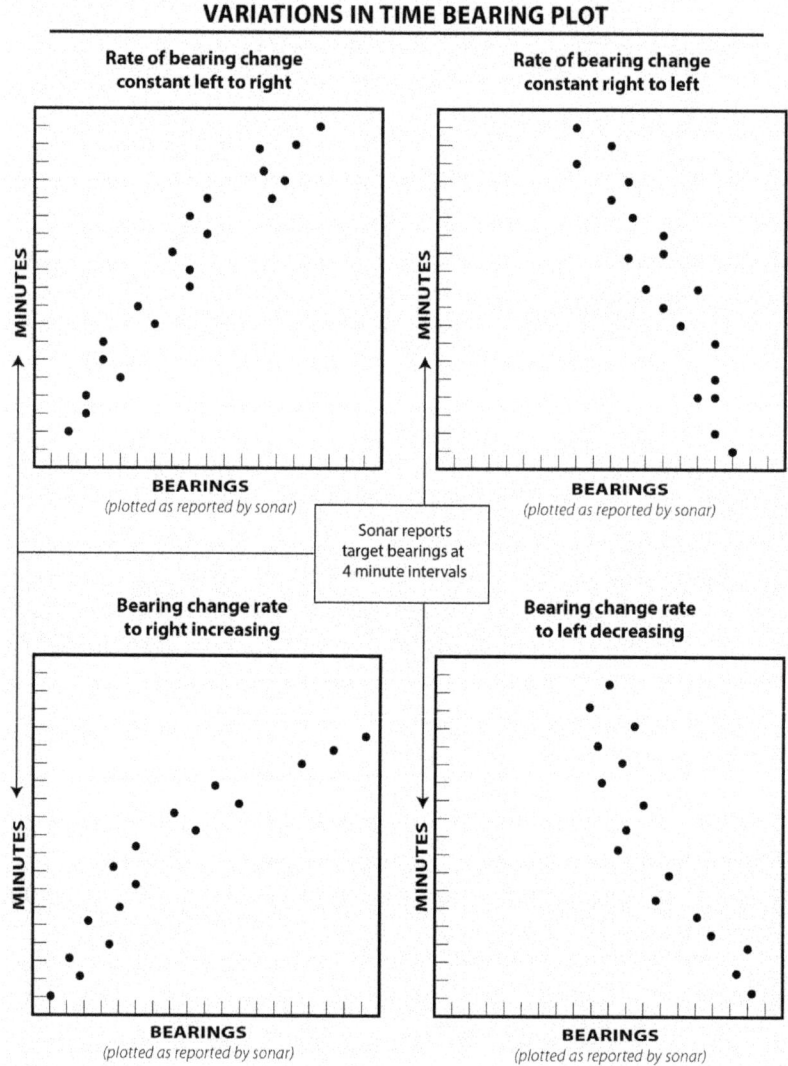

The time-bearing plot can illustrate target motion changes (speed and/or course) and can assist in estimating range (Submarine Research Center).

1. If true target bearing was drawing toward the bow, own submarine was losing true bearing and the target would pass ahead.
2. If true target bearing was drawing toward the stern, own submarine was gaining true bearing and the target would pass astern.
3. If true target bearing was remaining constant, the lead angle was correct and the submarine was closing the target.[7]

Within the limits determined by target speed and course, the submarine could control the rate of true bearing change by changing own speed and lead angle; however, the submarine had only a limited amount of control over the change in true bearing, since its own speed depended on battery state, need for silent running and sea temperature/salinity condition. The optimum tactic by a submarine, particularly early in the approach, was to maintain a steady bearing or nearly steady bearing, to ensure closing the target to an affective weapon range.

Running in parallel to the time-bearing plot, another team of plotters used the same sonar bearings at discrete intervals to geographically trace the progress of bearing drift. The bearing drift appeared as spokes in a wheel. Lieutenant Joseph Ekelund and his colleagues saw that with an accurate target speed ruled as distance on a plastic strip, the plotting party could align the strip with bearings in such a manner as to match the ruled marker with bearing progression. This was done by sliding the strip up and down the most recent bearing, assuming a 90-degree angle-on-the-bow, then tilting the strip at various ranges to see if the ruled speed marks would align with previous bearings. In so doing, target angle-on-the-bow would be shown, target course could be derived and range estimated. It was not an exact science, but successive attempts resulted in surprisingly accurate information, particularly when in the hands of plotters who were willing to trust the method. As the plot continued, the initial estimate could be verified to eliminate other possible matches. The Ekelund "speed strips" method was simple in the extreme, but surprisingly effective at a time when electronic computers were far in the future.

Normally, the optimum firing point for the bearings' only problem was about the same as for the normal periscope attack, with the exception that a greater stress was placed on obtaining near-zero gyros, optimal track angle and a short torpedo run to reduce the effect of not having a perfect solution.

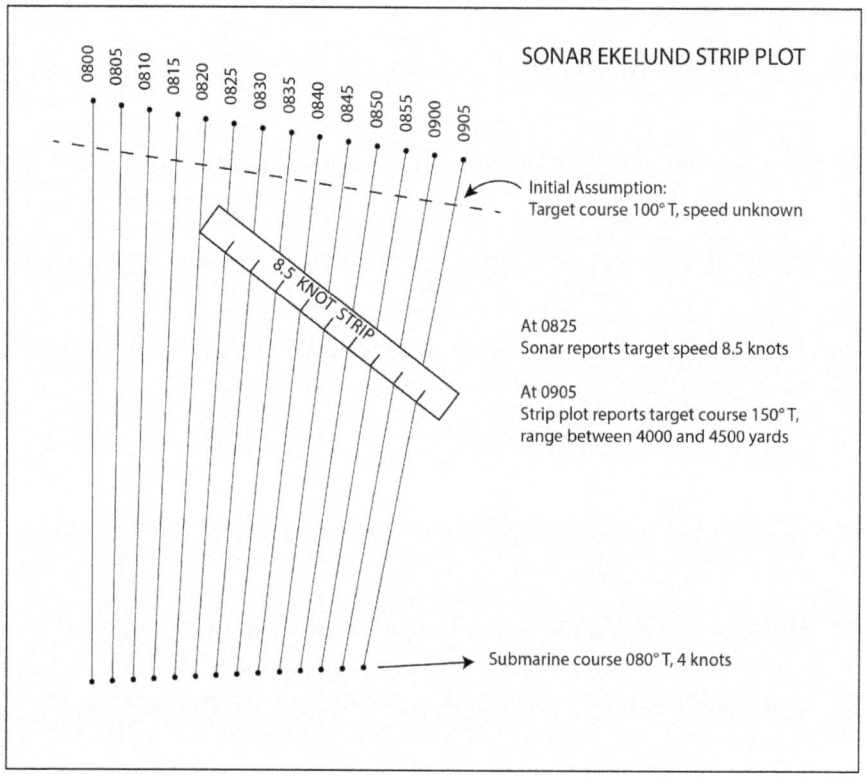

The Ekelund plot depended on accurate sonar bearings taken at consistent intervals. Sonar accuracy was seldom as vivid as portrayed above (Submarine Research Center).

Optimum track angles produced a minimized effective target length. The shortest possible torpedo run reduced the affect of inherent errors.

Whether the plots were run in the wardroom, pump room or engine room, the accuracy of problem analysis depended on the acuity of sonar bearings and the ability of sonar operators to identify the unknown submerged vessel as a Soviet submarine, and if so, the type of submarine with corresponding screw noise signature. If bearings could be pinpointed and if the screw noise signature could be correctly identified, the sonar operator had a good chance of obtaining an accurate turn count on the screw noise. He then could enter the turn count into his ship/submarine turn count conversion tables and render a probable target speed.

6—The Era of the GUPPY

Target speed was reported to the sonar supervisor, who integrated the information with any other data at hand and told the plot coordinator the best target speed. At precise time intervals target bearings were reported and plotted. An Ekelund plot might appear as follows:

In this example, the listening submarine is on course 080 and the 8.5 knot speed strip reflects sonar's best estimate of target speed. The grid of the strip aligns with the timed bearings to indicate a target course of 150, range about 4200 yards. Were this an actual approach and the target positively identified as hostile, the captain would either attempt to receive from ComSubLant or ComSubPac approval to begin a tracking mode or would have standing orders relevant to the situation. The captain, acting as approach officer, would be thinking of his TDC set-up (and later the Mark 101 set-up) in relation to the possible use of a Mark 37 torpedo.

During the Second World War the Mark 28 electric torpedo was an alternative to the straight-running, steam-propelled Mark 14 torpedo. Also during the war a purely defensive weapon, the Mark 27, had several unique features. It was the submarine's first swim-out torpedo. With longitudinal guide rails and a small diameter, the torpedo was pushed silently out of the tube by its propeller. The torpedo then followed a pre-set course to a point where its passive sonar was activated. It was an excellent evasion maneuver weapon. The Mark 37 torpedo design was largely based on the concept of the Mark 27.

In the bearings-only attack, the Mark 37, Mod 4 torpedo was the weapon of choice. The optimum firing point would be reached when the target was within the Mark 37 torpedo's enabling range of between 600 and 3,100 yards. The standard firing point thumb rule was 2500 yards. Target angle-on-the-bow at time of firing should not have been more than 60 degrees. The Mark 37 torpedo was a relatively slow electric torpedo and a large track angle indicated a probable divergent target course, with accompanying probability of the target outrunning the Mark 37's capacity to close the target. An angle-on-the-bow of less than 60° at time of firing and a range of 2500 yards or less would maximize the chances of the torpedo's acoustic acquisition. With a target submarine at a range of over 4000 yards, but with plot showing range decreasing and bearings reasonably constant, the captain would simply stay on course until the target was within range.

Once the torpedo had been launched, the submarine had to take evasive action on the assumption that own ship might be in the cross hairs of the target submarine. The captain knew the condition of his battery, which dictated how much speed he could use in an evasive maneuver. He balanced speed with cavitation noise emission at his depth and normally descended to find a positive gradient. Soviet ASW tactical doctrine of the 1950s called for use of active sonar much more abundantly than did American doctrine. If a Soviet submarine or surface vessel used active sonar in an attempt to locate the attacking submarine, the captain's best chance of hiding was to get under a layer. The following diagram illustrates the evasion maneuver.

The effectiveness of active sonar to detect an evading submarine is often thwarted by some form of a positive gradient found in about 75 per-

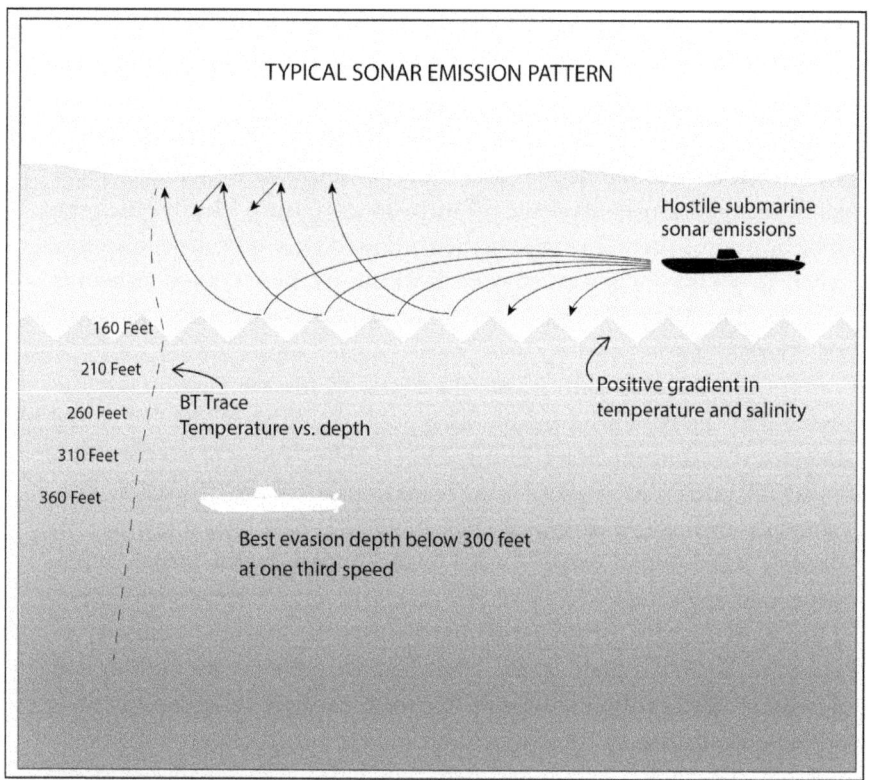

If the hostile submarine dove below the layer depth, the evading submarine could ascend above it and thereby remain hidden from active sonar (Submarine Research Center).

cent of ocean strata. The best depth for a submarine attempting to avoid detection by active sonar above a layer was to descend as quickly as possible. The avoidance of passive sonar was to maintain a slow speed to avoid cavitation. Avoidance of active sonar was to continually present a bow-on or stern-on aspect to the estimated bearing of the hostile submarine and to descend to a depth well below the positive gradient shown on the BT.

The evading submarine had a variety of maneuvers and tools at hand. The simplest was to release a mass of bubbles while turning the submarine and changing depth. This was the knuckle. At least one innovative boat found that by putting an electric razor to the UQC microphone, the sound in water was strikingly similar to an electric torpedo. This technique was intended to intimidate a hostile boat, but it never saw action against a Soviet submarine. The evasion arsenal included such tools as false-target canisters which could be ejected from the pyrotechnic ejector in the after torpedo room. These were used as the source of bubbles when performing a knuckle. The evasion weapon of last resort was the Mark 27 torpedo, normally carried in the after tubes. This torpedo was only 7 feet, six inches in length and 19 inches in diameter. As described above, it was swim-out launched by having a smaller diameter with guide rails that matched the 21-inch tube diameter. Its run was gyro controlled on a specified course, at the end of which its rudder assumed control, turning the torpedo in a wide circle. When its passive sonar detected a sound source it attacked that source.

While these measures could be deployed, the evading submarine's best initial tactic when sensing that a hostile submarine had detected its presence was to go to ultra-quiet. Each compartment had a silent running bill and an ultra quiet running bill. In the latter, all machinery and pumps were shut down with the bow and stern planes being shifted to hand power. When such a condition lasted for several hours the planesmen became so exhausted that they would be relieved by off-watch planesmen.

During the 1950s the Navy renewed its effort to silence its submarines. Sound isolation of equipment became the focus of each yard overhaul. Running the diesel engines while snorkeling put so much sound in the water that shore-based low-frequency installations could monitor snorkeling boats as they transited the Atlantic. Neoprene engine mounts were inserted and experiments were conducted to suspend engines within soundproof boxes. Each line carrying fuel, water, hydraulic fluid and electrical conduiting had flexible inserts to reduce machinery vibrations entering the hull. While improvements were made in sound emission control, the GUPPY boats could not overcome the cavitation of the traditional four-bladed screw. Crews relied upon simple solutions: shut down every piece of non-vital equipment, reduce speed and go deep. During a submerged encounter with a Soviet submarine, crew members talked in whispers.

In 1946, the Bureau of Ordnance contracted with Arma Corporation for the design and development of an integrated torpedo fire control system which would augment the capacity of the torpedo data computer Mark IV.

It is difficult, in an age when a computer can be held in the palm of one hand, to visualize the difficulties of engineering a computer when electronics consisted of vacuum tubes and wiring. The evolution of the modern computer, when it is reversed, starts with micro chips the size of a pinhead, chips the size of a postage stamp, circuit boards with transistors and finally vacuum tube-driven monsters the size of a living room. In 1946 computers were made of syncro-servo units, tiny motors driving gears and mechanical displays that required considerable interpretation.

The new system was to incorporate concepts which evolved out of long wartime use of the TDC. Ideas presented to Arma Corporation by experienced submarine officers included an analyzer that could produce a quick, initial target solution, reduction of hand-inserted data with accompanying automation of target data assimilation, and automatic shift of torpedo ballistic data for mixed torpedo loads. Torpedo officers saw the need for electrical transmission of tactical data to tube-loaded torpedoes. The spindle-set torpedo required a mechanical connection with the torpedo tube so that point-of-fire information could be relayed to the torpedo. Experienced submarine officers knew that as torpedoes became more sophisticated, more inputs would be required. As the number of spindles increased, the greater complexity meant greater chances of malfunction. Spindle retraction time would be increased even if all systems worked properly. The mechanical transfer of information had to be replaced by electrical connections. This concept became a necessity when the Mark 37 torpedo's design demanded instantaneous multiple inputs. Finally, there was the need for automatic torpedo firing and torpedo spread setting.

In 1913, Corbin, an authority on submarines at the time, predicted that submarine-to-submarine warfare would remain an impossibility. This opinion was to continue through the Second World War. In part, the opin-

6—The Era of the GUPPY

ion was predicated on the limitations of the steam torpedo. Also, sonar equipment prior to the Second World War could not furnish an accurate enough bearing to allow shooting a straight-running steam torpedo with any expectation of a hit. During the war, American submarines had sunk several Japanese submarines, but these attacks were periscope attacks against surfaced submarines. At the end of that war, a British submarine managed to accomplish the feat of hitting and sinking a submerged German submarine.

Arma Corporation tackled submarine officers' tactical frustrations in a series of TDC improvements ultimately leading to a synthesized system designated the Mark 101 fire control system. It was augmented by the Mark 106 system, which provided for electrically fed inputs to torpedoes. The design of the Mark 101 system was grounded in the several innovative additions that were serially added to the TDC. A review of these TDC components illustrates the progression of bearings-only fire control equipment.

An initial addition to the TDC was a receiver section, which was physically located between the position keeper and angle solver. It received corrected sonar bearing inputs and furnished information to a sonar dial display together with other information such as observed optical bearing, radar bearing, and target range. The receiver section permitted inputs of searchlight sonar bearings to allow integrated best bearing information to the TDC.

The position indicator Mark 6 was the display unit of the receiver section. The main function of the position indicator was to display to conning tower personnel the fire control problem being solved by associated fire control equipment in the attack center of the submarine. The position indicator provided information as it was being received from various sources, the most important of which was sonar. The system also provided for a sound bearing converter that accommodated the difference between the speed of sound through water and the atmosphere.[8]

Another addition was automatic screw noise baseline conversion in which a sonar baseline constant was permanently set into the TDC's internal mechanism at the time of installation. From these inputs the converter continuously generated sonar baseline corrections, which were angle corrections to accommodate the difference in linear length from the location of a submarine's screws to the middle of the target.

As the TDC improved system matured into a complete display of own ship movements, target movements and anticipated target turns, Arma engineers developed a console that would totally replace the TDC. The central function of the new Mark 101 display was the Mark 7 analyzer. It was basically an electric-mechanical navigational plotter. It received inputs of own ship's motion with target ranges and bearings which were displayed together with target course and speed. The accuracy of the solution was dependent upon the accuracy of sonar bearing change rate; the greater the change, the more accurate the solution. The Mark 7 analyzer provided an end-point type of solution, which required a range and a bearing. Two observations were required and a time lapse between bearing change observations of about 90 seconds was required for a reliable solution. The drop-last feature could be utilized to increase the time between observations and could thereby refine the solution. The bearings-only type of solution was used when only target bearings were available. Bearing changes of at least 4.25 degrees were required for a reliable solution. After the initial solution based on three bearings was obtained, and subsequent bearings were entered, the drop-last feature could be utilized to refine the solution. The Mark 7 analyzer was helpful in obtaining quick solutions for target course depending on the reliability of inputs being used. Fire control personnel often used the Mark 7 solution as confirmation of plot-obtained information.

As the Mark 7 analyzer operator entered a series of three target bearings taken at equal intervals as described above, he adjusted estimated target range, course, and speed as further bearings became known. Initial estimates from plots could be integrated into the Mark 7 solution. The system's analyzer could fit a straight-line constant speed track across the bearings. In effect, the Mark 101 system accomplished an Ekelund speed strip plot within its analog computing ability. The display information was still by dials, but the information was superior to that of the TDC even with multiple improvements.

The Mark 101 console was bulky and best suited to a dedicated space.[9] Some GUPPY III conversions housed the massive console in an engine room which had been converted into an attack center by removal of the engines. The GUPPYs were stretched and pushed in experimental efforts to house the Mark 101/106 and sonar interpretation equipment.

The electric setting of tactical data into tube-loaded torpedoes from Mark 101 fire control solutions was accomplished by the Mark 106 system.

The Mark 106 system also provided for tracking of multiple targets. This augmentation provided for more than one submarine in coordinated ASW attacks.[10] Of course, the modification of torpedo tubes from spindle settings to electrical settings had to be accompanied by equivalent modifications of the torpedoes themselves. The conversion to electrically set torpedoes meant that complex information could be entered immediately prior to firing.

The finalized system was first installed aboard an operating submarine in 1951. Its central feature was a control console which provided for automatic shifting of spread order from right to left as changes in angle-on-the-bow moved from right to left and vice versa; automatic application of corrections to torpedo tactical data and automatic spread solution and application were inserted into the angle solver. The almost exclusive purpose of these sweeping improvements was to provide fire control capability against submerged submarines.

Since range continued to be a difficult problem even for the Mark 101 fire control system, the submarine force entertained the possibility of placing two hydrophones at the extreme ends of the GUPPY. The concept was simple. With a 300-foot separation, assuming a beam aspect to the target bearing, a triangulation of signal strength might produce a focal point (range) if the target was close enough to allow a signal comparison. To test the theory the Naval Ordnance Laboratory at White Oak, Maryland, used two modified JT hydrophone arrays mounted on the deck of a GUPPY submarine.[11] One was mounted on the bow and the other at the extreme stern. This provided a triangulation of a submerged target at a range short enough to be computed by electronic trigonometry. The system was called "Passive Underwater Fire Control Feasibility Study, or PUFFS. Many GUPPYs of the late 1950s were equipped with PUFFS ranging equipment. Four of the *Tang*-class boats were also so equipped. These were all deck-mounted hydrophones which produced drag and were prone to environmental interference. The system was improved by moving the hydrophones into tanks, but the final designs on single-hull submarines had side-mounted passive sonar built into the basic structure of the hull.

In the early 1970s, a few Guppy III conversions, such as *Tiru* (SS-416), included a Mark 66 console for the newly-introduced Mark 48 torpedo. It used the BQS-4 azimuth range indicator. Another part of the system was a Mark 19 plotter for TMA estimates and PUFFS plotting. In these stretched conning tower conversions the PUFFS electronics BQG-4 display was installed. Also in a few attack center conversions were the BQS-4a and BQR-2b displays.[12]

The GUPPY submarine also was America's first attempt at electronic surveillance of Soviet communications. In the Atlantic, boats from New London and Norfolk put into Portsmouth, England, took on supplies, and headed north through the Irish Sea to the bleak and hazardous waters of the Barents Sea. On board were "spooks" from classified authority who carried black boxes as they crowded the radio space of the control room. Submarine captains received their orders from ComSubLant, who, when defining the special operation mission, tended to be a little vague as to respecting the international 12-mile limit. The Soviet Union claimed a 200-mile limit, which was ludicrous and therefore ignored.[13] The trip was made through state five seas, and those on the bridge of step-sail GUPPYs were strapped to the TBT as the boat plunged through one wave and crested the next. The after room suffered from screws lifting out of water and vibrating their struts. At two-thirds on two engines using the raised snorkel and with the sea coming from off the bow, the submarines plowed their way forward on the surface.

One boat keeping to an eastward course rolled 102 degrees from a beam wave. It was saved by the helmsman, who acted quickly and without orders by putting the rudder hard over, bringing the boat's bow into the sea. The submarine slowly righted itself, but the lookout and officer of the deck were drowned.

The USS *Cochino* was lost, and that story was told by Sherry Sontag and Chris Drew in their book, *Blind Man's Bluff*. The following abbreviated description of the event has been taken from that book:

> It was the need for stealth that convinced intelligence officials that submarines could be the next logical step in the creation of an eavesdropping network that would circle the Soviet Union. On its way to Murmansk the *Cochino* was rocked by waves as crewmen braced themselves, grabbing chart tables and overhead pipes. Others lunged to catch sliding coffee cups and tools.
>
> "*Cochino* was running submerged on the snorkel, but the rough sea made the inherently tricky business of snorkeling impossible. The forward engine room reported that water was pouring into the submarine through the snorkel. The commanding officer sent his executive officer to investigate as the engines were shut down from lack of air. About two minutes later, there was a muffled thud and the submarine shuddered. An electrician saw

sparks coming from the after battery compartment. He yelled for the compartment to be evacuated. Then, the commanding officer was informed of a fire in the after battery well. The submarine surfaced and was immediately swept by heavy seas. Another submarine, USS *Tusk*, in company with *Cochino*, was signaled by flashing light of the after battery fire and resulting casualties. Several crew members including the executive officer had been injured and remained in the after torpedo room of the submarine. All other crewmembers evacuated the after compartments to escape poisonous fumes. They crowded into the forward torpedo room.

The situation went from bad to worse as another crew member went over the side. After approximately two hours it became apparent to the captain that he would have to abandon his submarine. As fires raged below, USS *Tusk* came alongside. *Cochino* began to settle by the stern. A makeshift brow [gangplank] was cleated to both boats and *Cochino* crewmembers scrambled to the *Tusk*. Captain Benitez was the last person to leave his sinking submarine. The demise of *Cochino* was America's introduction to the dangers of the Cold War.[14]

During the 1950s some submarines were built and converted from fleet-type boats or GUPPYs in response to the need for sonar-specific missions. These included the K boats, which were small listening platforms designed only for sonar picket duty. Conversions from fleet snorkels or GUPPYs extended the bow to allow the larger BQR-4 array. These submarines played an important role in monitoring Soviet submarine transits.

GUPPY submarines were incorporated into ASW hunter-killer groups that included a helicopter-carrying aircraft carrier surrounded by a bent-line screen of ASW destroyers. In the van of these units were one or two submarines stationed about 20 miles ahead of the group. In addition, sonobuoy-equipped helicopters hovered on station in a 40-mile semicircle ahead of the main group. These units were very effective ASW threats to any Soviet transiting boats.

In the late 1950s, as an exercise test, a snorkeling GUPPY submarine zigzagged unannounced into an ASW hunter-killer search area. The submarine was detected at an estimated 23,000 yards. It was tracked by another GUPPY using only passive sonar, and the ASW submarine was able to close to a 2,000-yard range. The ASW submarine did not sight the target's snorkel until just at the firing point. In another 1954 exercise off Iceland, the *Cavalla*, a converted SSK, simulated a transit to a forward base. The exercise called for the submarine K-1 to be the target and *Cavalla* the attacker. Both relied entirely on passive sonar. K-1 used the new Target

Motion Analysis (TMA) technique and was able to successfully track *Cavalla*'s movements without *Cavalla* detecting K-1.[15]

Yard overhauls with equipment and hull modifications kept pace with new sonar and fire control technologies for the duration of the GUPPY era. As described above, a ten-foot extension of the conning tower provided space for the latest TMA equipment, but there were limits to what a fleet-type hull could accommodate. Extension of the conning tower with added weight of equipment meant a higher center of gravity. The safety tank, which had been designed to counter the effect of a flooded conning tower, was rendered useless. The enormous sail produced additional underwater drag and its broad vertical face when on the surface invited heavy rolls in high winds and rough seas.

Some GUPPYs of the 1970s also had a Prairie-Masker system, which pumped bubbles into the screw blades' leading and trailing edges. This system broke up the cavitation-producing collapsing bubbles, which quieted the boat when running at shallow depths.[16]

The GUPPY program lasted for about twenty-five years, from the late 1940s to the late 1970s. As sufficient nuclear-powered submarines came into the fleet, the number of diesel-powered submarines dwindled. The transition from diesel-electric powered submarines to an all-nuclear powered submarine fleet may have covered over two decades, but the engineering effort to perfect a superior nuclear-powered attack submarine was multidimensional and complex in the extreme. The driving force of the transition was the Cold War evolution of mission definition, which demanded prolonged transiting at high speed and acquisition of submerged targets at great distances.

The Cold War was a race of technology between the United States and the Soviet Union. Each country tried to embarrass the other by attempting to force the opposite country's submarines to the surface, thus exposing espionage efforts. It was commonly known, for example, that ComSubLant offered a case of Jack Daniels to the submarine that could force a Soviet Foxtrot boat to the surface. But, although the enthusiasm on both sides was extreme, the contest between the United States and the Soviet Union for world dominance never reached a level of open conflict.[17]

As a result, sophisticated submarine torpedo fire control techniques, computers with high-speed TMA solutions, and the ability to diagnose noise signatures coming from opponents' submarines never produced a single warshot torpedo fired from one submarine at another. It is remarkable that in 25 years of brinksmanship so intense that submarines were sunk, none did so from a torpedo attack. The casualties of the submarine Cold War resulted only from accidents in training exercises, equipment failures and aggressive surveillance collisions.

In a review of submarine torpedo fire control during the Cold War, it is appropriate to examine submarine development as a platform for torpedoes. Parenthetically, the decommissioning of the last diesel-electric powered submarine in the Navy's fleet was later to bring about an unusual arrangement with a foreign nation.[18]

7

From Tang *to* Nautilus

The German Type XXI design contributed many improvements to the fleet-type submarine that resulted in the GUPPY, but that class of submarine, with its many modifications, was burdened by the limitations of its original design. In 1946 the naval architects and engineers at BuShips analyzed the advanced submarine technology that German industry produced during the war. At the same time, the American engineers identified Type XXI weaknesses, and thereby produced an entirely new American class of submarine.

The Type XXI submarine had a figure-8 hull. A large-diameter master cylinder housing the operational functions of the submarine included a second, under-slung cylindrical hull. A cross section resembled a figure–8 double hull with minimum compromise of hull strength. Although American designers saw that frame strengthening could accommodate any compromise to such a hull configuration, they remained convinced that a single cylindrical hull was preferable. Through an increase in the diameter of the pressure hull, limits on the size and weight of machinery, and the elimination of the need for two engine rooms, a new class of fast attack submarine could have a relatively short hull.

The test depth of the new submarine was to be 700 feet. The increased test depth was to be accomplished by using high yield (HY 80) steel. A minimum length hull would provide a minimal friction area with resulting higher speed potential. The hull was streamlined and the sail was reduced in size by eliminating the conning tower. The submarine was double hulled amidships for ballast and fuel ballast tanks.

The final *Tang*-class design was 266 feet long and 16 feet in diameter. The new design incorporated six bow torpedo tubes with 16 torpedo reloads. The stern room was equipped only with two short torpedo tubes that would be used for defense using the Mark 27 torpedoes.

7—*From* Tang *to* Nautilus

Fitting the fire control equipment into the control room, to be called the operations compartment, would not be easy. It had to house the diving stand, hydraulic manifold, air manifold, helm, periscopes, and radio room. The final basic design placed the diving group on the port side, the periscopes in the middle on a raised platform and the fire control space on the starboard side with radio at the after end.[1]

It was difficult to design an attack center for the *Tang*-class boat that could accommodate the Mark 101 fire control system. Although the approach officer most often elected to conduct torpedo tactics from the raised periscope platform, he used the periscopes primarily for surveillance. This was due in part to the decreased height of the periscope above the sail, but of more importance was the reliance on sonar as the primary source of tactical information. When maneuvering submerged against a hostile submerged submarine, the basic concern was to achieve a quick and accurate estimate of target course, speed, range and depth. Passive BQR-2 and 4 sonar provided most target information, but a single ping was often a temptation to achieve an accurate range. The Mark 101 had the computer ability to anticipate a target turn, knowing the turning radius of Soviet submarines. It also had the capacity to control post–Second World War torpedoes, such as the Mark 27, which after being launched would travel on a gyro-set course, then circle at a pre-determined depth while listening for a sound source.

In 1960 the Mark 101/106 fire control system was modified to handle the Mark 37 torpedo. After leaving the torpedo tube, the torpedo could be gyro-controlled to a pre-set course or wire-guided by the fire control system to the sound source. Although the Mark 37 had a maximum range of 9500 yards, the tactical problem had to allow for the torpedo's run after having acquired the target from either passive or active on-board sonar. Most approach officers preferred a firing range of about 4500 yards.

True torpedo bearing, having been converted from relative bearing within the computer, and true target bearing of a target sound source were displayed on concentric dials on the face of the Mark 101 console. The first Mark 37 wire-guided torpedoes simply followed the sound source, but in doing so on a deflection shot, the torpedo followed a curved path that was inefficient. This problem was solved through a technique called corrected intercept, by which the system automatically calculated the projected impact point and aimed the torpedo at that point.[2]

In the after end of the *Tang*-class control/attack center were the radio room on the port side and the sonar station on the starboard side. Sonar displays including the BQR-2b indicator were adjacent to radio.[3] The Mark 101 fire control display and DRT were arranged along the starboard side of the attack center.

The Navy knew that the Soviet Union had a number of Type XXI submarines at their disposal and that the Soviets would be wasting no time reverse-engineering the German design. As they had done with the B-29 Superfortress in 1945, they would most likely dissect the German boats and copy them as nearly as possible. By contrast, the American Navy used the German design only as a starting point, while emphasizing the need to get the new design off the drawing board and into the construction phase as quickly as possible. The *Tang*-class boats would have a maximum battery speed of 18.3 knots submerged and a surface engine speed of 15.5 knots. These new boats would also be equipped with an automatic hovering system.

A submarine may be thought of metaphorically as a pyramid. The fire control system and its torpedoes are at the apex with the supporting systems such as navigation, propulsion, communication, and commissary near the base. Without each of the supporting elements performing as designed, the fire control system and weapons become irrelevant. In the case of the *Tang*-class submarine, this concept was illustrated by the failure of its propulsion system. Although BuShips had only sketchy intelligence as to the pace of Soviet design and construction based on the German Type XXI submarine, it had to assume that Soviet shipyards were in high gear.

The Navy placed great hope in the new General Motors 16–338 "pancake" engine. BuShips sought a lightweight, high-output engine, and the 16–338 seemed to fill the bill. The *Tang*-class submarine was to be considerably shorter than the GUPPY, and the single engine room was to accommodate both engines and generators. While the GUPPYs of the time had 53 feet of hull length devoted to main propulsion, the *Tang*-class boat was to have almost the same total horsepower output in 22 feet of hull length. To accomplish this, the Navy rushed ahead to purchase the radial diesel engine. The General Motors 16–338 engine had four decks of four horizontally arranged cylinders. These 16 cylinders turned on a vertical crankshaft that drove a generator hanging below the engine. Four of these engines with generators were crammed into the 22-foot compartment. The vertical

7—From Tang to Nautilus

distance from base of generators to pressure hull was approximately 20 inches at their narrowest point.[4]

Engineers of the Cleveland Diesel Engine Corporation, a division of General Motors, hadn't sufficient time to test the new type of engine in a submarine. It warned BuShips of this fact in a strongly worded letter. The only evidence of the engine's reliability was its use in a 110-foot submarine chaser that used the vertical crankshaft engine directly geared to a right angle drive to the propeller shafts. These proved to be passably reliable, but the demands of a submarine were much more severe.

Diesel engines run at specified speeds. The opposed-piston, twin-crankshaft Fairbanks Morse ran at 720 RPM and the General Motors

Exhausted Second Class Engineman C.D. Yates stares into space while anticipating the next breakdown of his GM 16–338 engines. November 1955 (Submarine Research Center).

equivalent engine at 750 RPM. The new General Motors 16–338 pancake engine ran at 1600 RPM, approximately twice the speed of the earlier Fairbanks Morse 1600 hp. 38D 8⅛ engine and General Motors 1600 hp. 16–278A engine. Engine room noise in *Tang* boats was excruciatingly increased.[5]

The Navy had a shipyard schedule to keep, and the result was the installation of unproven engines in both *Tang* (SS-563) and *Wahoo* (SS-565), the first two boats to be launched. On their maiden trips from their shipyards on America's east coast, through the Panama Canal to Pearl Harbor, the *Wahoo* was able to make the trip by constantly making repairs to broken parts. The *Tang* turned back for further basic repairs to its engines. It was the enginemen aboard the *Tang*-class boats who would pay the price for BuShip's blunder.

The layout of the submarine's "pancake" engine compartment was unusual. It was sound-isolated in a unique L-shaped (as seen from the port aspect) arrangement that housed the four engines, their suspended generators, and the main propulsion motors directly aft of the generators. A partial keel-fitted bulkhead separated the engine/generators from the propulsion motors. Above the main motors was the maneuvering compartment where electricians controlled electrical output from generators and batteries to the main motors. This compartment was sound-isolated from the engine compartment. The compartment design posed an inherent danger not anticipated by BuShip engineers.

Wahoo (SS-565) was conducting special operations in the Sea of Japan in November 1955. Using its automatic hovering system, the boat remained quiet at about 500 feet with Soviet destroyers on the surface. A fire broke out below the stern plane wheel in the area of the electric hover pumping motors. The flames were extinguished, but unknown to the diving officer the boat was heavy aft. This condition had been masked by the automatic feature of hovering. Depth control was lost as the planesmen switched to hand operation. The submarine took an up angle from the heavy aft/heavy overall condition. Water in the bilges of the engine compartment spilled over the baffle separating generators from propulsion motors. The submarine's up angle rapidly grew to about 40°, and being heavy overall, it slid backwards past its test depth. The electricians in maneuvering reported that a severe ground prevented applying full voltage to the propulsion motors. Blowing the main ballast tanks would surface *Wahoo* in the midst

7—*From* Tang *to* Nautilus

Sweat-soaked First Class Engineman C.H. Anderson and Chief Engineman Earl "Moe" Wineberg examine gauges in their attempt to keep *Wahoo*'s engines running. November 1955 (Submarine Research Center).

of the Russians. Captain Hanssen grabbed the 7MC microphone and demanded full power, hang the stator ground. His voice carried the urgency of the situation to those in maneuvering and they promptly complied by spinning up the voltage controllers. *Wahoo*'s downward plunge slowed, and while the propulsion motors pushed at flank speed, the boat began to rise. The submarine regained depth control and came to a depth where bilge pumps could evacuate the engine room. *Wahoo* was able to evade the Soviet surface forces while it slowly exited the area. At its deepest point the stern room was estimated by the electricians in maneuvering to have been at about 1,150 feet.[6] As noted earlier, the test depth of the *Tang*-class boat was 700 feet, giving it a theoretical crush depth of 1100 feet.[7]

In the late 1960s a story was told that while on a similar special operation in the Vladivostok area, *Gudgeon* was held down by Soviet destroyers for over 30 hours. When *Gudgeon* finally was sure it was in international waters, it surfaced. A flashing light message in plain English was sent from the Soviet destroyer in Morse code, "Thank you for the ASW exercise."

On page 258 of *U.S. Submarines Since 1945*, Norman Friedman recounted the story: "Captain Norman Bessac, later commanding officer of *Scorpion*, had reason to appreciate his nuclear powered submarine's agility and high speed endurance. He had been cornered by Soviet ASW ships off Vladivostok and was held down for more than 30 hours during which time Soviet destroyers dropped practice depth charges on the submarine. After surfacing the commanding officer took his boat away from the Vladivostok area."[8]

Another significant *Tang* problem was the boat's hydraulic torpedo loading system. This system had to be redesigned and modified in the next available yard overhaul.

In 1957 the Navy had had enough of the pancake engines. In a yard overhaul, about 9 feet of hull length was added, enough to accommodate two of the trusty Fairbanks Morse ten-cylinder, opposed-piston diesels. From that point on, the *Tang*-class boats performed well in a variety of demanding missions.

The idea of a controlled nuclear chain reaction to create heat for a steam-driven turbine came into being during the late 1930s. As American industry during the Second World War took on the problem of a fissionable material in quantities sufficient to create an atomic bomb, individuals in the Navy Department saw nuclear energy as a source of propulsion for ships and submarines. Rear Admiral Earle Mills, assistant chief of the Bureau of Ships, and Captain Thorwald Solberg, also of BuShips, had several conferences with Brigadier General Lesley Groves, head of the Manhattan Project. The three forward-looking senior officers outlined their collective opinion in a formal record of agreement that nuclear propulsion for ships was feasible. In the fall of 1944 a committee of the two naval officers and their staffs visited the Naval Research Laboratory, where they discussed with scientists Ross Gunn and Philip A. Abelson the possibility of a nuclear-powered submarine. What started as a concept was developed through 1945 into a detailed plan for the building of a nuclear power plant as a source of propulsion for a submarine.[9]

The advantages could not be ignored. They included an unlimited range, high submerged speed, no recharging of batteries, and the elimina-

7—From Tang to Nautilus

tion of an induction system by snorkel that brought with it moisture and fumes. By 1946 the Oak Ridge, Tennessee, facility was producing enough high-grade fissionable material to provide an experimental reactor with sufficient fuel. Hyman G. Rickover was able to receive the backing of the Chief of Naval Operations and ultimately of Congress in leading the many contractors involved in the construction of a nuclear power plant. Admiral Rickover saw the concept of a nuclear-powered submarine as his personal responsibility. This was a significant extension of his authority from nuclear power propulsion to the construction of a submarine to house the nuclear power plant. His driving force took a concept from the drawing board to a building program. The first nuclear submarine was to be designated SSN-571. It was to be named *Nautilus*, and the contract for its building was awarded to the Electric Boat Company of Groton, Connecticut.[10]

The first thermal reactor, called a pressurized water reactor, or PWR, was designated STR for submarine thermal reactor. The Electric Boat design for the *Nautilus* was essentially a *Tang*-class hull, lengthened, improved, and made considerably more complex by the machinery required for sustained underwater performance. The design called for a 3,500-ton submerged displacement with a hull length of approximately 324 feet.[11]

Running in parallel with the construction of *Nautilus* was the development of the S2W nuclear reactor at Arco, Idaho. The Arco reactor served both as a test vehicle and as a trainer for Navy personnel handpicked by Rickover.

The *Nautilus* inner area diameter was 28 feet. The submarine had a partial double hull with six compartments designated as the torpedo room, berthing quarters, central operating compartment, reactor compartment, engine room, and stern compartment. As with the *Tang* design, a large sonar chin mount was to house a BQR–4a passive sonar and an SQS-4 active sonar. *Nautilus* was to have a crew of approximately 90 enlisted men and 12 officers. Both the enlisted rates and officers were divided between those qualified as nuclear specialists and those in the more traditional rates of communication, weapons, navigation, and supply. To reduce the dangers involved in a reactor failure, an auxiliary diesel engine with generator provided a safety backup. *Nautilus* also had a snorkel and battery, the latter of which was approximately half the size of a GUPPY battery. The nuclear-powered submarine *Nautilus* was placed in commission on September 30, 1954, and was commanded by Eugene P. Wilkinson.[12]

The *Nautilus* proved that a fast underwater speed could outmaneuver an experienced ASW hunter-killer group. Not only was she difficult to find, but she was too fast for existing ASW torpedoes. She could break off and run, then re-attack at will. During the first two years of her experience in numerous exercises, *Nautilus* seemed to live up to all the expectations of the BuShips engineers.

As stated earlier, a submarine's fire control system and weapons become relevant to the submarine's mission only when they are supported by its fundamental design. While *Nautilus* had an advanced sonar and Mark 101 fire control system and while these systems were manned by competent personnel, they had only limited value in a submarine capable of high submerged speed, but encumbered by extreme noise emission at speeds greater than eight knots. Not only did the auxiliary machinery introduce noise, but vibrations in the sail, hull and superstructure increased in direct ratio to speed. If the vibration frequencies emanating from the sail and those from the hull were to harmonize, serious damage could be caused to the integrity of the pressure hull. It was reported that noise from vibrations when the submarine exceeded eight knots was so intense in the torpedo room as to preclude normal conversation. Of most critical concern was the rendering of passive sonar as useless at any speeds greater than eight knots.[13]

Admiral Hyman G. Rickover was successful in keeping the reputation of *Nautilus* intact. After all, he had almost single-handedly been responsible for the successful introduction of nuclear power into the United States fleet. Although *Nautilus* was recognized worldwide as something of a marvel, its vibration/noise difficulties had to be addressed promptly. The Navy brought one of its best problem solvers to address the vibration problem. John Craven, chief scientist for the U.S. Navy's Special Projects Office, was given the task of precisely identifying the vibration source or sources and recommending corrective measures.

After having been at sea for approximately a year and a half, *Nautilus* made her slow approach up the Thames River to the Electric Boat Company dry dock. As she approached, she was down by the bow and her reserve buoyancy was minimal. The commanding officer's concerns were initially addressed to retired Admiral Andrew McKee, who had immense experience in building submarines. Wilkinson had already complained to BuShips about the severe vibrations at high speed. The BuShips structural engineers were able to measure the vibration levels, but could not find their source.

7—From Tang to Nautilus

Flow studies were begun at the David Taylor Model Basin. Wilkinson, McKee and Craven worked side-by-side in creating an analysis method that would lead to correcting the vibration problem. When in dry dock the ship was examined carefully by this team of brilliant individuals.

Most submarines use a cylinder-shaped hull reinforced by girders of steel called stiffeners or frames. These girders are inside the pressure hull for that part of the hull where the hull plating is a part of the hydrodynamic shape of the submarine. For those portions of the hull where ballast tanks and superstructure completely surround it, the stiffeners are external to the hull, but are not exposed to water flow. In either case the stiffeners are attached at regular intervals to the pressure hull by welding. The metallurgic properties of the hull steel strike a balance between two possible failure modes: buckling and elastic failure. The interaction between the cylindrical hull and the ring stiffeners is vital to the submarine's ability to resist buckling and to maintain elasticity. Wilkinson, McKee and Craven discovered ring stiffeners within the superstructure that had torn away from the hull, twisted and eventually failed from fatigue. McKee had never seen anything like it, and Wilkinson thought of how close his submarine had come to complete failure. It was assumed that the massive hull structure of a submarine could not be seriously affected by hydrodynamic forces. Certainly, the devastation of heavy metal parts far exceeded anything previously experienced by submarine builders. Additionally, the submarine's thin ballast tanks showed severe signs of fatigue by longitudinal slits in the steel. Within the ballast tanks were high-pressure air flasks used for blowing the tanks on surfacing. These flasks had parted from their holding brackets and were hanging only by their piping.[14]

Craven's first job was to examine and understand what was happening to the sail, pressure hull, stiffeners, superstructure, and ballast tanks. Repairs were made to allow *Nautilus* to once again go to sea and with intricate measurement instruments, determine the hydrodynamic influences causing damage at successively high speeds. Eventually, the information gained from the near-fatal vibrations of *Nautilus* was to lead to a basic reassessment of what a submarine's hull should be.

When *Nautilus* had not yet entered service, the two fiscal-year 1955 SSNs, *Skate* (SSN-578) and *Swordfish* (SSN-579), as well as the two fiscal-year 1956 SSNs, *Sargo* (SSN-583) and *Seadragon* (SSN-584), became the first classes of U.S. nuclear fleet combat submarines. The *Skate* had a design des-

Submarine Torpedo Tactics

ignator EB264A. Both *Skate* and *Swordfish* were built at Electric Boat in Groton, Connecticut. The *Skate*- and *Sargo*-class boats had a hull length of 267 feet with a 25-foot beam. Their submerged displacement was 2,848 tons. Their blunted bow allowed a faired sonar system that housed an SQS-4, BQR-2b, and BQH-2. Like the *Nautilus*, the *Skate*- and *Sargo*-class submarines had Mark 101, mod 19 fire control systems. Their nuclear power plants were pressurized water reactors, type S3W.[15] These boats were basic *Nautilus* designs scaled down to approximate *Tang* dimensions. As a nuclear equivalent of *Tang*, *Skate* carried a pair of short stern countermeasure tubes in addition to her long bow tubes. In January 1957 the bow tubes of the *Skate*-class submarines were modified for Mark 37 wire-guide torpedoes. In addition, the power torpedo handling gear was modified to allow for sharp maneuvering while reloading.[16] By this time, *Nautilus* had made it quite obvious that high speeds were extremely desirable and the four follow-on boats had equal expectations.

The young nuclear-powered submarine fleet was not immune to accidents despite exceptionally well-trained crews and the most advanced equipment.

On June 14, 1960, during an oxygen charging evolution at dockside, a rupture in the charging hose caused a violent fire and an accompanying torpedo fuel explosion in the stern room of the *Sargo*. The captain, who had quickly returned to the boat after hearing the explosion, immediately had the after lines thrown off and the after group vents opened. The boat's stern settled to the bottom as seawater rushed into the open hatches, extinguishing the fire. The ignited oxygen leak had occurred at the fueling truck, traveled down the hose and into the submarine, where it fanned out to engulf the entire compartment, killing a crew member.[17]

Skate had a close call in the spring of 1962 while transiting from Key West, Florida, to Norfolk, Virginia. The boat's depth was 600 feet and its speed was approximately 20 knots. The quartermaster was not completely sure of the boat's position when he was relieved by a more senior navigator. Recognizing the breach of safety, the navigator ordered the fathometer switched on. It showed less than a hundred feet under the keel. He then grabbed the stern plane yoke and pulled. The boat took a 35° up angle, narrowly missing the bottom. The captain entered the control room as the angle leveled off. He ordered 200 feet and reduced the speed.[18]

On November 10, 1966, as the aircraft carrier *Essex*, under command of Capt. William B. Murray, was being refueled by USS *Salamonie*, *Nautilus*

7—*From* Tang *to* Nautilus

made several successful penetrations of the ASW bent-line screen. It then maneuvered into firing position and launched green flares as indication to those on the surface that it had taken periscope pictures of the *Essex* with telemeter cross hairs cutting vertically through the superstructure. *Nautilus* was inside the ASW bent-line screen and was close to the *Essex*, as heard by the senior sonarman. The screw noise became very loud, alarming the sonar operator. At that moment the captain yelled, "Flood negative! Take her deep!" The diving officer ordered negative flooded and full dive both planes. At that moment the bow of the *Essex* crashed into the port side of the sail. *Nautilus* was filled with the shriek of metal scraping against metal. The force of impact was so great that she rolled 45° to starboard and was pushed downward, losing depth control. The boat recovered, and signaled that she was surfacing. The bridge hatch could not be opened, but *Essex* described the damage via UQC. *Nautilus* made port on the surface accompanied by surface craft.[19]

The public's eye remained on *Nautilus* even as the *Skate* and *Sargo* boats worked with other Navy units in confirming the benefits of nuclear-

Nautilus after collision with surface vessel (courtesy Submarine Force Museum).

powered high submerged speeds. Nautilus traveled 1300 miles submerged from New London to San Juan, Puerto Rico, in 1955. Using SINS navigation, she covered 1383 miles under the polar ice to reach England in July of 1957. The submarine may have experienced some dramatic problems, but she unquestionably brought the Navy to the forefront of public admiration.

Despite occasional accidents and design problems, nuclear-powered submarines of the 1950s were a resounding success in terms of providing vital operational information that would become the basis of a new generation of high underwater speed submarines. The *Albacore* provided hull shape information and high speed data that were essential to future submarine design.

8

A Most Unusual Torpedo

The U.S. Navy paced the Army's missile research program by developing a guided missile that could be launched from ships and submarines. The basic idea of the German V-1 pulse jet flying bomb led to the first submarine-launched missile, called the Loon. The USS *Carbonero* (SS-337) and USS *Cusk* (SS-348) first launched the Loon at sea in February 1947. It had an affective 135 nautical mile range when using relay-guidance.

The Navy converted two Second World War submarines for the purpose of carrying guided missiles. The USS *Tunny* (SSG-282) was the first submarine to carry the Regulus missile. The submarine carried a large, pressurized cylindrical hangar about 15 feet in diameter aft of the sail. The hangar could accommodate two Regulus I missiles in a rotating ring. To launch the Regulus I, *Tunny* had to remain on the surface for the launch, which required approximately 45 minutes. During the early 1950s *Tunny* operated out of Point Mugu, California, while perfecting its Regulus launching capability. Working with *Tunny* was the USS *Barbero* (SS-317). It had a hangar nearly identical to that of *Tunny*. Both submarines were then moved to Pearl Harbor, from which they conducted special operations in the northwest Pacific during the latter 1950s and 1960s.

The Chance-Vought Regulus carried a 3000-pound warhead for 500 nautical miles with relay guidance. It was essentially a small turbojet aircraft, 42 feet long, with a wingspan of 21 feet. The missile was launched from an inclined ramp and required JATO assistance for launch.

The USS *Grayback* (SSG-574) and USS *Growler* (SSG-577) were commissioned as the first diesel electric submarines specifically designed to carry Regulus missiles. Both *Grayback* and *Growler* were home ported in Pearl Harbor, from which they conducted Regulus missile patrols in the northwest Pacific during the early 1960s.[1]

Of course the Regulus submarines of this era carried torpedo tubes, even if their notoriety was derived from their mission pertaining to guided missiles. In these tubes were to be found standard torpedoes of the day: the Mark 14 steam torpedo, Mark 16 Navol torpedo, the Mark 28 electric torpedo, and the Mark 27 evasion torpedo. The *Growler*'s torpedo tubes were no exception, although they played a key role in an event that has gone largely unrecorded.

What has come to be known as the "Great Totem Pole Caper" was in reality several thefts by at least three submarine crews over a period of two years during the 1960s. Each theft brought reprisals and threats at the highest levels of the Submarines Pacific organization and came even to the attention of Commander-in-Chief, Pacific Fleet. The following narrative is based on descriptions from Bill Gunn and Bob Harmuth, both officers of reliable memory. Their narrative has been attested to by other crew members of USS *Growler*. With Bob Harmuth's permission, the following paraphrased description of a most unusual "torpedo" is presented.

Adak, Alaska, is one of the westernmost islands in the Aleutian chain. The Navy had maintained a base there since the Second World War. While it is a desolate, wind-swept, cold, barren island, the Navy had tried its best to provide its occupants with some comforts of home. The base served both the air arm of the Navy and many ships that visited the port in the northern Pacific. A few of these ships were submarines, which were unfortunate enough to have assignments in the inhospitable waters of the northwest Pacific. Some amenities were distinctive to the climate and people of the region. For example, the base club and exchange offered booze at a very low cost, crab legs at next to nothing and fur overcoats at ridiculously low prices. The officers' club prided itself above all else on its genuine, hand-carved and painted Aleutian totem pole which stood proudly just outside the entrance.

Since flying officers and other members of the Navy's air arm were constant customers of the club, they had a proprietary feeling about the totem pole. The symbol of the Aleutian natives became their symbol. Several of the patrol planes had images of the totem pole painted on their sides.

It has been an age-old fact that submariners and airmen don't always see eye to eye on various subjects. This fact became most vivid when, in the course of an evening, the two groups of men drank to excess. They had to constantly remind themselves that they were in the same navy.

8—A Most Unusual Torpedo

USS *Grayback* and *Growler* were sister ships. They were nearly identical from the outside and the two skippers had the habit of announcing themselves as the opposite ship. This led to confusion on the Adak base and many of the pranks attributed to one submarine were actually carried out by the other. Although the confusion was intended for the Adak base organization, it often made itself apparent at Pearl.

One evening, *Growler* ran submerged after having been on a lengthy patrol. The officers and men were in a feisty mood after so long at sea. The boat was entering Adak, but in a somewhat unorthodox fashion. It was a Saturday night when they made Adak Island landfall through the periscope. *Growler* cruised along the northern edge of the island and then turned south into the harbor at the naval station. Lieutenant Bill Gunn had convinced the captain it would be fun to arrive unannounced and undetected on a sunny Sunday morning. What could be better than surprising the Airdales? That became the plan. The battery was fully charged and they would be taking on water the next day, so the captain decided to go below and wait for first light to enter port. It was showers all around and a long game of hearts in the wardroom. After all, it was Saturday night and they were going home.

Slowly, *Growler* moved through Kuluk Bay with no sign of activity on shore. The navigation was tricky when running submerged. She made her way into Scabard Bay, made a large circle and headed toward the fueling pier. Not a soul could be seen on the pier. The captain and officers had put on some old Japanese maritime hats with big red stars. They wore jeans and old foul weather gear. Most of the men had grown beards. All in all, they made a very shabby and haggard appearance.

When the boat was parallel to the pier the captain ordered the boat surfaced. The high pressure blow was left on a little longer than normal for effect. The deck hatches popped open and the rough-looking men appeared on the bridge and deck. With no name, no hull number and no flag, the *Growler* could have belonged to any navy. An old chief in a shack alongside the pier was awakened by the noise of the surfacing submarine. He stared at the boat with open mouth and waved his arms. "Ahoy, there! Who are you?" yelled the chief on the pier. With a megaphone, the captain answered in a flurry of made-up Russian. The chief ran back into the shack and a moment later the base alarm sounded. It echoed around the bay and caused immediate mayhem. A minute later three truckloads of Marines headed down the hill toward the fuel pier, followed closely by a couple of sedans which carried the commanding officer of the base and the duty officer.

By the time the sedans arrived at the pier, *Growler*'s captain had shifted into a proper uniform and the crew was in the process of doubling up.

"Who the hell are you?" demanded the base commanding officer.

"USS *Grayback*, returning from patrol," answered the *Growler*'s captain. "We need fuel, stores, and recreation."

"We can supply you with fuel and stores. As to the recreation, it's Sunday and it's nine in the morning," explained the base officer.

Growler's captain was persuasive, and both enlisted and officers' clubs were opened immediately after Sunday services. The duty section of the *Growler* worked while the majority of the crew played. It took a couple of days to get everything accomplished. Things had settled down and the crew was ready to go back to sea on the final leg back to Pearl.

On the night before *Growler* was to leave Adak, Lieutenant Bob Harmuth had gone below for second helpings of crabmeat when a commotion started topside. He climbed back up the ladder just in time to greet about ten of the crew who had returned in a stolen Navy truck carrying what appeared to be a huge log. Harmuth queried the men, but they mumbled and continued their task of carrying aboard a totem pole.

"It's our new torpedo," a less-than-sober seaman attempted. It was so long it took all ten men to carry the thing. Harmuth tried to prevent the men from bringing the brightly painted pole aboard. He stood his ground until a first class torpedoman explained, "Lieutenant Gunn told us to take it back to the boat, remove the wings and store the totem pole in a port torpedo tube. It's the captain's wish."

Harmuth scratched his head and reasoned that if the captain said it was okay then that's the way it was going to be. The men used the forward torpedo loading hatch to get the totem pole down into the torpedo room. There they inserted the totem pole into the tube using regular torpedo handling gear.

When the captain came aboard he announced that he was heading to his stateroom to sleep and he didn't want to be disturbed.

About midnight when the fueling was being topped off, a pickup truck roared onto the pier and halted next to the *Growler*. An officer emerged who was wearing an O.D. brassard on his arm. As he ran across the brow he hollered, "Okay, where's the totem pole?"

8—A Most Unusual Torpedo

Harmuth replied with military dignity, "I beg your pardon, commander?"

"I said, Mister, where's my totem pole?" repeated the officer.

Submarine officers relished such situations. They were not much intimidated by rank. Harmuth reminded the lieutenant commander of navy protocol.

"Excuse me sir, but you forgot to request permission to come aboard," reminded Harmuth. A discourse began on the necessity for an officer, coming aboard a United States vessel, to salute the topside watch and the colors. The Airdale lieutenant commander could not understand why he should salute a second class petty officer. He became very vexed when Harmuth reminded him that he must request permission from the third class petty officer to come aboard. Harmuth wondered if the officer had been absent the day this part of Navy orientation was covered at OCS. In frustration, the base officer finally brushed past the petty officer topside watch stander and stormed aboard to demand an interview with the captain. Harmuth escorted the man down the ladder and to the captain's stateroom, where the captain lay fast asleep. The man demanded to know where the *Growler* had hidden his totem pole. The half-awake captain told Harmuth to show the lieutenant commander through the boat and to satisfy him that no totem pole was in his submarine. Harmuth took his time moving from compartment to compartment. Finally, the officer was satisfied and made his way back to the captain, where he apologized for having disturbed him.

Growler got underway early the next day. On a spot in front of the Adak club was a large hole where the totem pole had once stood.

The evening before entering Pearl Harbor the officers and crew of the *Growler* were in high spirits. They played cards and talked about Waikiki. In the wardroom Bill Gunn asked the captain what he wanted the crew to do with the totem pole. Of course, the captain had known nothing of the caper and at first was put out. The pole had been stored in the only empty torpedo tube. The captain couldn't resist admiring the innovative skullduggery and he smiled with satisfaction. As *Growler* made its way into the channel the boat was met by Commander Submarines Pacific. The admiral came aboard, but without the usual smile. He climbed down the ladder and sat in the wardroom. After a few preliminary remarks the admiral demanded to know if *Growler* had the flyboys' totem pole. The captain replied that he did, expecting the admiral to be appropriately irritated. The admiral slapped the captain on the back and gave him a well-done.

The totem pole was hauled out of the forward torpedo room and manhandled to a truck, where it was loaded and carried to the next transport heading back to Adak. The captain wrote a letter of apology to the Adak base commander. It was very short.

The early missile boats didn't spend much time in port. They went to the shipyard, where repairs were accomplished, and took on stores at the SubBase finger piers. Then back out they went, back to the northwestern Pacific.

Growler had spent another patrol on station and now was back in Adak on its homeward-bound trip. On the last night in port, Bob Harmuth went up to the club. He stood in front of the club, where he expected to find the replaced totem pole. It was not there—just a hole in the ground. Perhaps it had not been returned; then again, it may have been stolen for the second time. Also in front of the club was a light standard, and tied to the metal light pole were two enlisted airmen who had been bound and gagged. Harmuth knew that there was going to be big trouble. His first instinct was to protect his ship. He told the men to hang tight, that he would only be gone for a short time. He then ran back to *Growler* to warn of the impending storm from the base commander. When he got back aboard, he asked the topside watch if anyone had brought a totem pole aboard. He got a noncommittal answer and went below to find out for himself. He asked the officers in the forward battery, each of whom he had to awaken for the questioning. Each denied any knowledge and so Harmuth felt relieved. To be sure, he went into the torpedo room and checked each torpedo tube. Each was labeled "war shot." The totem pole was not in a torpedo tube. That much was certain. He then called the base officer of the day and told him that there were a couple of his sailors tied up outside the club. Figuring that he had done about all that could be done to ensure that *Growler* was not implicated in another pole theft, he went to bed.

He had not been there long when the same base lieutenant commander came bursting into the forward battery compartment. He demanded that each torpedo tube be opened for his inspection. The captain wearily accepted the challenge and ordered Harmuth to get a torpedoman to open each tube in the boat for inspection.

The base officer stuck his head into each tube to see propellers and

8—A Most Unusual Torpedo

nothing else. His totem pole was simply not there. After Harmuth and the base commander had again gone carefully through each compartment, the lieutenant commander again apologized to the captain.

As it turned out, the pole had again been stolen by the crew of *Growler*. This time the men had opened up an empty fuel ballast tank, sawed the pole into sections so as not to destroy the artwork, and had placed the pieces in the tank. They had then secured the tank with the 48 bolts holding the soft patch. Of course, the captain had no knowledge of this second theft.

When *Growler* was back in Pearl Harbor and all was routine, the captain had a dinner party at his Makalapa home. It was to be a mild social event; nothing big, just the wardroom and a few other guests from SubPac staff.

The crew decided to give the captain a treat and so glued the totem pole back together and mounted it on the captain's front lawn. When he returned from the boat to get ready for the party he immediately saw the implications of what was before him. He was furious at whomever was responsible. By this time the totem pole had become so infamous that every boat commander tried to stay clear of the whole thing. He was mad at the executive officer, who knew nothing of the incident. He was mad at the officers for not telling him about the pole, but they too knew nothing; and he was mad at the crew for ripping off the pole and thereby creating huge political problems for the boat's commanding officer.

At this point it should be noted that descriptions of what took place thereafter were not consistent. Some *Growler* crewmembers blamed the latest theft on the *Grayback*. Others thought it might have been the *Barbero*. In any event the totem pole was transported back to Adak, repainted, and set into a solid concrete slab in front of the officers' club. One final note: When *Growler* went back to Adak on the next patrol, her officers could not find their boat's plaque, which should have been above the bar in the officers' club. Each patrol squadron and each submarine had a plaque, but *Growler*'s was not to be found. After searching the bar area, the *Growler* officers found that it had been nailed to the underside of the pool table.[2]

The USS *Growler* was stricken from the Navy list of ships in August 1980. The submarine is now a part of the USS *Intrepid* Sea-Air-Space Museum in New York City, along with an example of a Regulus missile.

9

Skipjack, *the Convergence of* Nautilus *and* Albacore

When *Nautilus* displayed her underwater speed, she came close to causing her own demise by the failure of her external framing and other superstructure weakness. In addition, she discovered that when she increased speed, own ship's noise obliterated the capacity of her BQR-2 passive sonar to detect possible targets. The emerging principle was that high underwater speeds and effective torpedo fire control (which depended on accurate sonar bearings), were incompatible.

Submarine officers in both the American and British navies discussed a variety of engineering problems arising from high underwater speeds. They agreed that the purpose of any hull design was to achieve the most volume-efficient form, one in which total volume was made as small as possible so as to reduce the power needed to propel the submarine. However, that principle was too simplistic since it may not have been compatible with the need for efficiency of pressure hull structure to accommodate internal machinery. Submarine officers saw the problem of high-speed hull design as a system of compromises surrounding the need for effective sonar information while running at high speed.

Even when in a non-combat situation, such as transiting, a submarine still needed to know whether there were other vessels, and particularly other submarines, in the vicinity. Also, continuous information on topographical features of the seabed or under-ice was critical to safety.[1] Thus, it had either to transit at a slower speed or to slow at regular intervals to check the submarine's immediate environment. Neither option appealed to forward-looking submarine officers. For this reason it was desirable that the design of a high-speed submarine should carefully define the maximum speed at which acoustic sensors could be relied upon. Such definition dif-

9—Skipjack, *the Convergence of* Nautilus *and* Albacore

fered in the tactical situation, but a speed-to-sonar efficiency curve seemed a mandatory tool for any high-speed submarine.

As early as 1945 a United States naval officer, Lieutenant Commander Charles N. Hendrix, had drawn up a page of ship characteristics that proposed a radical, high-speed submarine design, incorporating features that included a single propeller, return to flood valves, automatic depth control, upper as well as lower rudders, and abolishment of the conning tower. He also advocated a dedicated space for torpedo fire control along the lines of a surface ship's combat information center. His farsighted imagination preceded by several years serious discussions of future submarines.[2]

In July 1946 the Bureau of Ships responded to the ideas of both engineers and submarine officers by requesting the David Taylor Model Basin at Carderock, Maryland, to undertake a series of various high-speed hull form tests.[3] The series was referred to as Series 58. It called for a rational design based on empirical data devoid of historical attitudes as to what a submarine should look like. At first, the experimenters looked to the dirigible's shape as a possible starting point, but this was dismissed as contrary to their determination to start from scratch. During the next few years, several high-ranking Navy officers began supporting the development of a high-speed underwater research craft having the basic hull design revealed from the David Taylor Model Basin Series 58 project. The resulting USS *Albacore* (SS-569) was a revolutionary design, because it departed from any previous submarine design. The *Albacore* was intended to provide information required for future submarine design by acting as a test vessel in regard to hydrodynamics at extremely high speeds.[4]

It was obvious to submarine officers during the late 1940s that reducing the transmission of onboard noisemakers and reducing fluid-flow noise, particularly over the parts of the hull where the sonar was located, was essential if the submarine was to remain undetected while maintaining maximum passive sonar acuity. Running at ultra-quiet entailed reducing speed to the minimum, consistent with maintaining depth control. Ultra-quiet also meant shutting down virtually all operating machinery, including ventilation and air conditioning.[5]

One of the considerations in developing a high-speed submarine was the placement of ballast tanks, either interior to the pressure hull, which posed difficult engineering problems, or the traditional external saddle tanks, which produced a much larger speed-reducing wet area. There were advantages to the traditional external ballast tanks. For example, the external second hull gave a measurable resistance to damage from a beam aspect explosion. The complete, wraparound outer envelope also provided space for fuel storage in diesel electric submarines.[6]

There was agreement between naval engineers and submarine officers that the major component of passive sonar would continue to be located in the bow, which was essential not only to have good forward-looking information, but also as far abaft the beam as possible. The most prevalent idea of bow arrangement was a sonar array embedded within an outer envelope of the hull, covered with an acoustic window of noninterfering material. Modifying this basic concept were other contending demands for space in the bow of the submarine, but in nearly all preliminary designs, these were treated as secondary to the interest of sonar as the primary source of information for torpedo fire control. The dependence of the submarine's safety on the effectiveness of its sonar meant that the bow configuration had to be, as far as possible, designed to the needs of the sonar equipment. Exactly how this requirement might affect the ideal form for minimum hydrodynamic flow resistance remained unsolved until these concepts were brought to reality through the construction of the USS *Albacore* (SS-569).[7]

The *Albacore* design began in 1949 as a proposal that both hull shape and control surfaces be responsive to hydrodynamic demands at high speeds. The *Albacore* designers had a free hand to pursue speed by using a hydrodynamic-ideal form, even though it might prove to be unsuited to the needs of operational submarines. To achieve high speed, the *Albacore* hull would house the largest possible propulsive power in the smallest possible hull that would comply with the dimensions of the David Taylor Model Basin demonstrated shape. The boat would use a 7,500-horsepower Westinghouse propulsion motor. To save space, the motor and engine controls were combined so that a single crew member could operate them. Since *Albacore* was to be diesel-electric powered, it was designed with saddle fuel tanks. The boat had no snorkel, although provisions were made for its future installation. Ballast tank vents in previous submarines were hydraulically operated. This was efficient, but required space, which *Albacore* couldn't provide. The solution was space-saving electrical control switches. High underwater speeds demanded quicker planes' depth control. This led designers to adopt one-man, aircraft-type controls that integrated planes and rudders.[8]

9—Skipjack, *the Convergence of* Nautilus *and* Albacore

The *Albacore* was commissioned on December 5, 1953. She quickly demonstrated that she was the most agile and maneuverable submarine yet constructed. Her pressure hull was fabricated of low-carbon, high-yield steel, but her test depth was held to 600 feet because of unknown factors associated with speed. Despite this, her ship's log indicated that on at least one occasion *Albacore* descended to 1,400 feet in trials. At such high speeds, the submarine could descend below test depth in a matter of seconds. An inattentive planes operator could quickly lose control.[9]

To reduce the turbulence generated as water flowed over the hull, all projections were removed except for a streamlined sail and control surfaces. The submarine had been planned to achieve a submerged speed of approximately 27 knots and its performance came close to this prediction. In 1956 *Albacore* achieved speeds in excess of 25 knots on the half-hour rate.[10] The submarine utilized two General Motors 16–338 "pancake" diesel engines, the same as those used in the *Tang*-class submarines. With a 500-cell battery, the power output was equivalent to 7,500 horsepower. The *Albacore* had a length of 150 feet with a 30-foot beam. This length-to-beam ratio was unheard of in previous submarines. The final *Albacore* design length-to-beam ratio was 7.5 to 1. It was a fat, teardrop-shaped hull. Her single propeller was increased from 11 feet to 14 feet in diameter.

The *Albacore* was in service for nearly 19 years. During this time she was modified in phases to cover several specific maneuverability projects. One experiment centered on placing control surfaces aft of or foreword of the single propeller. Another experiment that was the basis for most future submarines was the relocation of the small bow planes to the sail to reduce flow noise at the bow. These planes had been useful only when operating near the surface and at slow speeds, both of which did not fit into the *Albacore* agenda.

In 1962 through 1965 the submarine went into dry dock to be lengthened to 210 feet with installation of contra-rotating propellers mounted on a small-diameter shaft within an outer shaft. A second 4,700-horsepower electric motor drove the second propeller. These alterations provided basic information to the Bureau of Ships regarding underwater maneuverability, speed, and noise emission. The *Albacore* attained the highest speed achieved to that time by a submarine, using its contra-rotating propellers. With that configuration the *Albacore* achieved approximately 36 knots.[11]

Dive brakes were fitted to prevent exceeding test depth at high speeds.

High-speed turns had some unexpected problems, the worst of which was *Albacore*'s tendency to snap roll when large rudder orders were used. When the submarine turned, her sail acted as a hydroplane, rolling the boat in the direction of the turn. As the boat rolled, the rudders inclined to the horizontal orientation, where they acted as planes, exacerbating the problem. A dorsal rudder on the sail's trailing edge only tended to act as a brake and had no positive effect on the snap roll tendency. The longitudinal center of gravity was approximately at the sail, while the linear midpoint of the hull was well aft of that point. This tended to slew the stern away from the turn direction, which meant the hull itself was acting as a plane. The correction design included going to an "X" stern plane and rudder configuration. The ultimate correction in later submarines would depend on computerized planes-rudder synchronization similar to that in aircraft.

In 1962 a digital, multi-beam sonar was installed to improve her passive sonar's ability to detect other vessels including submarines. As in later single-screw submarines, a plastic sonar dome carrying a BQS-4 and BQR-2 sonar in combination with the new 14-foot slow-turning quiet propeller greatly improved sonar acuity.

The interiors of all free-flooding spaces were coated with Aquaplas, a heavy spray-plastic coating that absorbed vibration and dampened water flow noise. The sail planes were increased in size and proved to be beneficial in controlling depth at slow speeds.[12]

The success of the experimental *Albacore* led to a proposal that a similar hull form be applied to a full-scale attack submarine. The result was the fast attack submarine *Barbel* class, which consisted of *Barbel* (SS-580), *Blueback* (SS-581), and *Bonefish* (SS-582). They had a length of 219 feet with a 29-foot beam, giving their hull shape a ratio of 7.5 to 1, consistent with the theoretical dimensions of the best hydrodynamic shape revealed through the David Taylor Model Basin experiments.[13]

The bow sonars were the active SQS-4 above and passive BQR-4 below the torpedo tubes. Both active and passive sonars were housed within a sound-permeable glass-reinforced plastic dome. The first of the series, *Barbel* had its bow planes mounted on the bow, but they were quickly moved to the sail in order to provide the bow sonars with better detection potential.

The sonar room occupied the middle deck space just aft of the mast housings and directly below the attack center. The attack center was equipped with a Mark 101, Mod 19 fire control system, upgraded from that

9—Skipjack, *the Convergence of* Nautilus *and* Albacore

found on the *Nautilus*. Since the *Barbel*-class submarines were diesel powered, they had external ballast tanks and fuel ballast tanks that were integrated with the basic hull design. Each boat in the series had a submerged displacement of 2,640 tons. Fitted with two diesel engines, the two small electric motors generated only 3,125 horsepower when snorkeling or on the surface. Their 252-cell G1A battery produced 4,700 horsepower, giving the submarines a submerged speed of approximately 19 knots at the half-hour rate. This comparatively slow submerged speed was the result of carrying the weight of advanced combat equipment and a snorkel system. The fire control equipment with the related operators, by themselves, made the *Barbel* boats significantly larger than the *Albacore*. Their test depth was 700 feet, unchanged from the *Tang*-class submarines.[14]

Each of the *Barbel*-type boats had six 21-inch torpedo tubes with 16 reloads. No stern tubes were fitted because of the single propeller and the tapered stern. The submarines' speed and maneuverability were considered sufficient to alleviate the need for stern tubes. *Barbel* retained a small walking deck aft of the sail.

The three *Barbel*-type submarines were completed in 1959. No others were built for the Navy because of the decision made in 1956 that all future combat submarines would be nuclear powered.

In early 1955 preliminary designs for the first standard operational nuclear submarine were begun.

While the *Barbel* was a diesel-electric-powered submarine with an *Albacore* hull, the nuclear-powered USS *Skate* (SSN-578) and her sister ship, USS *Swordfish* (SSN-579) were similar in length and beam to their *Tang* predecessors. The *Skate*-class submarines had twin screws and were thereby able to carry a pair of short stern countermeasure tubes. The design was modified several times during construction. In January 1957 the design was amended to include a wire guidance feature for the six bow tubes. Freedom to maneuver at high speeds while reloading torpedoes was accomplished through the installation of powered torpedo-handling equipment.

The *Skate*-class submarines had the basic Mark 101 fire control system integrated with BQS-2 and BQR-4 sonars. *Skate* was later updated with a Mark 101, Mod 19 fire control system, which controlled its primary weapon, the Mark 37 torpedo. Her traditional four-bladed twin screws were powered by an S3W pressurized-water nuclear power plant. The *Skate*-class submarines were the last submarines to be built with pre–*Albacore*–type hulls.

Submarine Torpedo Tactics

Engineers and naval architects at the Bureau of Ships and Electric Boat Company worked cooperatively in the design of a new attack submarine that would combine nuclear propulsion with the *Albacore* hull. The work concentrated on combining many new concepts into one new class of submarine. Innovative concepts were thrashed out with differing opinions. One such argument took place between Admiral Hyman Rickover and Captain Donald Kern. Rear Admiral Rickover held sway on nearly every question of nuclear submarine design. He opposed the adoption of a single propeller for nuclear submarines.[15] Captain Donald Kern, in the Bureau of Ships, engaged the admiral in heated arguments over the question of twin-screw versus single-screw propulsion. The conflict centered on the safety of a single-screw submarine operating under the ice. The admiral finally acquiesced to the single-screw design despite his misgivings about the hazards of a large single screw being damaged by ice.[16] All future nuclear-powered submarines would be equipped with single screws.

One of the design problems with the *Albacore* hull form had been how to locate the required pair of sonars, SQS-4 and BQR-2, within the streamlined *Albacore* bow without the elimination of torpedo tubes. The designers at Electric Boat first elected to simply reduce the normal six-tube arrangement to four tubes. They later agreed to the provision of three tubes on each of two tiers, bringing the total to the standard six tubes. Those *Skipjack*-class boats built at Electric Boat Company were equipped with the latter torpedo tube arrangement.

In October 1955, six weeks after the Portsmouth Naval Shipyard had received the order from BuShips to build *Barbel*, the Navy awarded a contract to Electric Boat for construction of *Skipjack*. The Navy was so confident that *Skipjack* would be a revolutionary submarine, it let contracts in rapid succession for six such submarines. These new fast attack submarines were the USS *Skipjack* (SSN-585), the USS *Scorpion* (SSN-589), both built at Electric Boat Company in Groton, Connecticut; the USS *Scamp* (SSN-588), built at Mare Island Shipyard in Vallejo, California; the USS *Sculpin* (SSN-590) and USS *Snook* (SSN-592), both built at Ingalls Shipbuilding in Pascagoula, Mississippi; and USS *Shark* (SSN-591), built at Newport News Shipyard in Newport News, Virginia.[17]

Skipjack, the first boat in the series, was placed in commission on April 15, 1959, with Lieutenant Commander William W. Behrens in command.[18] The *Skipjack* immediately demonstrated the success of her design. She

9—Skipjack, the Convergence of Nautilus and Albacore

achieved just under 33 knots submerged with her original five-blade propeller. This was 15 knots faster than the previous *Skate*-class submarine. However, the *Skipjack*'s speed and maneuverability was paid for in noise emission. It was clear to both submarine officers and those at BuShips that while *Skipjack* lived up to design expectations, the problem of noise emission would have to be a high-priority correction.

Machinery weight had been reduced from the *Skate* class, giving *Skipjack* a submerged displacement of only 3,500 tons. The wide hull provided four decks, each of which was crammed with equipment, berthing, galley, mess and storage. Fore to aft compartments were generally arranged with the torpedo room forward, officers' berthing with operations on the upper level, crew's mess and berthing, the reactor compartment, the maneuvering room (with reactor controls and turbine throttles), and stern room. Its power plant was an S5W pressurized water reactor. It also had a 126-cell battery, primarily used for silent running. *Skipjack* had a test depth of 700 feet with an estimated 1.5 safety margin, or, 1050 foot theoretical crush depth. During a dive while in a hard starboard turn at a speed in excess of 20 knots, the stern plane controls jammed and *Skipjack* plunged at an angle of almost 30 degrees. She exceeded her test depth before recovery with no damage to the boat.

The *Skipjack* had a 15-foot, five-bladed propeller that turned approximately 7 RPM for every knot of speed. On her initial trials, her maximum speed had been 30 knots, achieved with her fast-turning, five-blade propeller. However, even at 20 knots the blade rate produced unacceptable levels of cavitaton. Her screw was subsequently changed to a seven-blade, slower-turning propeller which reduced her speed while reducing cavitation and shaft noise.

Underway analysis revealed that the submarine had six identifiable noise sources: those from main propulsion and auxiliary machinery, especially pumps in the reactor plant that circulated coolant fluids; unbalanced rotating machinery and poorly machined gears; flow-induced propeller blade vibrations; flow of water around the submarine's hull, sail and control surfaces; movement of torpedo tube doors and shutters; and crewmen opening and closing hatches and using tools.[19]

In *Skipjack*'s first yard overhaul, dynamic vibration absorbers and rubber mounts were fixed to all machinery. Flexible couplings were fitted to the twin turbo generators. All major auxiliary equipment was sound isolated by sound-absorbent shielding, floating mounts and flexible piping connections. Crew members were trained in techniques of moving through the submarine while making as little noise as possible.

Skipjack devised two noise-limiting modes of operation. In each mode the need for various power demands were balanced against the need for reduced noise emission.

The mode of quiet operation that allowed retention of propulsion by the reactor was the "Reactor Creep." Both turbo generators were kept on line in this mode, while screw turns were reduced and depth was altered to comply with Reactor Creep noise emission limits.

The most extreme noise-limiting mode was "Battery Creep." In this mode the reactor was put on standby, and propulsive power was drawn from the battery. Only one of the two turbo generators was kept on line. All hands were restricted to their bunks except those on watch. At Battery Creep, the only steady-state machinery noise generated was from the indispensible main lubricating oil pump.

The *Skipjack* submarines had, for their time, elaborate sonar suites, with SQS-4 active sonar and the BQR-2 consoles arranged side by side. This compartment was on the deck below the attack center. The *Skipjack*'s attack center arrangement consisted of a Mark 101, Mod 19 series of display consoles adjacent to the periscopes on the starboard side of the operations compartment. Aft of the periscopes were the radar PPI scope and plot. A DRT plot was forward of the Mark 101 consoles.

During their years of operation the *Skipjack*-class boats proved to be exceptionally maneuverable with speeds adequate to attack and evade hostile submarines. In many exercises, these submarines provided services both as targets for ASW forces and as effective sonar platforms for hunter-killer ASW missions. The *Skipjack* and her sister submarines were the first real nuclear-powered fast attack boats. They should be remembered, not only for their speed and high maneuverability, but for their contribution to reduction of self-noise and their improved sonar acuity with commensurate fire control capability.

The *Skipjack* class of submarines was so successful after BuShip's silencing efforts that the basic design provided engineers with the pattern for the next generation of fast attack submarines, the *Los Angeles* class. The USS *Los Angeles*, with its S6G pressurized water plant producing 30,000 horsepower, was to have a submerged speed of 33 knots, the same as *Skipjack* in 1959.

10

The Sturgeon-*Class Submarine*

In March of 1967 the USS *Sturgeon* (SSN-637) was launched at the Electric Boat Company yard in Groton, Connecticut. It was the first of a 37-boat series ending in 1975 with the USS *Russel* (SSN-687). Within that series of nuclear attack submarines were two significant variants: the *Glenard P. Lipscomb* (SSN-685) and the *Archerfish* (SSN-678).[1] The succeeding series of submarines was the *Los Angeles* class, starting with hull number 688.

The *Sturgeon* had a length of 292 feet and had a surface displacement of 4,229 tons. The boat's design was similar to the *Thresher* class, but was larger with improved equipment-silencing measures. Within a larger sail, several electronic countermeasure masts were added. The sail planes were strengthened for possible under-ice operations. They could be rotated so that the trailing edge could be vertical for breaking through overhead ice. Her crew consisted of 83 enlisted men, 12 chief petty officers and 12 commissioned officers. The boat was powered by an S5W reactor which provided a top 25-knot submerged speed. Her test depth was 1,300 feet, according to Norman Freedman.[2]

Sturgeon had a conformal bow which housed its BQQ-2 active and BQQ-7 passive sonar sphere. The sonar was centered on a 15-foot diameter axis with 1,241 hydrophones. The main advantage of the system was its ability to distinguish between target screw noise and noise generated by own ship machinery and ambient sea return. The sphere occupied the most forward position of the bow, requiring the Mark 63 torpedo tubes immediately aft of the array to be canted outward at approximately 15 degrees. Considerable tests were run to determine the maximum speed that *Sturgeon* could make when firing torpedoes from the canted tubes. The concern stemmed from the fear that a torpedo leaving the tube would encounter strong lateral pressure on the forward part of the torpedo that might produce a twisting motion with a resulting hang-up in the tube. It was found that submarine speeds up to 18 knots would not interrupt a smooth torpedo departure.

The boat carried a normal mixed load of torpedoes, including Mark 14, Mod 6, Mark 37, Mark 37NTS, Mark 48 and Mark 48 ADCAP. Its powered torpedo handling equipment was capable of rapid reloads.

In 1965 a submarine-launched rocket-propelled torpedo, armed with a nuclear warhead and having a range of about 30 miles, was placed aboard some of the *Sturgeon*-class submarines that used the analog Mark 113 fire control system. It was called the SUBROC (UUM-44A). This weapon was launched from a submarine's 21-inch torpedo tube and was 21 feet in length. Its W55 nuclear warhead had dial-control of up to 5 kilotons of destructive power. After launch, it then ascended to the surface, where its booster was ignited, sending the warhead in a ballistic arc to a point approximating the range of the target. It descended to a preset depth and was detonated by a hydrostatic igniter. Since the SUBROC was analog it could only be controlled by the Mark 113 fire control system. This meant that only some of the *Permit* (SSN-594) and *Sturgeon* (SSN-637) submarines could carry the missile. Those boats in the classes having the updated Mark 117 fire control system could not carry the weapon. By 1980 the SUBROC was obsolete by virtue of its outdated mission.

Following the SUBROC was the Sea Lance (UUM-125B), which had a conventional warhead, but in other respects was similar to the SUBROC. It was a solid-propellant rocket with a lightweight booster, but had a short life, being canceled in 1990. Neither of these weapons were ever used against an adversary, and all were removed from *Sturgeon* submarines during the 1980s.[3]

The *Sturgeon* boats were on operational status until the mid–1990s. The *Sturgeon* was decommissioned in August of 1994, and its sail was later installed at the entrance to the Naval Undersea Museum at Keyport, Washington. A section of the museum was devoted to the boat's operations compartment, including periscope, diving stand and fire control consoles.

During the 30-year operational period of the *Sturgeon*-class submarines, the undersea Cold War contained many confrontations. A few of the *Sturgeon*-designed boats were specially modified for unique operations. One *Sturgeon*, the *Parche* (SSN-683) underwent considerable modifications at the Mare Island Naval Shipyard in California. The shipyard period lasted from January 1987 to May 1991. The hull was lengthened by about 100 feet to accommodate special search and recovery equipment.[4] Polmar and Moore reported that the special gear included a claw device for sea floor retrieval.

She was assigned to the same type of special operations that *Halibut* had undertaken in the Sea of Okhotsk. The added section of the boat housed a chamber for divers to exit and return to the submarine. The operations in the Sea of Okhotsk took place in the 1970s and were abandoned when the Soviets were tipped off to the operation. The exact nature of *Parche*'s operations has never been revealed.

Another *Sturgeon*-class submarine, the USS *Narwhal* (SSN-671), powered by an S5G reactor, was modified to further quiet the propulsion system. The reactor was fitted with a special circulating water system that cooled the core by natural convection when at lower power settings. In addition, low-speed, direct-drive turbines eliminated the need for reduction gears. Both of these modifications contributed to a significantly lower propulsion noise emission. Circulating water by convection for low-power output in the S5G reactor was adopted in future system designs. The *Thresher*/*Sturgeon* interior design and equipment layout served as a model for much of the space and equipment allocation for Polaris missile submarines.

The sail plane strengthening and rotational potential served the submarines *Whale* (SSN-638) and *Pargo* (SSN-650) well when these boats were assigned to find and surface at the North Pole. The photographs and filming of these events made national coverage and were important, nonclassified public relations triumphs of the Cold War; however, considerations of under-ice operations limited the nature of prolonged under-ice submergence. Connectivity was poor and sonar ice return made any attempt to recognize a possible target nearly impossible. Certainly, trailing a Soviet adversary under the ice was abundant with great risk.

The *Sturgeon* boats were initially provided with Mark 113 analog fire control systems. The earlier Mark 112 fire control system had been merely a Mark 101 with an analyzer designed to solve fire control problems using bearings-only solutions, but it had been limited to single-target problem solving. The Mark 113, Mod 10 was digital, with four-target TMA capability. The interface between sonar information and Mark 113, Mod 10 fire control analysis was a huge step forward in getting a quick solution. Using the TMA range estimate defined by the improved Mark 113 system, a preliminary solution for target course and speed could be constantly modified as amplifying sonar data was entered into the fire control system. The solution depended on bearing changes that were significant, and that meant that contacts at appreciable range had to close before TMA solutions were accurate enough for weapons placement. The fire control coordinator monitored both sonar information and the fire control analysis by looking over the shoulders of fire control team members.

An example of how the system aided in the trail of a Soviet submarine was the 1969 patrol of the USS *Lapon* (SSN-661), a *Sturgeon*-class submarine. *Lapon* was equipped with BQQ-5, BQS-20, BQR-20, and BQR-22 sonar arrays, which were mated with the boat's Mark 113, Mod 10 fire control system. The following narrative represents typical trailing scenarios that demanded patience, concentration and dedication from sonar operators and fire control technicians.

Commander Chester M. Mack commanded USS *Lapon* while on patrol near Iceland. On September 16, 1969, SOSUS detected a *Yankee*-type Soviet submarine north of Norway.[5] It was heading out from its home port of Murmansk toward open ocean. A second SOSUS picked up the Soviet submarine as it passed the mouth of the Denmark Strait, which separates Greenland from Iceland. If Mack could intercept the *Yankee* before it made it past the gap into the open ocean, where it would be far more difficult to find, *Lapon* would be able to attempt a trail.

Only one day went by before the *Yankee* passed to the east of *Lapon*. The sound of the submarine was so faint that *Lapon*'s sonar almost failed to detect it over the noise of nearby fishing trawlers and noisy marine life. A slight flicker on the oscilloscope betrayed the Soviet submarine. Keeping track of the *Yankee* wasn't going to be easy. Ambient noise meant that *Lapon*'s sonar was only effective to about 1,400 yards. Sonar found and lost the Soviet submarine several times over the next few days. Then, on the fourth day, the *Yankee* showed up again. This time *Lapon* was able to follow.

Mack increased speed and raced ahead as he tried to place himself in a position which he hoped was the destination of the Soviet commanding officer. He estimated the Soviet's course and probable patrol area near Portugal's Azore Islands. Almost as soon as *Lapon* settled into her new position awaiting the arrival of the *Yankee*, she became ensnared in a fishing trawler's net. After a six-hour struggle, *Lapon* was able to get free.[6]

10—The Sturgeon-Class Submarine

This time Mack was determined not to lose the Soviet submarine. The water in that portion of the Atlantic was relatively quiet and she again picked up the Soviet boat. Mack decided to get behind the Soviet submarine and trail the boat within 3,000 yards of he *Yankee*'s stern. At ranges more than 3,000 yards it was probable that sonar would lose contact. *Lapon* was so close that all someone had to do was drop a piece of equipment or slam a watertight door at the wrong time and even the Soviet's second-rate sonar equipment would detect the American submarine.

Lapon's sonar watches began listening for any flaws in the Yankee's construction, anything that would give them clues as to what was happening inside the other submarine. Her sonarmen zeroed in on certain frequencies, particular noises made by the *Yankee* submarine as it moved through the water.

Lapon positioned itself just to the left of the *Yankee*'s stern. This allowed its sonar watch stander to anticipate the Soviet submarine's next turn. When the noise source became momentarily weaker, the submarine was starting a right turn. When the noise source became stronger, the submarine was beginning a turn to the left. The small amplitude fluctuations were corroborated by equally small Doppler changes: attenuation for a turn away, and up Doppler for a turn toward. Additionally, *Lapon* was able to identify specific machinery noises that indicated activity within the submarine. These sounds acted as predictors of the submarine's turning intentions. Each time the *Yankee* turned, *Lapon* turned with her, trying to stay behind, just off to one side, shielded in the stern-wash of the *Yankee*'s propeller noise.

Once a day the *Yankee* engaged in a wild, high-speed maneuver that *Lapon*'s sonarmen called "The Yankee Doodle." The Soviet submarine performed a figure 8, ending up facing 180° from where she had started. She would then make another 180° turn series that would bring her back to her original course.

Had the *Yankee* sonar been better, the maneuver might have been effective. But Soviet sonar was inferior to that of *Lapon*'s, which allowed the American submarine to stand clear and listen as the Yankee submarine went through its wild twists and turns.

Lapon continued on through the rest of the *Yankee*'s patrol until the Soviet submarine came to a northerly course that would take it directly back through the Denmark Strait and to its home base in the Barents Sea.

Submarine Torpedo Tactics

Lapon broke off on November 9, 1969, having accomplished the longest time for an American submarine to track a Soviet submarine without being discovered.[7]

A year later, in June of 1970, USS *Tautog* (SSN-639), another *Sturgeon*-class submarine with similar fire control and sonar equipment as *Lapon*, was operating in waters frequently traveled by Soviet submarines as they transited in and out of Petropavlovsk. This port was the major Soviet submarine base in the northern Pacific. *Tautog*'s captain, Commander Buele G. Balderston, drove *Tautog* through the Soviets' sonar net, beneath a group of ships and submarines, expertly dodging them while keeping his submarine just below the surface. Only the tips of the antennas and periscope broached through waves. He used the periscope sparingly, never for more than a few seconds at a time. The diving officer kept the submarine level at the shallow depth even though *Tautog* was getting heavier. The reason for the heavy-over-all condition of the submarine was the captain's constraint not to use overboard discharge pumps during delicate tracking operations.

Tautog remained in the Soviet-crowded area for more than two days, accumulating substantial electronic data from Soviet communications. Balderston drove *Tautog* toward Petropavlovsk while his crew became comfortable with being so close to Soviet activity.

An exiting Soviet *Echo II*–type submarine was picked up by *Tautog* sonar that showed on the sonarmen's screens the submarine's trademark: twin screws with four-bladed propellers.

The submarine moved south from its home port, as *Tautog* fell in behind. The *Echo* submarine was noisy and appeared to be an easy target. Relying on passive sonar, *Tautog*'s sonarmen concentrated on identifying the various machinery noises of the Soviet submarine. The trick to trailing a submarine, as it moved through its evasive maneuvers, was to slow and increase the range until the *Echo* submarine turned back to its base course. *Tautog* remained close to the stern of the Soviet submarine as the functions of the operations compartment became routine.

Sonar operators who had been on watch for over 12 hours were allowed some sleep while less senior operators took their place on watch. One such junior sonarman relayed information to the executive officer, who was command duty officer whenever the captain rested. *Tautog* followed the *Echo* submarine at approximately 12 knots at 200 feet.

10—The Sturgeon-Class Submarine

It seemed to the young sonarman that *Tautog* was slowly overtaking the *Echo* submarine and becoming dangerously close. He reported this to the executive officer, who sent for Captain Balderston. Both officers examined the image on the sonar display, which traced a sonar-generated signature of the *Echo*. The image created by the Soviet submarine was bright and filled the screen. The only interpretation possible was that *Tautog* was very close to the *Echo*.

The executive officer now stood next to Commander Balderston as both studied the sonar plots in operations. Another officer and his fire control team made sure that the Mark 113 fire control solution was accurate as it traced the *Echo*'s bearing, speed and distance from *Tautog*. The fire control officer reported that the target's indicated range was too close for torpedoes to arm.

The American sonarmen could not say with certainty the *Echo*'s depth. They guessed that the *Echo* had risen to a depth near the surface and was probably above *Tautog*. As the captain was about to order a deeper depth, the image on the sonar oscilloscope disappeared, and the senior sonarman pressed the "speak" button on his sound-powered phone to so report. At that instant, no one knew the proximity of the Soviet boat. The 6,000-ton *Echo* submarine's stern smashed into *Tautog*'s sail with such an impact that it sounded through the hull like two trains colliding. With a chopping sound, the *Echo*'s propellers ground through *Tautog*'s shears with a force that knocked crew members from their bunks. As the American submarine rolled 30° to starboard from the impact, it was also forced downward. The impact knocked equipment to the deck, threw crew members against bulkheads and tossed dishes around the crew's mess. Meanwhile, officers not on watch jumped into the operations compartment, wanting to be of some assistance. The captain ordered that the collision alarm not be sounded, but that the ship should be rigged for collision by word of mouth through sound-powered phones.

By this time the senior sonarman had switched places with the more junior operator and had placed the headset over his ears. He heard what was being recorded on the running tape as the buckling sounds of a submarine's pressure hull. After the noise had stopped, the senior sonarman pushed a button which stopped the endless tape from recording over the telltale sounds.

Tautog was damaged but remained watertight as it kept to a shallow depth while proceeding at 12 knots eastward. *Tautog* arrived at Pearl Harbor on July 1, 1970, and was maneuvered into a shipyard dry dock where a shroud was draped over her sail. The event remained top-secret and crew members were ordered by the captain to never reveal any aspect of the event.[8]

Fire control systems aboard *Sturgeon*-class boats were updated throughout the 30-year period of operations. At each overhaul, new consoles or modifications to existing equipment were installed. In the 1980s, submarines began receiving the Mark 118 fire control system. Although this system had been installed on *Sturgeon* (SSN-637) prior to its decommissioning in the mid–1990s, the Mark 118 is described in the following chapter since its installation on the *Los Angeles*–class submarines was of more significance.

Toward the end of the Sturgeon production series the Navy began work on a new submarine design. The design effort came to be known as CONFORM for Concept Formulation. It proposed that the new type submarine be produced to counter the ever-developing Soviet improvements. The new design effort would not be bound by prior innovations in hull or reactor. The sole exception was the special convection feature of the S5G reactor. With modified hull design, the S5G reactor was thought capable of driving a boat at a submerged speed of 30 knots.[9] The eventual result was the 688 class of submarines, which is described in the following chapter.

11

The Los Angeles–*Class Submarine*

Corbin's 1913 prediction cited earlier held a couple of assumptions leading to the conclusion that a submarine-vs.-submarine contest would be like "a fight between two gangs of deaf men in a large field on a pitch black night. Some might spend all their time groping about vainly trying to find some one to 'go for' while others, colliding by accident against another human being, would be in utter ignorance as to whether he was friend or foe. The end of the scramble would probably be that little damage to either side was done and that damage might very likely be inflicted by friend upon friend."[1]

Today's nuclear-powered submarine isn't deaf, and during the Cold War it used its sonar to keep track of its opposite Soviet submarine. On the other side of the coin, American submarines attempted to prevent other submarines from hearing them.

During the 1970s, BuShip engineers doubled their efforts in making those submarines on the front line quieter than ever. This was in response to the Soviets, who had achieved considerable success in quieting their submarines. The Soviet decision to initiate a major quieting effort came from John A. Walker, its spy in the United States Navy, who passed on American advances in acoustic technology. Warrant Officer John A. Walker sold secrets to the Soviets from about 1967 until his arrest in 1985.

Another severe setback came in 1983 when the Toshiba firm sold sophisticated, nine-axis milling equipment to the USSR through Königsberg Company, a state-owned Norwegian arms firm, which also sold advanced computers to the Soviets for the machining of quiet propellers.[2]

Despite these blunders of economic greed and Soviet espionage triumphs, American submarines stayed ahead of their Soviet counterparts. This was particularly true in the Navy's program to suppress equipment and screw noise emissions. Post–Cold War information from Soviet records indicates that the Russian Navy was seldom able to detect American attack submarines operating in the Barents Sea. No doubt, technology played an important role in America's continued dominance in the undersea environment, but it was the training of submarine technician crew members and the grit of captains and crew members that gave the American boats the edge over their Soviet adversaries.

What the fleet-type submarine had been to the Second World War, the *Los Angeles*–class boat became to the Cold War. After many confrontations between Admiral Rickover and BuShip engineers working with operational submarine commanders, a large attack submarine came off the drawing boards.

The *Los Angeles* design was a follow-on to the *Sturgeon*. The design was successful because it incorporated the best features of every class boat that had come before it. Its designers were not limited to what had come before, but were free to maximize the interface between systems. This was most evident in the relationship of sonar and torpedo fire control.

Commissioned in 1976, the USS *Los Angeles* (SSN-688) was destined to become the Navy's standard nuclear-powered attack submarine of the Cold War. It was large for an attack submarine, being 360 feet in length and having a submerged displacement of 6,900 tons. Its S6G reactor gave the boat a designed speed in excess of 30 knots.[3] The *Los Angeles*–class boats more than matched the performance of the best Soviet submarines. The initial series of *Los Angeles*–class submarines housed the same sonar and fire control arrangement (Mark 113, Mod 10) as the *Sturgeon* class.

In the 1930s, the submarine was seen as the best weapon to counter threats from hostile submarines intending to attack the main body of a formation of capital ships. By stationing a submarine with adequate communication ability in the van of such a formation, any hostile submarine could be located and destroyed before it was able to launch a weapon. During the Cold War a carry-over of this concept was that long-range sonar on a submarine stationed 20 or 30 miles off the bow of a carrier group could ensure the safety of the carrier and its protective surface ships. This was a valid concept for ASW, but the *Los Angeles* proved to be so effective at locating and trailing Soviet submarines that its primary mission remained that of challenging the best designs of the Soviet Navy in close-quarter adversarial roles.

BuShips produced plans for a submarine having multiple acoustic sen-

11—The Los Angeles–Class Submarine

sors which could reach beyond the less-efficient sonars of the Soviet Navy. The bow of the *Los Angeles* class was to have a wraparound hull array stretching along both sides of the torpedo compartment. Within the vertical staves of the hull array at the bow would be a spherical array. Another, high-frequency passive sonar was to be located in the forward curvature of the sail. Mounted on the hull's curvature, both fore and aft, were two synchronized sensors that were the upgraded version of the PUFFS range-finding sonar. Specific sonar systems such as PUFFS (passive underwater fire control feasibility study) and wide-aperture array sonar could provide bearing information even if triangulation was not possible.[4] Finally, provision was made for a towed array, which added to the submarine's total sonar capability, and also gave protection for its stern. All in all, the *Los Angeles* was to be an acoustical giant with a suite dedicated to the displays of the various sonar systems.

The *Los Angeles*–class submarines carried the Mark 48 torpedo. As emphasized earlier, while it streamed a wire to the submarine after being launched, its gyro placed it on the bearing to the target. The wire only came into play if the target's position and movement suggested a change was needed to correct the torpedo's gyro course. In such case the fire control technician made the alteration through the wire. It was first introduced in 1972 as the ultimate submarine torpedo, replacing the Mark 37 torpedo, which had been in service since 1956. Over 5,000 Mark 48 torpedoes were produced in several mods and remains to this day as the Navy's standard anti-submarine weapon launched from a submarine.[5]

The "688" boats, as they had become known, had been designed to have speed, deep submergence capability, comprehensive sonar and an advanced fire control system, all of which would be upgraded several times throughout the life of the submarine's basic design. While their Soviet counterparts were not lacking in basic design, they never equaled the American boats in silent operation, sonar capability, fire control computer systems and training of crew. These factors kept the *Los Angeles* boats ahead of their adversaries.

Thirty-one *Los Angeles*–class boats were built from 1976 through 1987. Actually, no two were exactly alike. Each new 688 attack boat had improvements over its earlier versions. As each substantial combination of changes was made, the boats having those improvements were referred to as within a certain "flight." Submariners came to know the comprehensive-

Submarine Torpedo Tactics

CONTROL BUTTON PANEL

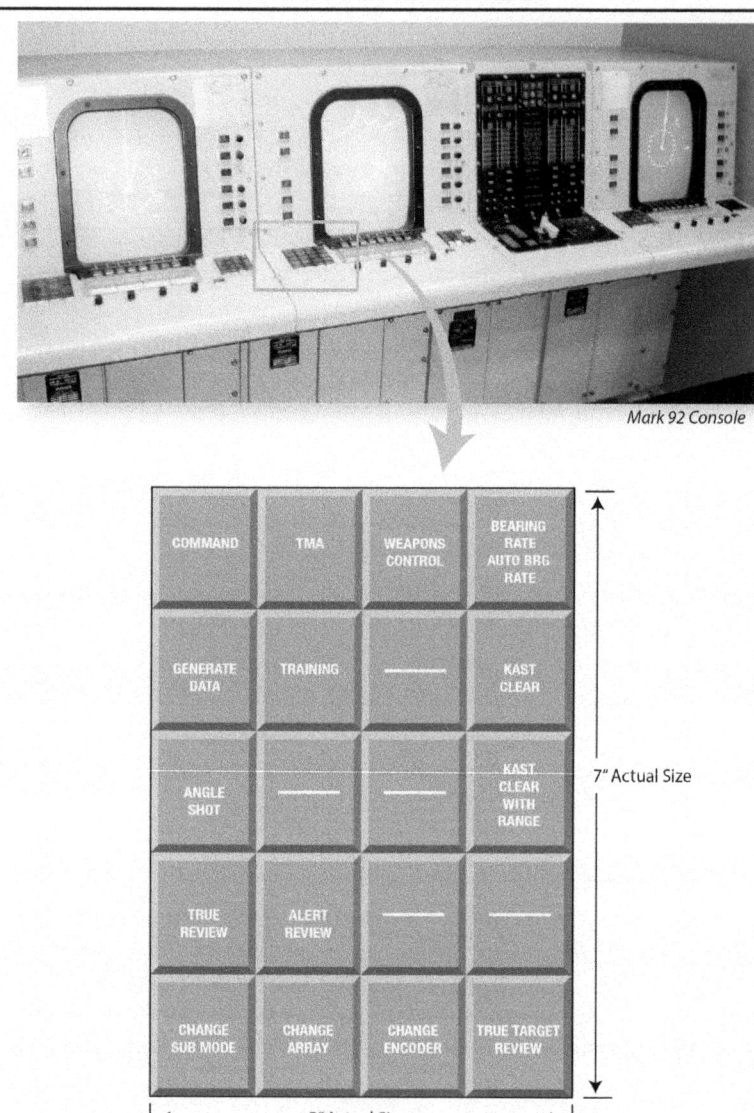

Mark 92 Console

7" Actual Size

5" Actual Size

Two Sonar Information Display (SID) consoles are on each side of the Mark 92 Target Motion Analysis (TMA) computer console. The pushbutton panel for integrating sonar inputs to computer appears below (courtesy Naval Undersea Museum, Keyport, Washington).

11—The Los Angeles–Class Submarine

ness of improvements in the *Los Angeles* boats by their flight number. Thus, *Los Angeles*–class submarines with high hull numbers were in Flight Four and had improved fire control capability over those in early 688 class submarines.

The port side of the operations compartment in all *Los Angeles* submarines was devoted to depth control while the starboard side of the compartment was occupied by fire control equipment. Forward of the fire control equipment was the sonar room with four two-screen display consoles for the BQQ-5, BQS-15 and BQN-134. This space also contained a performance-monitoring console with attendant video display.

The consoles in the attack center were a Mark 92 attack control console at the forward end, then a Tomahawk weapon control console in the 719 boats and three Mark 81 weapon control consoles for torpedoes and torpedo tube–launched Harpoon missiles. The other consoles and related analyzers made up the various components of the digital Mark 118 fire control system.

The Soviets' most important shipyard facility was at Murmansk. It was more than a shipyard; included within its vast area were a Soviet submarine training school, repair facilities for its submarine fleet, and housing for its crew members, who were the elite of the Soviet Navy. The nation's submarines were lined up along the piers at the edge of the Murmansk River, a wide estuary with a surprising depth. Also operating out of Murmansk were many Soviet surface vessels, most of which were members of ASW formations. These put to sea on a regular basis with accompanying submarines to conduct various exercises designed to hone the skills of ferreting out American submarines that the Russians knew were stalking their classified movements in the Barents Sea.

The *Los Angeles* boats carried out a variety of missions including special operations against America's lingering foe, the Soviet Union. In February 1992 the USS *Baton Rouge* (SSN-689) ran submerged off the coast of Murmansk in the Barents Sea as it conducted special operations. At that time the collapsed Soviet Union still had a powerful navy and continued to conduct training exercises off its home port. Sonarmen in the *Baton Rouge* picked up a *Sierra*-class submarine as it maneuvered submerged while training its crew. The *Sierra* changed depth and engaged in high-speed turns through a series of drills in the relatively shallow water. As a safety measure the Soviet submarine kept its fathometer operating to keep track of the water beneath its keel. For unknown reasons the *Baton Rouge* lost contact with the *Sierra* submarine, but its fire control computer generated the *Sierra's* range at a safe distance. Without warning the American submarine was slammed upward. The diving officer fought to regain depth control as men stood up after having been thrown onto the decks. Immediately after the event, the special operations people in radio monitored plain-language Russian as the panicked submarine skipper reported that he had hit a trawler, which must have sunk. It never entered the Russian's mind that he could have hit an American submarine. And even if he were to have been suspicious, it was better for his career to report the event as a collision with a trawler.[6]

The *Baton Rouge* stayed submerged and quietly limped out of the area. After reporting the event to ComSubLant, it made its way back to an American port.

By the end of the 1980s *Los Angeles*–class submarines were being produced in several shipyards and were serving in both oceans. At that time they were to have an important addition. Starting in the late 1960s, there had been interest in providing U.S. submarines with both anti-ship and land-attack nuclear cruise missiles. Precision guidance was becoming available for cruise missiles that would have small nuclear warheads capable of destroying discrete targets. An attack submarine that could be equipped with nuclear warhead missiles was intended to counter the increasing number of large Soviet surface ships that were going to sea on a regular basis. It was also to be an additional weapon for attacking the Soviet homeland. Admiral Rickover visualized a future diverse fleet of submarines including attack class boats, with cruise missiles as well as ballistic missile submarines.[7]

In July 1985, the USS *Providence* (SSN-719) was commissioned. While this was a *Los Angeles*–class submarine, it was considerably changed from the earlier *Los Angeles* boats by virtue of its twelve vertical launching tubes in the bow. Aft of the sonar dome and forward of the horizontal torpedo tubes, which were canted outward from the boat's longitudinal centerline, the twelve vertical launch tubes were able to fire Tomahawk missiles. The four 21-inch torpedo tubes and power torpedo handling gear were customized for the Mark 48 and Mark 48 ADCAP.

Additionally, the submarine's power plant was upgraded to the S6W plant. The steam turbine throttle and control rod coordination of propulsive power continued to be as effective as it had been with the S5W plant.

11—The Los Angeles–Class Submarine

Additions and improvements in sonar and fire control equipment continue to be controlled by a government appropriations and allocation system that results in a variance in equipment from submarine to submarine.

The material acquisition process within the Department of Defense, together with government oversight of spending accountability, induces a prolonged and convoluted process from definition of a need to dockside delivery of equipment. The process begins with a perception of threat or capability gap. Scientists are summoned to respond with technological designs, from which bids are assembled with specifications. Contracts are let and construction begins. Congress must appropriate the necessary funding for the initial cost estimates. The wording of the funding documents limits the Navy and contracted company to strict funding specifications down to the smallest detail. Those responsible for scheduling improvements are constrained by cost, scheduling and performance standards. These interrelated constraints are balanced against each other with the result that each submarine's schedule of modernization is singular to that submarine according to yard overhaul schedules. Thus, there are those boats coming out of overhaul that have the latest technology available, while other submarines must wait their turn for modernization.

In describing the Mark 118 fire control system and that of its predecessors, it is not accurate to assume that one is the successor to the other. It is more accurate to view the succession of improvements as a phasing-in of improvements over a period of time consistent with the overall needs of the submarine force. The acquisitions process is iterative, especially for complex systems with long lead times for development. Often, as a new system is being fielded, its replacement system is in one or more phases of the DOD acquisitions process; this helps to maintain a technological advantage for current threats, and to meet future needs as they arise. For the submarine force, this concept applies to all technology onboard, from the smallest gadget to the submarine itself.

There were twenty-four improved (719) *Los Angeles*–class submarines built from 1985 through 1996. As the Cold War between the United States and the Soviet Union dissolved into history, the versatility of the *Los Angeles* 688-class boats proved to be invaluable in meeting the changing threats aimed at the United States. The fire control system of the Mark 118 configuration varied slightly from boat to boat, but the basic system as found in the early *Los Angeles* submarines was essentially the same as that in the *Sturgeon* boats.

The consoles in the attack center were a Mark 92 attack control console at the forward end, and three Mark 81 weapon control consoles for torpedoes and torpedo tube–launched Harpoon missiles. Other than the Tomahawk guidance control equipment found on the later 719 boats, the other consoles and related analyzers made up the various components of the digital Mark 118 fire control system.

A pair of Mark 81 consoles were normally manned by two experienced fire control technicians who were trained in tracking multiple targets. One of the technicians would have been responsible for a MATE TMA solution for one target, while the other monitored a digital screen that showed changing submarine and target motions. The two-man team acted in combination to mutually support or question the fire control solution of the opposite team member.

The Mark 92 attack control console was the heart of the system. The operator watched the developing tactical situation on his screen. He used pushbutton inputs to modify the emerging TMA solution. The Mark 92 was the last stop of the fire control system. It was normally manned by an officer, who was responsible for pushing the button that fired the weapons.

Most of the *Los Angeles* submarines operating in the mid–1990s were equipped with the Combat Control System Mark 2, Block 1C. It had a problem-solving time of about 2 seconds, utilizing inputs from its analyzers, and continuously reading sonar input signals. If the input data from sonar didn't conform to previous data, a new analysis of target range, bearing, course, and speed would be carried out by averaging the new data with the previous data. The solution from the previous analysis was thereby projected ahead to form a corrected solution. Its computer could identify four target coordinates by forming a matrix of target bearing, range, course, and speed by its micro-circuit ability to solve these simultaneous dimensions in a linear equation. Dr. Friedman describes the systems in use during the mid–1990s as the Mark 134 fire control system.[8]

The basic difference between the Mark 118 system and subsequent improvements was the latter's ability to quickly adjust to manually inserted data and solve for revised TMA solutions without loss of its previous computer solution. The CCS (Combat Control System) Mark 2 Mod 3, as used in the *Ohio*-class fleet ballistic missile submarines, was separate from

11—The Los Angeles–Class Submarine

and completely different from the CCS Mark 2, Block 1C in *Los Angeles* submarines. Both systems had increased processing speed, but their functions were not alike. A product of the mid–2000 decade, the CCS Mark 2, Block 1C system was a considerable upgrade from the Mark 118 fire control system. The number of targets that could be simultaneously tracked was greatly increased, non-sonar sensor data could be easily integrated, new algorithms provided quicker TMA solutions, and the interface between sonar and fire control was enhanced. These new qualities meant that fire control personnel had to keep up with increased flow of data. Their training on the new system was exhaustive. While intended for encounters with hostile submarines, the system was so flexible it became an indispensible tool for conning the ship while submerged in densely populated areas having the potential of other submarines transiting the same area. As such, the fire control system was an important part of the submarine's safety.

Both versions of the *Los Angeles*–class boats performed many tailing and surveillance missions against Soviet submarines and surface ships. Although they never had to fire their weapons against their Soviet adversaries, they proved themselves as most capable in the continuing contest between United States submarines and the many newly designed submarines of emerging, powerful nations having unknown intentions.

One of the most innovative and daring of all U.S. surveillance missions during the Cold War had been carried out not by a *Los Angeles*–class boat, but by an earlier Regulus II submarine of a bygone era. The boat was the USS *Halibut* (SSN-587), which was the nuclear-powered version of the *Grayback* and *Growler*.

In the early 1970s Captain James F. Bradley, Jr. was the person in charge of submarine intelligence gathering. His job focused on the USS *Halibut* (SSN-587). This submarine was a one-of-a-kind boat, capable of unusual missions. It had been built to launch the Regulus II guided missile, which had been replaced by the Polaris. Without a mission, its unique structure of having a large hangar bay built into its bow lent itself to operations that might involve deep submergence vehicles or deep-water divers requiring a SeaLab type of pressurized lock.[9]

Halibut had been commissioned in January of 1960, so the boat was already obsolescent when it was called upon to conduct the most dangerous and rewarding special operations of the Cold War. She was 350 feet in length, 40 feet longer than a fleet-type boat, and she had a surface displacement of 3,845 tons. Her appearance was like an oversized *Tang*, except she had a bulge on her forward deck that belied her spacious watertight hangar. Her S3W reactor provided enough power for about 12 knots submerged and her fire control system was a Mark 101, Mod 20, which was upgraded to a Mark 113 system. Although she only had four torpedo tubes forward, they were Mark 60s, which could electrically control several types of torpedoes including Mark 37s and Mark 48s.

Bradley sat at his desk remembering the days of his childhood aboard flat-bottom steamers that plied the waters of the Mississippi. As a boy he was allowed to join the officers in the pilothouse, where he observed different signs that had been placed along the shore. Most of the signs marked mileage and locations, but there were a few that warned of a cable crossing. The purpose of these signs was to prevent an anchor from falling on a cable.

He had been dreaming about a possible cable tap almost from the moment he had been assigned to his current job. He and his staff had spent hours talking about the possibilities for using *Halibut* to tap into the Soviet communication cable across the Sea of Okhotsk. Since the Soviet submarine base at Petropavlovsk had to communicate with Moscow through Vladivostok, it was reasonable to assume that such a tap would bring vast amounts of intelligence. The *Halibut* was at that time in the Mare Island Naval Shipyard being fitted with a portable version of SeaLab.

Bradley's office continued to be the clearinghouse for all submarine spy missions. *Halibut*'s hump on the forward deck was advertised to house a Deep Submergence Rescue Vessel (DSRV). In fact, it was a divers' decompression and lockout chamber. It was where divers would begin breathing a mixture of gases allowing them to exit the submarine at deep depths.

Halibut's commanding officer, Commander John E. McNish, advised his crew to say nothing whatever about the submarine, its mission, or the purpose of the hump on *Halibut*'s bow. The submarine got underway from Pearl Harbor and made an uneventful, slow transit to the mouth of the Sea of Okhotsk. *Halibut*'s 1950 reactor had to overcome the drag of carrying the fake DSRV on her after deck. Moving north past the Aleutian Islands, the submarine evaded Soviet surface ships as she transited the Bering Strait. She maneuvered slowly through a channel that eventually brought her into the Sea of Okhotsk. The search for a sign indicating a cable crossing began along several locations predicted to be amenable to a cable lying on the bottom of the sea.

11—The Los Angeles–Class Submarine

Halibut then deployed her "fish," which was a towed scanner with a video presentation in the submarine. Eventually the "fish" indicated the possibility of a cable lying on the sea floor. Captain McNish gave the order for *Halibut* to approach the submarine cable and drop its specially constructed fore and after keel anchors, which would place the submarine athwart the cable. The length of the anchor chain kept the submarine positioned only a few feet above the cable. The divers exited the submarine and, using pneumatic guns to blow debris from the cable, began attaching the tap. About 5 feet long and looking much like a fat cucumber, the device had a recorder with rolls of tape allowing months of listening. The tap operated from induction, causing no harm to the cable.

Leaving the pod in place, *Halibut* retrieved the divers and silently made her way out of the Sea of Okhotsk and onto a course taking her to Pearl Harbor. After several months, *Halibut* returned to the cable site, retrieved the listening pod and returned to Pearl Harbor. The tapes were analyzed at the National Security Agency at Fort Meade, Maryland.

According to the NSA, the information gained was invaluable and plans were made for further incursions using a more sophisticated listening pod that would allow transmission of conversations in real time. This new pod was much larger, but it, like its older brother, straddled the cable without revealing its presence.

Halibut made another trip back to the Sea of Okhotsk to place the new pod in position. Captain McNish admonished his men to never divulge any information about *Halibut*, or the missions that had been accomplished during the 1970s.

The cable-tapping missions continued with upgraded pods that gave U.S. intelligence officers ongoing access to the most classified Soviet secrets. These missions came to an abrupt halt when the traitor John Walker betrayed the missions to his Soviet spymasters. Of all the top secret information given to the Soviets by Walker, the revelation of *Halibut*'s cable taps was the most damaging.[10]

The Cold War ended not as a result of American submarines, but because our production of technology drained the Soviet Union's economic ability to keep up with its American adversary. It did not take long for terrorism on a worldwide scale to make new demands on the Navy and its submarines.

12

The Ballistic Missile Submarine

In the autumn of 1955 an organization called the Special Projects Office was established and headed by Admiral William F. Raborn. To staff this new organization Admiral Raborn picked 40 naval officers and a similar number of civilian scientists. The group was housed in the old Munitions Building on the Capital Mall in Washington, D.C.[1] The group's mission was to develop a sea-launched version of the Air Force's Jupiter missile. It quickly became apparent that the liquid-fueled Jupiter missile would be inappropriate for a submarine-launched system. The central concept for development was an intermediate-range missile that could be launched from a submerged submarine. As described in Chapter 8, the Navy had already invested great resources in the Regulus missile program. The first generation of Regulus I was put on station as America's first deterrent. Operating off the Kamchatka Peninsula, fleet-type submarines *Tunny* (SS-282), *Barbero* (SS-317), and *Carbonero* (SS-337) were pushed into service as America's initial guided missile program. The Regulus II effort was provided by *Growler* (SS-577) and *Grayback* (SS-574), but all of these missiles required the submarine to surface. Admiral Raborn called the proposed Navy's system for a submerged launched missile, the Polaris.

In 1956 the National Academy of Sciences conducted a summer study to determine the probable Soviet advances in submarine launched missiles. The group agreed that a Russian submarine with a solid-fuel ballistic missile was the most logical course of scientific development. Edward Teller, father of the hydrogen bomb, confidently predicted an acceptable weight-to-yield ratio that no one had dared conceive. Those in the Special Projects Office declared that if the Russians could produce such a system, American scientists would dedicate themselves to the identical task.[2]

On February 8, 1957, the Chief of Naval Operations issued a requirement for a 1,500-nautical-mile missile launched from a submarine to be operational by 1965. This range was stipulated to enable a submarine in the Barents Sea to target the Soviet capital of Moscow. The February 1957 schedule with a goal of 1965 was followed by a series of revisions and accelerations in the Polaris program.

In December 1957, three months after Sputnik, the Polaris program was shortened from a nine-year completion date to four years and was assigned a priority level of Brickbat 01. This was the highest scientific development priority of the United States government. The Special Projects Office was ready to move ahead full-steam in the development and deployment of a fleet ballistic missile submarine and its Polaris missile. In doing so, the Special Projects Office retained complete oversight of every program within its mission.[3] The manifold problems facing the scientists included a missile that would weigh less than the most optimistic prediction; a range that would encompass a large land target area from water deployment sites; a propellant of adequate impulse that could be safely stored in a submerged submarine; a capability for launching with an absolute certainty of success, under all conditions of sea state; a warhead guidance system of light weight and accuracy never before achieved; a navigation system for pinpointing the submarine's precise position; officers and crew trained to operate the most sophisticated weapon system ever deployed; and a submarine life support system to sustain a crew for two or more months without access to external supplies.

Since the development of such a diverse set of scientific demands involved many parallel-running programs, the Special Projects Office originated a progress evaluation and reporting technique referred to as "PERT." This planning and reporting model served various research sites throughout the United States, particularly in the northeast and western states. It also involved companies and institutions including Lockheed, Westinghouse, North American Aviation, Sperry, General Electric, the Massachusetts Institute of Technology and the Lawrence Livermore Laboratories.

As research continued, subtle differences between the fast-attack mission and that of the ballistic missile submarine became more apparent. The differing submarine designs came directly from an analysis of their missions. The designers of attack-type submarines wanted pressure hulls that could withstand depth charge explosions. Therefore, these submarines had to be resistant to shock. Machinery had to be shock-mounted and rugged. Piping had to be flexible. The attack submarines had to be able to recover from a variety of damage scenarios and had to be highly maneuverable at flank speed for short periods of time.

On the other hand, the missile submarine would have to be quiet at low speed, as it lay in wait with missiles ready. In recognition of its requirement to remain at great depth, the significance of hull integrity became a central construction effort. The special steel used in *Skipjack* was intended to be duplicated for the hulls of the Polaris submarines. The term HY 80 referred to its 80,000-pound-per-square-inch yield strength. A deterrent missile submarine had to be kept as far removed from harm's way as possible. In so doing, it had to venture into shallow water only when it was positioned for launch. Otherwise, it had to remain in deep water and at great depth. Being vulnerable to attack from a hostile hunter-killer submarine, it had to remain as silent as possible and as deep as possible for prolonged periods. Such a submarine's pressure hull, having a collapse depth of 2,200 feet, would have to withstand almost 1,300 pounds per square inch, a figure several times higher than previous hull designs.[4] The skipper of a Polaris submarine would not worry so much about localized pressure from an exploding torpedo, as he would about his submarine's ability to withstand deep submergence for long periods of time. As the Navy continued development of the attack submarine as its primary anti-submarine vehicle, it accelerated development of the guided missile submarine as its primary means of Cold War deterrent.

The Special Projects Office made rapid progress in solving the problem of how to launch the Polaris missile. Its chief submarine designer was Captain Harry Jackson. He estimated that an air-blast launch would be possible from a submerged submarine. He saw the missiles as not too different from antenna masts that had used compressed air for raising and lowering. Calculations verified Jackson's opinion that it was possible to eject a missile on a column of air. He estimated that a missile, once launched, could be ignited while rising. This was a key concept from which the ballistic missile became a reality.[5] Such missiles would be short enough to fit vertically in a pressure hull with beam measurements approximating those of the *Skipjack* and later classes of submarines.

Additional concepts completing the launching system came quickly. Each missile was to be stowed under a neoprene diaphragm until the missile was ready for launch. The space above the diaphragm would be flooded with water when the deck doors were opened for launch.

12—The Ballistic Missile Submarine

The launch sequence would consist of pumping water out of the space above the diaphragm into a compensating tank, while the space so vacated and that below the missile would be pressurized to match sea pressure. The deck door could then be opened. When ejection air, at 4,000 PSI, entered the silo beneath the missile, the rising missile would puncture the diaphragm and continue to accelerate upward, leaving the submarine. The missile would rise to the surface and leap into the air from inertia. Its propellant would ignite when the missile's upward motion was equal to gravity's pull. For an instant, the missile would be suspended motionless, then its engine would ignite, driving it upward toward its target. Jackson's calculations and scenario for launch paved the way to accelerated research, design and construction.

By 1957, the previous schedule of production was no longer acceptable. Jackson began to look for existing or partly built submarines suitable for modification as interim Polaris platforms. They soon fixed on several *Skipjack*-class boats nearing completion. Two of these boats, already on the launching slip, were cut in half so that a 141-foot-long section could be installed. They would be similar to that planned for the keel-up construction of USS *George Washington* and others in her class. The new midsection was wider than the *Skipjack*'s tapered stern. This necessitated fitting a conical-shaped section to accommodate the two hull ring dimensions.

Five submarines were completed to *Skipjack*-modified *George Washington* design. The improvised boats may not have been as perfect as the *George Washington* design, but they were able to put to sea much sooner than the boats being built from the keel up.

The first five SSBNs were modified *Skipjack*s. Their missile compartment insert was of high-tensile steel rather than the HY 80 steel used in the *Skipjack* hull. The resulting depth limitations were regarded as tolerable in view of the need to complete the first line of missile submarines as quickly as possible.

The FBM submarines built from the keel up were superior to the *Skipjack* modified series, in that equipment and hull form were mated without compromises. The *Ethan Allen* (SSBN-608), *Lafayette* (SSBN-616) and *Benjamin Franklin* (SSBN-640)-class boats (all of which were post–*George Washington*–class submarines) had many improvements including better habitability for crew, quieter machinery and upgraded missile fire control systems.

Submarine Torpedo Tactics

The improved *Ethan Allen* class was larger, incorporating the hull features of the *Thresher* and with much superior depth potential. They had improved sonar equipment that provided information to Mark 113 torpedo fire control systems.[6]

The SSBN missile guidance system is completely separate from that of the torpedo fire control system. There is little similarity between a fire control system for torpedoes and that for guided missiles. Torpedoes are tactical weapons whose fire control systems relate to relative motion of own ship and that of the target. Targeting requires pinpoint accuracy with destruction of a target having dimensions approximating that of own ship. In comparison, the guidance system for ballistic missiles launched from a submarine relates to long-range, sea-to-land weapons capable of massive retaliatory destruction of multiple geographical targets. The land targets are stationary, requiring no TMA solutions. The *George Washington* and *Ethan Allen*–type boats have Mark 80 missile guidance systems while the *Lafayette* and later classes have the Mark 84 systems. The *Ohio*-class submarines have the Mark 88 missile guidance system.

During the period of the *George Washington*'s deployment, its Mark 80 guidance system relied upon the Submarine Inertial Navigation System (SINS) to accurately define the boat's position. Today's missile guidance system relies on inertial shipboard gyros that are periodically calibrated from satellite information. However, the absence of satellite information does not preclude a launch. Since the land targets are fixed and their locations pre-programmed into the missiles, it only remains for the launching submarine to await the signal from appropriate authority to launch its weapons. The security measures for both communication of targeting instructions and on-board decision-making to launch were extreme.

Torpedo tubes in ballistic missile submarines were canted outward and were aft of the dedicated sonar bow which housed the BQS-4 and BQR-2b, which were later upgraded to BQQ-5, BQS-20, BQR-20 and BQR-22 globular arrays. The *George Washington* and *Ethan Allen* submarine classes originally had Mark 112 torpedo fire control systems, but were later upgraded to the Mark 113 systems. The consoles for the Mark 113 system were located on the starboard side of the operations compartment in the approximate arrangement of the *Skipjack* line of consoles. The torpedo fire control computers and displays were updated as modifications to the Mark 113 system continued through the 1960s. The Mark 113 fire control system was an analog system. Previous systems such as the Mark 101, with limited capacity to analyze target motion, relied upon a physical plot analysis to prepare an initial target estimate. In the Mark 113, the automated analyzer became the basis of the system. The torpedo director for wire-guided weapons relied upon the Mark 75 attack director, which was a component of the Mark 113 fire control system. The Mark 75 component could function independently by using a manual TMA solution. The computer solution was a continuous relative-motion display from own ship to target in terms of target range, bearing, and depth.

The Mark 113 operator could monitor the progress of the TMA solution, just as the operator of a Mark 101 had watched the movement of the dials to tell when a position keeper solution had settled sufficiently for firing. The Mark 113 computer could smooth bearing inputs it received through averaging and drop-last methods, sending the data electrically as automatically-corrected inputs.[7]

The Mark 78 analyzer used target motion information effectively as it interacted with other information in the Mark 113 fire control system. To solve the analog-digital interface problem in the Mark 113 fire control system, a simple analog-to-digital converter was installed. The same solution was accomplished for the Mark 78 analyzer, a key component of the system. By the mid–1980s the computer was now so powerful that operators could interact with a running TMA solution using manual adaptive TMA (MATE) evaluation techniques. Operators determined target course, speed, and range by trying alternatives and matching sonar bearings with best solution for target course, speed and range. The analog BQQ-2 sonar was replaced by the digital BQQ-5. The new system, which incorporated the Mark 78 analyzer, was the Mark 117 fire control system.

Admiral Raborn, as the director of the Special Projects Office, continued to have overall responsibility for ballistic missile submarine development and construction as well as missile development.[8]

The *George Washington* was placed in commission on December 20, 1959, under Commander James B. Osborn and John L. From, Jr. The need for two commanding officers lay in the Polaris submarines' introduction of a new operating concept. Each submarine had two 135-man complete crews. One crew was called the blue crew, the other the gold crew. One crew took a Polaris submarine to sea on a deterrent patrol for 60 days, after which the submarine returned to port for repairs and replenishment. After a transfer of personnel, the alternate crew took the submarine back to sea for the next 60-day patrol. While one crew was at sea, the other took advantage of shore time for rest, leave, and training.

The next generation of missile was the Poseidon. The impetus for the Poseidon missile came from indications that the Soviet Union was developing an anti-ballistic missile system that would be able to defeat the planned number of U.S. strategic missiles in a nuclear strike. Whether or not this intelligence had merit was irrelevant since the need for larger, longer-range and greater payloads was apparent. The resulting missile was the Poseidon C-3 with enhanced payload, range, and separate target attack capability. While the conversion of the Polaris submarines was required to carry this larger missile, the changes were relatively minor, and in the 1970s all 31 ballistic missile submarines were converted to launch the Poseidon missile.

Submarines built after 1977 would carry the new, longer-range Trident I missiles. Ballistic missile submarines built in the 1980s were to have enlarged silos to accommodate the full-size Trident missiles.[9]

Twelve of the *Lafayette*-class submarines were converted to carry the Trident C-4 guided missile. The C-4 missile with a diameter of 74 inches had a range of 4,000 miles and 8 Multiple Impact Re-entry Vehicles (MIRV) of 100 kilotons each. This multiplied the effectiveness of each missile by a factor of eight, giving each Trident-carrying submarine the potential to destroy 128 targets.[10]

The lead Trident submarine, USS *Ohio* (SSBN-726), was launched at Electric Boat on April 7, 1979. She was the largest submarine built by any nation up to that time. The *Ohio* was commissioned on November 11, 1981, and went to see on her first Trident missile patrol in the northern Pacific on October 1, 1982. She carried 24 C-4 Trident missiles. The ultimate U.S. submarine-launched ballistic missile was the Trident D-5, which had a greater payload than previous missiles. This missile introduced greater range and more accuracy than previous submarine-launched weapons.

The missile guidance system could place each of the eight MIRV warheads within a circle 560 feet in diameter at a range of 4,000 nautical miles. With MIRV warheads, the Trident submarine could destroy 192 targets at one time.[11]

The *Ohio*-class ballistic missile submarines of the 1980s had Mark 88 missile guidance systems and Mark 118 torpedo fire control systems with

12—The Ballistic Missile Submarine

BQQ-6 spherical passive sonar arrays. The *Ohio*-class submarines had four deck levels for most of the submarines' pressure hull length and could operate at depths consistent with that of *Los Angeles*–class submarines. The Trident C-4 could be fitted into existing Poseidon silos.[12]

The fire control system Mark 118 console consisted of a pair of digital Standard Information Displays (SIDs) flanking a Mark 92 attack control console (pictured in previous chapter). The Mark 92 attack console was used to send commands to the torpedo room watch, and to launch torpedoes and countermeasures remotely from the attack center. Although one SID operator was responsible for target motion analysis and the other for weapon orders, the SIDs were fully interchangeable and either SID operator could conduct an entire attack from initial TMA to the launch.

The Mark 118 Fire Control System was simpler than the Mark 113 since its weapon was exclusively the Mark 48 and 48ADCAP torpedoes. It also had an emergency torpedo preset console as a backup in case of a SID/ACC failure.

The Department of Defense had had a tendency to allocate funds for computer hardware at a level of importance that had outpaced its allocations of funds for fire control software. The result had been bulky analog computer consoles for the Mark 101 and Mark 113 systems that often fell short of accurate solutions. The inadequacy was most apparent when advanced sonar equipment produced small target bearing rate changes for contacts at ranges not anticipated in the computer designs. The Mark 118 system's software was a significant improvement over previous computers.

When digital computers replaced the older analog versions, and preset software algorithmic functions were introduced, the fire control technician's trust in computerized solutions was increased. The Mark 118 system of the early 1990s, with its Mark 92 console, included an improved system of pre-set functions called KAST for Kalman Automatic Sequential Target Motion Analysis. The improved version was the CCS Mark 2, Mod 3. that performed multivariant regressions based on sonar information at a level of reliability similar to the CCS equipment in the *Los Angeles* attack-class boats. Each contact was processed automatically using KAST to give a quick estimate of relative motion.

The fire control technician could quickly bring to his computer screens the best KAST solution. He then compared this solution with that of his various paper plots running in parallel to the computers. He could also refine data for a particular target using techniques such as Manual Adaptive Target Motion Analysis (MATE). The MATE system was an additional computerized application of the Ekelund target course and ranging (strip) method.[13]

Each KAST solution, augmented by MATE analysis presented on a screen, was subjected to verification by the fire control technician's confidence in the quality of sonar's information, his analysis of plot information, and his ability to synthesize these inputs as corroborating or contesting the KAST TMA solution.

In examining the reliability of computers in the fire control process, a first impression may be that the introduction of computers was the ultimate answer to obtaining accurate solutions. One's impression of their miraculous applications is sobered by the reality of the problem to be solved. Despite their sophistication, they are often overmatched by the multi-dimensions of the problem. They are required to solve linear problems that are defined only in terms of multivariant options. The computer is called upon to estimate and predict target motion in the exactitude of range, course and speed from sonar inputs that reflect only changes in bearings. It attempts solutions (in algorithmic sequence) by holding one variable constant and electronically manipulating the other two. It runs through its instructions sequentially. Failing to find a fit, it shifts its constant to another variable, holding that and commencing the same type of analysis. It continues its search systemically in accordance with its pre-set structure. Seen from a broad perspective, the computer uses the primitive time-bearing plot and Ekelund hand manipulation of bearing alignment to reach the most probable target course, speed and range. Of course, it accomplishes the search for a fit at lightning speed. When it settles on the most probable combination of course, speed and range it presents its solution on a screen, but in doing so it is only presenting what its pre-set algorithm defines as a "most probable" solution.

As described above, a computer's KAST solution is subject to critical evaluation by the fire control technician. He must have an understanding of and appreciation for the capabilities and limitations of his fire control equipment. Additionally, he must be able to integrate his processes with those of sonar. He also must have an intuitive sense of the problems confronting his sonar team members.

The Mark 118 fire control system was replaced in accordance with the

12—The Ballistic Missile Submarine

scheduling of yard overhauls. The new CCS Mark 2, Mod 3 console looked much the same as previous equipment, but the new software gave the *Ohio*-class submarines improved TMA processing speed, refined TMA algorithms, increased number of automatically tracked targets, and serial mission capability.

The Mark 48 torpedo was a three-speed, electrically driven, "wire guided," active/passive acoustic homing torpedo. It was launched by hydraulic impulse, which started its engine. As the wire payed out, the fire control equipment monitored the weapon's course, speed and depth. It was not wire guided, but continued on a pre-set gyro course to a point where its sonar could assume control of the weapon. If the torpedo should digress from its pre-set course, the wire guidance could override the course instruction to enter a new course in response to target motion changes after the time of launch. It carried a 330-pound HBX head and had a range of about 9000 yards.

As nuclear attack and guided missile submarines were being produced in the 1960s, attention was given to providing them with sophisticated defensive systems that could alert a submarine when in the proximity of a hostile submarine. The Submarine Acoustic Warfare System (SAWS) was installed on the growing fleet of submarines. SAWS I was first installed in the *Sturgeon* class, and an improved SAWS II was installed on *Los Angeles*–class submarines. More sophisticated processing in SAWS II drastically cut alert processing time.

Each version of SAWS had a Countermeasure Launcher Acoustic Module System (CLAM), which consisted of vertically mounted, 3-inch-diameter ejection tubes and their decoy devices. Another, larger countermeasure device was the Mobile Submarine Simulator (MOSS) that could be launched from a torpedo tube. Because a submarine had to be able to fire a MOSS at a moment's notice, from a SAWS alert, one torpedo tube was dedicated to that purpose.[14]

The human factor of Cold War submarine operations cannot be ignored. A torpedo attack on a hostile submarine or surface ship required enormous onboard decisions and precise calculations, while the decision to launch missiles from a submarine carried with it the certainty of not only huge loss of life and property, but the possibility of worldwide conflict. The types of underwater warfare of the fast attack submarine and the guided missile submarine were disparate in missions and methodology, but crew members were subjected to the same hostile environment of undersea warfare. The Cold War between the United States and the Soviet Union was a period of great stress for every submariner on both sides of the competition for dominance.

Stress and boredom were relieved as much as possible by excellent food, an ice cream machine, endless card games, contests and a juke box that played five tunes for a nickel.[15] A most unusual method of breaking the monotony came from a unique piece of equipment in the fleet ballistic missile submarine, *Thomas A. Edison* (SSBN-610), an *Ethan Allen*–class submarine. The *Edison* was the only Cold War submarine to have a real piano. While other boats had some electronic instruments, the *Edison* possessed, for its entire career, a genuine Steinway upright piano.

The Steinway piano was purchased by one of *Edison*'s first commanding officers for $1,500, according to John Fletcher, an officer on board *Edison* at its commissioning. The piano was to be housed in the crew's mess, but its exact location was left undefined until the boat was completed. Steinway and Sons agreed to construct the spinet-type piano and consulted with Electric Boat Company on its construction. The piano, identified as serial number 370862, model 100, in ebonized satin lacquer, was delivered to the shipyard as *Edison* was nearing completion. The boat was in the water, but still had its access patch over the operations compartment open. The piano was lowered by crane through the soft patch, through radio, which had to move some equipment, and onto the mid-level deck of crew's mess. It competed for deck space with serving tables as well as a slot machine, which was later installed in Holy Loch. It was eventually located on the forward bulkhead, to the left of center line on the port side. The piano was bolted to the deck using only its two legs as bolt-down points. The bulkhead provided ample fore and aft stability.

The crew's mess on *Edison* was aft of operations-torpedo attack center and forward of officer berthing. The commanding officer's and executive officer's staterooms were immediately aft of crew's mess. Crew's berthing was on the lower level beneath the piano. Several constraints arose that limited piano playing by crewmembers. These were voiced by officers aft of the piano and enlisted men below it, who claimed that sleep was more important than music. Nevertheless, crew members of the *Edison* reported that the piano got plenty of use by anyone who had reasonable talent. During Sunday services the piano served as instrument for hymns sung by crew members. The piano also played a central role in special recreational events, since nearly all crew member performances featured so-called musicals.

The concept of a piano was contradictory to a basic submarine principle, to remain undetected by being quiet. Patrol operations meant stealth, and during these times the piano's keyboard cover was locked shut.

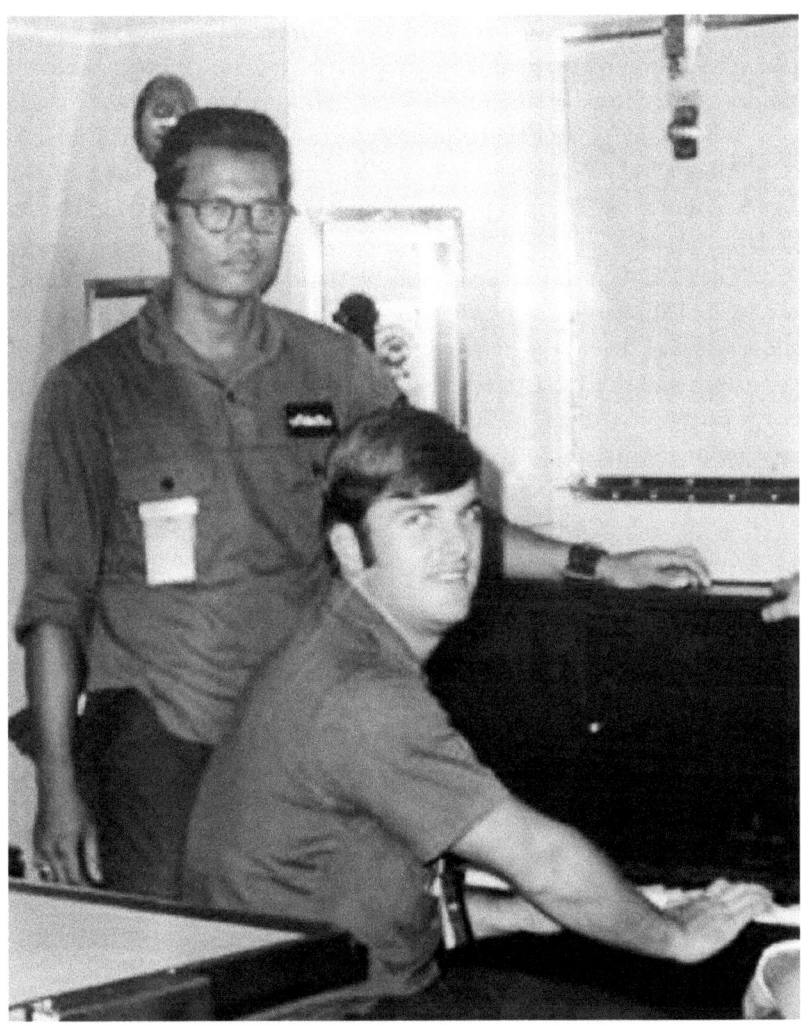

Second Class Storekeeper Fred Staley plays Steinway piano while First Class Stewards Mate Lorenzo Vincente listens (courtesy Fred Staley).

On prolonged patrols the piano went out of tune. It was found that a certain torpedo wrench fit the string pegs and sonar provided a frequency generator for the proper tones. It was the torpedomen who did the tuning at sea which drove to distraction those eating in crew's mess.

When *Edison* was decommissioned, the fate of the piano was uncertain. After a long period of warehouse storage, the piano was retrieved by Steinway Company, which repaired and refurbished its by-now famous piano. It is currently the permanent property of Steinway Incorporated and resides in the Steinway Museum in New York. It remains the only piano ever to be an integral piece of equipment in an American submarine.

All in all, there may have been spells of joviality and breaks from the rigors of undersea deterrent patrols, but nothing could dispel the stress of such operations.

The Cold War ended abruptly in 1990 with the economic collapse of the Soviet Union, but deterrent patrols have continued. Four ballistic missile submarines have been converted for special operations of SEAL team incursions and other classified missions. Guided missile submarines currently carry a mixed load of Tomahawk, C-4 and C-5 missiles as a specific mission might dictate.

13

The Seawolf *and* Virginia *Submarines*

By 1980 the building programs for the *Ohio*-class deterrent-missile submarine and the *Los Angeles*–class attack submarine were in place, and it was expected that these two superior type submarines would continue to keep pace with Soviet submarine technology. This was not to be the case. The Soviets did not seem to be standing still. Coming off the ways at Russian shipyards were impressive-looking, advanced submarines. With small, hull-integrated sails, these submarines appeared to be completely new, rather than merely variations of old designs.

Advancing Russian submarine and weapons technology alarmed the United States Navy. The Russian *Akula*-class submarine was one of the stealthiest, fastest, and most potent submarines ever built. She was many times quieter than previous Russian fast attacks, which made detection at tactically advantageous ranges a challenge for American boats. *Akula* also had advanced sonar arrays and could carry high-speed torpedoes that potentially could be nuclear-warhead capable. Thus the worst-case scenario played out for American war planners. They faced the following facts: *Akula* could detect a *Los Angeles* submarine at the same time she was counter-detected, or perhaps, prior to being detected by *Los Angeles*; *Akula* could quickly launch a high-speed torpedo with a very destructive warhead; and the combination of enemy torpedo speed and radius of warhead blast created a sphere around *Akula* in which *Los Angeles* could not successfully evade destruction, due to her lack of speed and tactical advantage.

Work was begun on a completely new submarine. It would have to be quieter and faster than the Russian *Akula*. Actual concept development for the USS *Seawolf* (SSN-21) began in June 1982. At about the same time, Admiral Rickover was forced into resigning his office as submarine nuclear propulsion director. After more than 30 years of his monopolistic control, it was time for a change. The resulting release from constraints of what had become adherence to outdated concepts accelerated innovation in submarine design. What emerged from conferences of submarine commanders and high-ranking officers came to be called the SSN-21, so named for the twenty-first century.[1]

The *Seawolf* design focused on speed, stealth, and advanced electronics suites to answer the *Akula* challenge. The level of stealth engineered in *Seawolf* was unprecedented for nuclear-powered submarines. Indeed, *Seawolf* was quieter at speed than *Los Angeles* was sitting next to the pier. In her engine room, *Seawolf* housed a massive reactor and main engines that could propel her faster than any previous submarine and faster than Russian torpedoes. Her sonar suite employed new technologies like a wide-aperture array (WAA), advanced spherical/towed arrays, and integrated sonar/FCS displays.

But it wasn't just the sub-on-sub ASW mission of *Seawolf* that drove innovations in her design. Like *Los Angeles* before her, *Seawolf* could be called upon to support carrier battle groups and strike groups, conduct land-attack missions with Tomahawk missiles, and wage full-scale war against the Russian surface fleet. *Seawolf* was built with state-of-the-art communications equipment and the capability to carry up to 50 torpedoes, rather than the nominal 17 torpedoes that *Los Angeles* could carry. From a broader perspective, present-day war planners and area Combatant Commanders (COCOMS) frequently deal with maintaining a certain number of assets in theater at any given time. The term "assets," used in this context, covers everything from whole units such as aircraft carriers, to weapons such as Tomahawk missiles. This combat strength imperative, among other objectives, drives both the number and type of ships, airplanes, and submarines being deployed to various parts of the world. The ratio of payload/weapons to platforms, including ships, aircraft and submarines, is relatively fixed. As the demand for weapons in theater increases, the number of platforms to support the weapons must also increase.

Keeping a high number of assets forward-deployed is very costly, especially when one considers the typical lifecycle of Naval ships. For instance, the typical *Los Angeles*–class submarine only spends about 5 percent of its hull life on "mission"; the rest is spent in overhaul periods, training with friendly assets, transiting, regular pierside maintenance, and port calls.

At the time *Seawolf* was being designed, only minimal progress was being made toward improving the lifecycle requirements of submarines to

13—The Seawolf and Virginia Submarines

support more hull life on station. The *Seawolf* design could cut costs by maintaining the amount of weapon payload in theater. It was estimated that if Russia were to sortie its fleet toward the United States, one *Seawolf* submarine on station could sink as many Russian surface ships as nearly three *Los Angeles*–class submarines. The *Seawolf* torpedo room, with 6 tubes and an automated, quick-reload system that was operated by pushbuttons instead of manually, as was the case of *Los Angeles*, was purpose-built to rapid fire at a rate sufficient to cripple or destroy the Russian fleet. This was one reason why only 29 *Seawolf* class submarines were planned. The Navy predicted that the United States would need that approximate number to provide adequate on-station coverage at any given time.

Those involved in propulsion design signaled the need for noise reduction as the road to getting rid of the outdated propeller. They pointed to the success of the British submarine *Trafalgar*, which had been equipped with an external ducted fan. The new type submarine also would have a new combat system, including improved passive sonar, vertical and horizontal weapon launchers and faster fire control computers. Although fiber-optic interior connections between sonar, fire control and weapons was envisioned, the complications of installing such a system made their inclusion questionable. The new S6W reactor would produce 30 percent more power than its *Los Angeles*–class predecessors. But to house the new reactor, the new SSN-21 would weigh almost 9,000 tons.

It would have a ducted impeller propulsion system of American design, but similar to that of the HMS *Trafalgar*. Although the Navy desperately called for better quality low-carbon steel, American foundries were not able to match the strides of their Soviet counterparts. It appeared that America's metallurgists would be able to cold-roll HY-130 low-carbon steel, but the SSN-21 building program could not wait for the design and building of machinery to fabricate the new material. The *Seawolf* would have to be built from HY-100 steel, with a test depth consistent with *Los Angeles*–class boats. This was an example of the many agonizing compromises that had to be made if the new class submarine was to become a reality. The *Seawolf* (SSN-21) went to sea on her initial trials on July 3, 1996, and was commissioned on May 19, 1997. The sea trials revealed problems in the Tomahawk launch system, propulsor, and sonar. It would have been too optimistic for such a multiple-innovative submarine not to be flawed in some respects. The boat returned to the Electric Boat Shipyard in Groton,

Connecticut, where the individual problems were identified, redesigns were made, equipment was replaced and failed systems repaired.

Construction of the *Seawolf* had rested predominantly with the Electric Boat Company. Its design and construction involved entirely new systems that had to be integrated with one another. This meant countless meetings with engineers responsible for specific functions. Each competed with the other for space and accessibility. Cost overruns and delays caused huge concern within the Navy, while congressional committees became disenchanted with the cost of the building program. When *Seawolf* finally went to sea, its performance far surpassed what designers had anticipated. The submarine was 353 feet in length with a beam of 40 feet. Her S6W reactor, coupled with her revolutionary propulsor, drove her at sustained submerged speeds in excess of 25 knots.

Two other submarines in the class were built, the USS *Connecticut* (SSN-22) and the USS *Jimmy Carter* (SSN-23). The *Jimmy Carter* was to have special operations capability, which meant that it would assume some of the research previously conducted by USS *Parche* (SS-683), an *Archerfish*-type submarine commissioned in 1974. It would also have compartmentalization for SEAL operations. In both of the follow-on submarines, the Navy's goal was to produce a multi-mission submarine that was substantially less expensive, with an ability to be modified as new technologies became available. Each had the new fire control system A/N BYG-1, which afforded full integration of sonar and fire control, multiple target tracking at super-rapid TMA simultaneous solutions, and full integration of sensor information from sources other than sonar.

The end of the cold war brought the *Seawolf* program to an end. Mission requirements had to be retuned to drastically changing world threats. The Navy had to shift its focus to more asymmetric warfare and littoral operations.

While the submarine was a success and the follow-on submarines USS *Connecticut* and USS *Jimmy Carter* were starting construction, engineers went to work on a new and more cost-effective submarine with construction costs that would not exceed four billion dollars per boat. This figure was cast in stone, since the Navy guaranteed Congress that a submarine that would be at least as advanced as the *Seawolf* class could be built with the four-billion-dollar cap as a realistic ceiling. The new submarine was to the first in the *Virginia* (SSN-774) class.

13—The Seawolf *and* Virginia *Submarines*

The new class of submarine would be distinguished from the *Seawolf* by many qualities, the first being its method of design and construction.

Traditionally, submarines had been designed and built using long lines of drawing boards and full-scale wooden mock-ups of equipment placement within compartments. It was a time-consuming process of trial and error.

Virginia would be designed entirely by computer. Engineers met and discussed the integration of systems while viewing screen projections of computer models. The hundreds of compromises involved in the interface of the various systems could be hashed out without going beyond computer-generated images. By itself, this approach meant huge savings.

Virginia's internal layout was modular, with specific space allocations for each piece of equipment. Not only would this minimize cost, it would allow system improvements to be made in the future, providing the revision did not alter the space dimensions.

In 1998 construction began. Once again, the approach was groundbreaking in bringing together the Electric Boat Company and the Northrup Grumman Newport News Ship Building Company. In the past these two rival companies had competed for funding of new construction. For the first time the two companies would work cooperatively to allocate specific construction components of the same submarine. The Newport News facility built the stern, habitability and machinery spaces, torpedo room, sail and bow section; Electric Boat built the reactor compartment, turbine compartment and operations center with depth control equipment, communication, sonar suite and fire control consoles. The hull structure contained isolated, individual, internal deck structures and integrated enclosures, which accommodated standard 19-inch and 24-inch width equipment for ease of installation, repair and upgrade.

Fabrication of hull plates and welding of plates into sections made use of robotic cold-rolling for curvature and robotic welding of plates as they were formed into the basic hull shape. Intricate cutting of heavy metal plates was accomplished by diamond abrasive water jets, eliminating the problem of HY-100 elasticity loss through flame cutting.

The equipment to be placed in the submarine was contracted to those companies specializing in the respective domain, but the specifications for equipment construction reflected the requirement to keep within the space allocated to the project. In doing so, the internal structure as originally designed was never compromised.

Submarine Torpedo Tactics

The *Virginia* is 377 feet in length with a 34-foot beam. It weighs 7,800 tons and is powered by an S9G pressurized water reactor providing an estimated 25,000 shaft horsepower to a ducted propulsor.

The *Virginia*-class submarine was a vast improvement over the *Los Angeles*–class attack submarine. But, for all of its many improvements in weapons, communication, sonar and fire control, its method of propulsion was the most revolutionary. Progress had been made in producing single, large, hollow, multi-bladed and complex-curved screws. These were much more efficient than those of the mid-twentieth century. They produced less cavitation and were therefore quieter. Yet even these had their limits. Exit flow continued to be non-linear and entrance flow was made turbulent by planes and rudder vortices. This often set up a "beat" and presented a serious problem in sound emission and signature identification.[2]

The *Seawolf* and the subsequent *Virginia*-class submarines are propelled by a propulsor rather than a propeller. This is a relatively new term in the submariner's lexicon and so deserves some explanation. At the beginning, let it be said that the primary reason for developing a means of propulsion other than a screw was to eliminate cavitation noise that is an unwanted byproduct of forward thrust.

A submarine screw provides thrust by accelerating a rearward water flow at the stern of the hull. Because it is a rotational thrust, the exit flow is both outward and to the rear. That portion of the thrust that is other than rearward is wasted. The problem confronting the designer of submarine propellers is one of maximizing that portion of thrust that drives the submarine forward while eliminating, or at least reducing, the adverse effects of rotational outward flow. The propulsor solves many of the problems inherent in the traditional screw. It effectively multiplies the number of blades into something akin to an aircraft's jet engine's impellers, but its greatest departure is the inclusion of a circular ring at the extremity of the blades. In most propulsors this ring or duct is fixed to the hull with impeller blades spinning within it. In such case the tolerance between blade tips and inner duct liner must be as close as possible in order to eliminate outward thrust called blade edge vortex. The circular duct's interior shape is contoured to accelerate water flow before striking the impellers. A similarity can be drawn between the interior shape of an aircraft's jet engine intake and that of the ducted ring for an impeller.[3]

To gain an appreciation of how the duct accelerates water flow, one might visualize an aircraft's wing. The wing's contour provides lift by accelerating air flow over its top surface. The propulsor's contour does the same thing, except that water is incompressible so the acceleration is more pronounced. The duct's inside curvature resembles an aircraft's wing upper surface that has been bent into a ring.

The cavity between the duct's outer and inner surfaces is open to sea, allowing the duct's light weight skin to withstand sea pressure at maximum depth. The duct is tapered to a point at the nozzle, where the exit aperture diameter is about one-third that of the intake diameter. To gain an understanding of the dimensions involved, the intake diameter is about 27 feet and the length of the propulsor is about twice that. As enormous as a commercial jet aircraft's engine may seem, the propulsor on the *Virginia* class submarine is over three times that size.

Water flow along the submarine's hull is accelerated by the conically shaped after body. As the hull decreases in diameter, the passing water rushes to fill the void. Thus, water entering the propulsor at the submarine's stern has already been accelerated. The inner shape of the duct forces the water into its impeller blades with great force. The multiple blades bite into the fast-moving water and thrusts it rearward and outward.[4]

The accelerated exit flow from a propulsor must be as free from outward thrust spiraling as possible. A stator made of multiple static blades is placed at the after end of the duct. These blades are mounted to introduce a counter spiral current to that of the impeller blade thrust. This serves to straighten the exit flow. The stator assembly produces drag, so the efficiency of producing a quiet, linear, rearward flow is thereby slightly reduced. To further complicate the design of a propulsor, rigid stator blades cannot be tuned to the varied thrusts of exiting water produced by variations in impeller speed. The answer is to match stator blade pitch to that of impeller speed. This is accomplished by a hydraulically powered assembly within the propulsor's tail section that pivots stator blade pitch to match impeller speed. One can easily imagine the synchronized action by tilting the multiple slats in a window's Venetian blind.

The final exit flow of water from the propulsor is linear, without cavitation and strong in propulsive thrust.

Virginia's impeller is turned by a shaft that extends through the hull at the centerline of the submarine's stern. Shaft revolution speed was controlled by two technicians who operated energy output controls. One con-

THE PROPULSOR

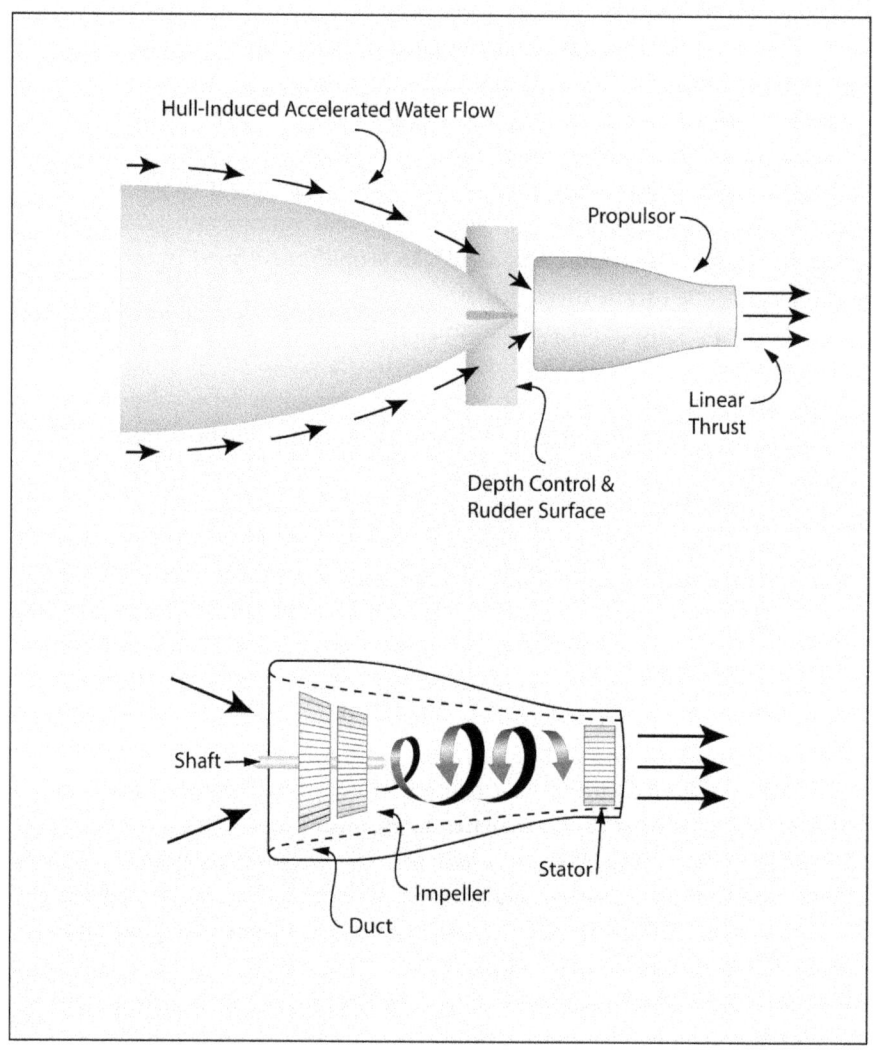

The submarine propulsor is a ducted multi-bladed impeller which accelerates rearward water flow. Stator blades at the propulsor's after end straighten the axial spin into a linear thrust (Submarine Research Center).

trolled turbine speed and shaft rotation direction, while the other manipulated the reactor's control rods, the position of which determined the heat output of the reactor. These two operators worked as a team in the smooth control of the submarine's speed. Much of the manual propulsion control has been assumed by computer controls monitored by technicians.

The nuclear fuel core of the reactor in *Virginia* has a 30-year life, approximating the life of the submarine. The reactor relies upon natural convection rather than pumps when at low power to further reduce its acoustic signature.

In place of the traditional optical periscopes are twin extendable photonic masts. Each contains high-resolution cameras with infrared capability. Each mast also has an infrared range finder and Electronic Support Measures array. Inputs from these sources are transmitted by fiber-optic links to computerized signal processors. Since the time required for a mast to be exposed is a matter of a few seconds, the risk of detection is minimal. The command center personnel are able to examine the data on screens.

The communication mast and system uses high data rate (HDR) multi-band satellite communications system that allows simultaneous super high frequency linkage with land and sea communication centers.

The advanced sonar system includes a suite with monitors covering 360 degrees of hydrophone array. The bow-mounted passive and active arrays are complemented by a stern wide aperture array, side-mounted arrays, and a TB-29A thin-wire towed array, as well as a second TB-16 towed array. The sensors are integrated by an AN/BQQ10(V4) sonar processing system. Attempts were made to produce a bow passive sonar array that would conform to the bow hull shape, but the design never reached beyond the drawing board. To deviate from the well-tested spherical array would place a questionable conformal sonar in a type of submarine which incorporated many innovations. The AN/BQQ 10 sonar, which is an upgrade of the BQS-6 and BQR-7 sonars, is spherical in shape, requiring the bow to be computer-formed to accommodate the system. Of greatest importance, the multiple sonar sensors feed information to displays and auto-tracking computers of the integrated A/N BYG-1 system, the fully developed form of the Submarine Advanced Combat System (SUBACS). The integrated bow-mounted passive and active sonar, wide aperture passive array panels fitted to the sides of the submarine, and an advanced towed array sonar, were the basic components of the integrated combat system.

The boat's command and control systems module was constructed by Lockheed Martin Naval Electronics and Surveillance establishment. This module integrates all of the submarine's sensors and has common displays for navigation and weapons control including the AN/BYG-1 combat control system. The new fire control system is an integral part of the Combat Command and Control System, which is the central system of deployment for such diverse operations as intelligence gathering, anti-ship, and anti-submarine attack, land missile attack, and insertion of SEAL teams.

The submarine's weapons include 26 Mark 48 and Mark 48 ADCAP torpedoes for four canted tubes, as well as 12 vertical launch tubes for Tomahawk missiles. Additionally, the submarine carries an integral lock-out chamber for SEAL egress and entry. In the conduct of SEAL operations in littoral waters, the submarine can hover for prolonged periods only inches from the sea bed. Its navigation system and hover equipment keeps the boat in one geographical position, compensating for current and gradient changes.

For protection, the *Virginia* has the AN/WLY-1 acoustic countermeasures system from Northrup Grumman. The system uses range and bearing data from fire control to launch countermeasure devices including UUV and AUV vehicles. *Virginia's* electromagnetic signature is minimized by onboard, computer-controlled degaussing.

As of fall 2013, nine *Virginia*-class submarines have been built and are operational. These are the Block I series of *Virginia* (SSN-774), *Texas* (SSN-775), *Hawaii* (SSN-776) and *North Carolina* (SSN-777). The completed Block II series are the *New Hampshire* (SSN-778), *New Mexico* (SSN-779), *Missouri* (SSN-780), *California* (SSN-781), *Mississippi* (SSN-782 and *Minnesota* (SSN-783).

Under construction are the Block III series submarines: *North Dakota* (SSN-784), *John Warner* (SSN-785), *Illinois* (SSN-786) and *Washington* (SSN-787).

Those *Virginia*-class submarines that are operating with the submarine force have proven themselves to be superior to any previous design. They are replacing the *Los Angeles*–class submarines with a significant weapons/payload advantage. This means that fewer submarines will be needed for future missions.

As each submarine is built, the cost is gradually being reduced from the four-billion-dollar original estimate.

13—The Seawolf and Virginia Submarines

Although the *Virginia* looks on the surface similar to previously designed submarines, she is fundamentally different by virtue of architecture and sound-isolated compartmentalization. The various functions of *Virginia*, including its sonar sensors, countermeasures, navigation, weapon control, communication and depth control are integrated into a single command organization. Good sonar performance also depends on cutting self-noise, always a high priority issue in submarine design. Each equipment unit rests on sound-isolating mounts in a single unit. The new submarine was designed to have machinery that had been produced from the ground up with quiet operation as its number-one achievement. The use of standardized space dimensions for each piece of equipment will continue to drive down production costs.

The dedication of the submarine's designers to reduce noise emission has produced an acoustic signature equal to or better than the SSN-21. *Virginia*'s outer hull has an anechoic coating, which absorbs rather than reflects active sonar impulses from other submarines or surface ships. The submarine's control suite is equipped with computer touch screens for ballast control and auxiliary machine operation. Its steering and diving are manipulated through a single dual-axis control column that is computer assisted.

In summary, the *Virginia* is a remarkable submarine in terms of its weapons potential, integrated combat command system, variable mission capability, low noise emission signature and advanced sensors.

14

The Future of American Submarines

It is impossible to predict the future, but it is possible to extrapolate current trends and thereby to indulge in reasonable speculation. A few glimpses into the future result from advances in technology, but most are simple extensions of recent trends. Of the latter is the growing use of unmanned submersible vehicles.

Small diesel submarines being produced in nations of fluid leadership are particularly effective in littoral waters not hospitable to most American nuclear-powered submarines. If the United States is to continue to protect its submarine assets, it must devise a means to counter the small, ultra-quiet submarines of foreign countries. The answer may lie in an entirely new concept involving an innovative use of torpedo tubes.[1] Unmanned Underwater Vehicles, or UUVs, are vessels that are able to operate underwater without a human occupant. There are two types of UUVs: remotely operated vehicles (ROV), which are controlled by a remote human operator in a mother submarine; and autonomous underwater vehicles (AUV), which operate independently of direct human input. One of the missions for the UUV and AUV is the detection and destruction of underwater mines. Such vehicles can inspect hundreds of square miles of ocean floor quickly and without the need to place humans in danger. Some UUVs may be tethered to a remote mother submarine or surface vessel, and the intricacy of such a tether is the Tether Management System (TMS). The tether incorporates a bundle of cables that carry electrical power, video and data signals between operator and vehicle. This cable bundle adheres to a strength cable, which enables the controller to haul the vessel to its garage bay in event of emergency.

The future submarine must be able to quickly respond to a threat as described above. It will do so by employing a variety of payloads including

14—The Future of American Submarines

UUVs, AUVs, long-distance torpedoes and distributed sensors, all of which need a fire control system able to integrate a large number of variant data into a comprehensive display, understandable by the fire control technicians. The A/N BYG-1 system has been designed to handle a variety of close-aboard tactical situations involving variable weapons in response to multiple targets. Its calculating speed utilizing sensor information from UUVs and AUVs will allow the future submarine to defend itself before an intruder can do damage.

A specialized AUV is the Anti-submarine Continuous Trail Unmanned Vessel. ACTUV is an unmanned miniature submarine designed to acoustically acquire a quiet submarine, to station itself close to the hostile submarine, and to transmit to its mother submarine the course, speed and depth of the hostile submarine. An ACTUV can be programmed to patrol and investigate large tracts of undersea domain. The vessel is designed to operate autonomously, providing a forward deployed and rapid-responding sonar module of miniaturized efficiency. In addition to its own sensors, an ACTUV could be deployed in conjunction with other ASW forces. Air-dropped sonobuoys, surface ship sonar and other assets can communicate with the ACTUV in detecting a hostile submarine. Once having acquired a target, the ACTUV's sonar can shift to a very high frequency, low-power type of active sonar to maintain contact. Multiple ACTUVs can be stationed around an American Trident submarine, which monitors the activities of its satellite ACTUVs. One of the more thorny problems of ACTUV design is immediate and reliable communication to its mother submarine without revealing its presence to the hostile submarine it is tracking. These multiple robotic patrol craft will be able to defend the Trident deterrent submarine from approaching threats without the hostile force being aware that it is being tracked.

One can expect that the present Advanced Seal Delivery System (ASDS) will be expanded as a primary means of attacking and destroying terrorist forces near the shoreline. The current ASDS vehicles are small submarines in themselves, carrying up to ten Seal team members and two crew members. Each ASDS weighs about 55 tons and can be attached to an attack submarine's after deck. It is propelled by a small impeller thruster and has other small, trainable thrusters to minutely control its position in relation to the ocean's floor. With fore and aft anchors, it can accurately place itself at a desired geographical position, where it can rest as its SEAL team exits the submersible via individual underwater breathing apparatus. The ASDS has two periscopes which fold onto its deck. While the concept of the ASDS has been a reality since 2003, its use in the future is almost a certainty in view of the increasing threat of terrorism from foreign countries.[2]

A major source of noise in a nuclear-powered submarine is its method of reducing high–RPM turbine energy into slow-turning shaft revolutions. Even the most advanced mechanical gearing, employing every device for reducing noise and vibration, falls short of perfection. The problem might be solved by eliminating the reduction gears and transmitting nuclear power-produced electrical energy into an electrical grid that is able to transform the energy into low-speed rotational energy. Future *Virginia*-class submarines may well be equipped with this new concept.

The size of the crew manning *Virginia*-class submarines is not significantly different from earlier types of nuclear boats. Even the fleet-type submarine of the Second World War and the GUPPY operated with crews of over 100 men. Only the much smaller German 212 and 214 boats being produced in the twenty-first century have automation-reduced crew size. The United States Navy relies on the quality of its training programs resulting in competent crew members who operate the complex systems of the *Virginia*-class attack submarines. Looking into the future, it is probable that more and more equipment will be automated and only monitored by crew members. If the German 212 and 214 class submarines act as an example, it is reasonable that the submarine of the future will have significantly fewer crew members, with much of its equipment being operated by computers.

Submarine propulsion has evolved from the three-bladed propeller to the ducted impeller propulsor. As installed on the *Virginia*-class submarine, the propulsor is a fixed extension to a single shaft. Rudders and stern planes are placed outward and forward of the propulsor. One design possibility is the option of a vectored thrust propulsor. Small submarines such as DSRVs and ASDSs use trainable thrusters to give them finite control of close-quartered movement. It is possible to detach the propulsor's nozzle and to mount it on gimbals, thus maneuvering the ship by vectored thrust, as is done in modern fighter aircraft. Although the principles of vectored thrust in many fighter aircraft is a common reality, it is not one which can be easily translated into the submarine's environment. Placing additional weight at the extreme end of the submarine might present many unknown architectural problems.

One might wonder why those responsible for submarine design don't follow the example of Tom Clancy's Soviet submarine *Red October*, with its through-hull caterpillar drive The purpose of fiction is to entertain. It is not bound by scientific realities. Placing a propulsor within the hull of a nuclear submarine involves a mountain of problems. Assuming an inlet in the bow and a nozzle at the stern, the internal ducting would be subject to sea pressure and therefore would have to be constructed of the same strength steel as the hull itself. The problems of cold rolling such a tight curvature, of fabricating framing strengtheners and of manufacturing the foundry equipment to accomplish the task are staggering problems by themselves. Add the difficulty of shaft gearing and sea pressure seals, and the engineering problems become too complex for serious consideration. But that is not the primary problem. By reducing the hull's internal dry volume, the boat would necessarily have to be increased in width and length as compensation. This, in turn, means greater hull friction with commensurate reduction in speed and increase in noise radiation. All in all, such a prospect seems unlikely. Still, in examining the potential of a future submarine, one must not forget that fiction often portends reality.

Among the more sophisticated sensors in addition to sonar is the ability to detect sources of electrical energy. Since small, electrically driven submarines using fuel cell propulsion emit high internal voltage, a system to detect an internal electrical source would be of significant value to future submarines. Research laboratories are studying those fish with the ability to make this kind of subtle detection. While the concept may seem too difficult to replicate, it is a serious Line of Effort (LOE). Were such a system to become a reality, the viability of the fuel-cell submarine would diminish.

The Navy is examining its traditional method of organizing ASW effort. The emerging concept is to consider every undersea encounter from the perspective of an integrated effort. The objective is to create a single point of command responsibility for all undersea activities, including surface vessels, submarines and ASW air units. In so doing, the integrated command could bring all assets quickly to bear on a potentially hostile situation. The central concept of such an organization is that submarines, accustomed to operating independently, can quickly assemble other resources to assist it in an undersea confrontation. The revised ASW organization is currently known as the Integrated Undersea Future Strategy (IUFS).[3] The idea behind this planning is to maximize submarine potential at minimum cost. As such, the submarine building program must look to the future, estimate the type of threats to the United States that will be present in the next fifty years, and determine what type of submarines will be needed to counter these threats. The conversions of a few *Ohio*-class ballistic missile submarines to multiple task platforms (AGSSN) are examples of the efforts likely to be expanded in the future.

The government has not changed its reliance on the FBM submarine as a deterrent to nuclear threats from unfriendly nations. The position of the *Ohio*-class submarine remains unchallenged as one of America's sources of military strength. But the effectiveness of the deterrent lies in the credibility of the government to use the poised weapon. If a hostile nation perceives a reluctance to "push the button," the deterrent is correspondingly weakened. The willingness of the government to retaliate must be strong in the eyes of those hostile leaders who work toward our demise. This consideration reaches beyond the command domain of the Navy.

An analysis of the submarine force may reveal that ever-increasing costs of construction and operation preclude a continuance of its current thinking. The Navy may examine alternatives to traveling the same path of building faster, quieter and more efficient submarines at costs that may become prohibitive. As the United States Air Force places greater emphasis on using unmanned drones for many specialized tasks, so too might the Navy. The future may include a cost-saving program of totally unmanned submarines, remotely controlled through satellites from shore installations.

Those submarines on the drawing boards will have *Virginia*-type propulsors, modular equipment, multiple stern control surfaces, wraparound sonars, thin-wire trailing sonars, larger bow wide-aperture sonars, vertical weapon tubes and expanded integrated sensor consoles capable of handling multiple targets. The space devoted to deployment of UUVs and UAVs as well as advance torpedoes may be increased. As electronic circuitry continues to decrease in size and increase in a variety of applications, an extrapolation of current electronic problem solving in an advanced multiple weapon combat system might appear as super-fast, completely computerized TMA using fiber-optic digital data from synthesized multiple sonar receptors. The role of the fire control team would be to monitor the TMA

14—The Future of American Submarines

process to ensure that the sophisticated solutions have the ring of reasonableness.

In looking to the future, it is natural that the historian should look to the past. The American Navy's submarine force has had a long and admirable service. Although the place of the submarine in the United States Navy is accepted without question, there remains to this day the stigma of a hidden threat that is somehow viewed as immoral by some of the public. Perhaps this stems from the original British contention that the "damned thing is downright ungentlemanly." But whatever the case, it is the men who have served in the "ungentlemanly" machines that must be remembered.

One cannot help but be moved by the magnitude of self-sacrifice in those American submariners who have preceded us. They who served in submarines found a virtuous commitment in doing so. "Riding the boats" has been a mark of valor that can never be erased. The experience for most was so profound that later civilian life became just a footnote. Nothing in the future can detract from what they did and what they continue to do.

Appendix A—A Glossary of Submarine Torpedo Fire Control Terminology

Angle-on-the-bow—The angle formed by the line of sight and target track. The angle is port or starboard through 180 degrees.

Approach course—The course or courses taken by the submarine during the approach phase.

Approach officer—The officer, normally the captain, who conducts the approach and gives all helm and speed orders to close and attack the target.

Approach phase—The period during which the submarine maneuvers to close to a position for commencing the attack phase.

Assistant TDC operator—The officer whose station is in the conning tower at the angle solver section of the TDC. He has two primary duties: to assist the TDC operator in obtaining the course and speed of the target, and to ensure that the proper gyro angle is set on each torpedo when it is fired.

Attack phase—The period during which the submarine maneuvers for a firing position.

Breach doors—Inner torpedo tube doors giving access to the torpedo room.

Contact phase—The initial submarine observation of a possible target, normally hull-down over the horizon with only smoke or mastheads visible.

Distance to the track—The perpendicular distance from the submarine to a forward extension of the target's track.

DRT—Dead reckoning tracer, a glass-topped table with a light under the glass, the "bug," which is a projected spot of light that indicates the ship's

Appendix A

position. It is controlled by the ship's master gyro compass for own ship's movement and underwater log for own ship's speed.

Final bearing and shoot—Order from the approach officer to members of the fire control party to commence shooting as soon as the next bearing is obtained.

Fire—An order from the approach officer to the firing key operator to fire the tube previously designated.

Firing course—The course of the submarine at the instant of firing.

Generated bearing—Relative bearing obtained from TDC position keeper.

Gyro angle—The angle between the longitudinal axis of the submarine and the final torpedo track measured right or left from the bow, from 0° to 180°.

Intercept point—The point at which the torpedo crosses the target track.

Lead angle—The angle between the true bearing of the target and the true course of the submarine.

Muzzle doors—Torpedo tube doors opening the tubes to sea.

Navigation plotter—The officer whose station is in the conning tower at the DRT. His primary duty is to maintain a navigational plot of the target or targets designated by the approach officer. He furnishes the TDC operator and the approach officer with values of target course and speed obtained from the plot.

Normal approach course—The submarine's course that will take it to its firing point in the shortest possible distance. The course is equal to the true bearing of the target, plus or minus 90° in the direction to close the target's track.

Optimum approach course—The submarine's course to the firing point that considers changes in target's speed or course. It is normally about 10 degrees ahead of the normal approach course.

Outer doors or shutter doors—Torpedo tube doors that comply with the submarine's hull curvature. These doors open inward to expose the muzzle doors to open sea. Muzzle doors and outer doors are linked to open and shut simultaneously.

Parallax—The angular correction compensating for the longitudinal distance between the torpedo tube muzzle doors and the periscope. The concept of parallax correction is not treated in this study.

Periscope assistant—The periscope assistant is normally a quartermaster who raises and lowers the periscope on orders of the approach officer, places the periscope on the bearing designated by the TDC operator, announces the relative bearing when signaled by the approach officer, and announces the stadimeter range when approach officer announces, "Range mark!"

Plan of attack—As early in the approach as possible, the approach officer should inform his fire control party of the target or targets to be attacked.

Relative and true bearing—Relative bearing is the compass rose with 000 at the bow and 180 at the stern. True bearing is the compass rose aligned to the Earth's north and south poles.

Salvo—A number of torpedoes fired at short intervals at the same target.

Set—A word used by the torpedo data computer operator to inform the approach officer and assistant torpedo data computer operator that the latest and best target information is set in the TDC and the submarine is ready to commence shooting.

Shoot—An order from the assistant TDC operator to the firing key operator to fire a torpedo. It also informs the approach officer that the designated spread is applied to the torpedo to be fired and that the TDC correct solution light is on.

Speed determination—The torpedo data computer operator is responsible to mentally calculate the speed and target angle-on-the-bow. Methods of mental calculations are a function of the TDC operator's capacity to quickly manipulate spatial relations including angles, distances and speeds. The TDC operator must also provide some or all of the following information when requested by the approach officer: generated range, generated angle-on-the-bow, generated true bearing, distance to the track, torpedo course, normal approach course, optimum approach course and indicated gyro angle.

Spread—A salvo of torpedoes fired to hit different points along the length of the target or its length extended. A salvo of torpedoes is spread to compensate for errors in the estimates of target course, speed, and range. These errors might also be caused by inaccurate fire control estimates or TDC errors, particularly if the target maneuvers at the firing point.

Spread offset angle—A change in target bearing applied to the gyro angle order of each torpedo of a salvo to cause successive torpedoes to hit at different points along the target length or extended track.

Sweep around—A 360° horizontal swing of the periscope to identify contacts other than the target.

Appendix A

Target length—The length of the target may be obtained by estimate based on intelligence, by observation considering angle-on-the-bow, or with use of the horizontal telemeter scale.

TBT (target bearing transmitter)—High-power binocular telescope with telemeter marks mounted on a compass card repeater slaved to the master gyro. The TBT is mounted on the forward rail of the bridge and is equipped with handles for slewing. The right handle has a button which sends the signaled bearing of a target to the TDC.

TDC operator—The officer whose station is in the conning tower at the position keeper section of the TDC. His primary duty is to operate the position keeper and, using all available information, to obtain the most accurate values of target course, speed, and range that can be determined.

Telemeter—Periscope reticules that assist in determining target range when target length (corrected for angle-on-the-bow) or target masthead height are known.

Turn count—A sonar estimate of target speed indicated by the rhythmic pulses of the target's screw.

Appendix B—Evolution of Submarine Torpedo Fire Control Equipment

Class of Submarine/ Mission/Era	Fire Control System	Improved Capability from Previous System
H, K, and L Classes Harbor Defense World War I	None	Navigational plot and proximity to target.
H, K and L Classes Fleet and harbor defense World War I	Torpedo Director	First device using mechanical slides for triangulation. Mark 1 sets torpedo speed, gyro off-set and tube alignment to provide line of sight at impact point. Poor adaptation to submarines.
R, S Classes Independent cruise 1920s and 1930s	Is/Was Banjo	Hand-manipulated overlapping plastic disks provided quick solution for best course and speed to target. Mechanical device for calculating torpedo spreads. Reduced time to calculate torpedo gyro course.
Fleet-type class Independent cruise World War II	Torpedo Data Computer	Electro-mechanical console with display position keeper, and angle solver for torpedo spreads. Automatic generation of target course, speed and range. Hand inputs from periscope, radar and sonar. Mark 4 with analyzer-automatic inputs from radar and sonar. Angle solver section for auto spread of torpedoes.
GUPPY, *Tang* and *Nautilus* Espionage Cold War	Mark 101	Improved single target display. Analog TMA solution from bearing change rate. Control of Mark 27 and Mark 37

205

Appendix B

		torpedoes and wire-guide feature. Auto generated target course, speed and range integrated with hand inputs from bearing change rates.
Skipjack, *Barbel* Independent cruise Cold War	Mark 113	Analog analyzer replaced by combination analog/digital computer. Improved system with analyzer could track up to 3 targets simultaneously. Semi-programmable computer for bearing rate interpretation limited to medium range targets. Drop-last feature smoothed sonar bearing change rates.
Sturgeon Attack *Los Angeles* Attack *G. Washington* FBM ASW and ISR Deterrent Post Cold War	Mark 118	Fully digital console consisting of Mark 92 analyzer/display. Two SID displays with Mark 92. Interchangeable SIDs tracking individual target TMAs. CCA exclusive for Mark 48 and Mark 48ADCAP. Improved software for faster TMA solution.
Ohio FBM Deterrence Post Cold War	CCS Mark 2	Improved processing speed over Mod 3 Mark 118. Refined TMA algorithms. Increased simultaneous tracking of multiple targets. Serial mission capability.
Los Angeles 688I (Improved 719) ASW and ISR Post Cold War	CCS Mk 2 Block 1C	Greatly increased number of simultaneous targets tracked. Increased integration of non-sonar sensory data. Greatly increased processing speed. New TMA algorithms. Increased integration of sonar/FCS interface. Greater demand for intra-crew data flow. Parallel mission capability–operator intensive.
Los Angeles 688I *Virginia* SSGNs ISR/SOF Post Cold War	A/N BYG-1	Full integration of sonar & FCS. Multiple target tracking in excess of multiple operator capability. Full integration of non-sonar sensors. Simultaneous multi-mission system.

Chapter Notes

Chapter 1

1. Edwin Gray, *19th Century Torpedoes and Their Inventors* (Annapolis, MD: Naval Institute Press, 2004), 7.
2. Ibid., 8.
3. Ibid., 62, 63, 154.
4. Ibid., 156, 157.
5. Ibid., 183.
6. Ibid., 186.
7. Ibid., 184.
8. Joseph M Califf, *Notes on Military Science and the Art of War* (London: James L. Chapman, 1898), 138, 139.
9. T.W. Corbin, *The Romance of Submarine Engineering* (Philadelphia: J.B. Lippincott, 1913), 134, 135.
10. Gray, 164.
11. Ibid., 21, 22.
12. Murray F. Sueter, Commodore, Royal Navy, *The Evolution of Submarine Boat, Mine and Torpedo* (Portsmouth, UK: Grieve, Mathews and Seagrove, 1907), 305–309.
13. Oliver Krausz, *Ruestung und Ruestungserprobung in der deutschen Marinegeschichte—Die Torpedoversuchsanstalt* (Bonn, Germany, Bernard und Graefe in der Moench Verlagsgesellschaft mBH, 2010), 48, 49. Translated by Irmgard Diekmann.
14. Ibid.
15. Eberhard Roessler, *Die Torpedo der deutschen U-boote* (Herford, Germany: Koehlers Verlaggesellschaft, mbH, 1984), 35–37. Translated by Irmgard Diekmann.
16. U.S. Navy Special Publication 1–X11, "Specifications for the Manufacture of Bliss-Leavitt Automobile Torpedoes U.S.N. 5 m. × 45cm., Mark III" (Washington, D.C.: Navy Printing Office, December 1903), 2 and 7.
17. Thomas Wildenberg and Norman Polmar, *The Ship Killers: A History of the American Torpedo* (Annapolis, MD: Naval Institute Press, 2010), 42.
18. Ibid., 42.
19. Ibid., 197.
20. J.L. Christley, *United States Naval Submarine Force Information Book* (Marblehead, MA: Graphic Enterprises, 2000), 22.
21. Wildenburg, 42.
22. Ibid., 42.
23. Roessler, 38.
24. Ibid., 38.
25. Califf, 142.

Chapter 2

1. The firm of Howaldtswerke in Kiel, Germany, is today the world's largest producer of affordable submarines. Its Type 214 has fuel cell propulsion for total submergence, high speed, and endurance up to two weeks. The Type 212 has a crew of 26 and the machinery spaces aft of the control room are totally automated. The facility at Kiel includes a giant pressure tank which allows hydraulic testing of hull sections before the submarine is assembled.
2. Richard Humble, *Undersea Warfare* (London: Hartwell Books, 1981), 17.
3. Ibid., 17.
4. Ibid., 18.
5. Ibid., 19, 20.
6. Ibid., 21.
7. Ibid., 22.
8. www.uboat.net/history/ww1/part2.htm.
9. Humble, 23, 24.
10. Lowell Thomas, *Raiders of the Deep* (Annapolis, MD: Naval Institute Press, 1955), 30, 31.
11. John Terraine, *The U-Boat Wars, 1916–1945* (New York: Putnam's, 1989), 239.

12. Norman Friedman, *U.S. Submarines Through 1945: An Illustrated Design History* (Annapolis, MD: Naval Institute Press, 1995), 72. Electric Boat sold a few boats from its H Series to England, Italy and Russia immediately prior to the First World War.
13. Ibid., 63, 64.
14. Ibid., 48.
15. Bill Lightfoot, *Beneath the Surface: World War I Submarines Built in Seattle and Vancouver* (Newcastle, WA: Greenboard Press, 2005), 147.
16. Clay Blaire, Jr., *Silent Victory* (New York: J.B. Lippincott, 1974), 21.
17. Friedman, 78.
18. Lightfoot, 197.
19. Ibid., 198.
20. Ibid., 199.
21. Ibid., 200.
22. *NavPers 16165, Submarine Periscope Manual, Bureau of Naval Personnel* (Washington, D.C.: Navy Printing Office, 1946), 5.
23. Wildenberg and Polmar, 214.

Chapter 3

1. Joseph Martin, *Submarine Qualification Notebook* (original copy held by Submarine Research Center), unnumbered page.
2. Ibid.
3. Peter Paderfield, *War Beneath the Sea: Submarine Conflict During World War II* (New York: John Wiley and Sons, 1973), 30.
4. Friedman, *Through 1945*, 166.
5. Ibid.
6. John D Alden, *The Fleet Submarine in the U.S. Navy* (Annapolis, MD: Naval Institute Press, 1979), 14.
7. E.W. Jolie, *A Brief History of U.S. Navy Torpedo Development* (NUSC, Technical Document 5436, 1978), 29.
8. Edward Jones and Lyle Cummins, "Growing Pains in Submarine Design," *Submarine Review* (July 2009): 49.
9. Jolie, 30.
10. Friedman, *Through 1945*, 349.
11. The exception is low powered transducers, which have been and continue to be used for communication with other submarines and surface ships.
12. Friedman, *Through 1945*, 131, 156.

13. Alden, 16, 36, 39, 47.
14. Friedman, *Through 1945*, 186, 187.
15. Jolie, 34. The last submarines built with riveted hulls were the Portsmouth boats, *Plunger* (SS-179), *Pollack* (SS-180), and *Pompano* (SS-181).
16. Jones and Cummins, 56. The M.A.N., short for Mannheim-Augsburg-Nuremberg, was manufactured in the United States under license. It and the H.O.R., short for Hooven-Owens-Renschler, were the best engines available to American submarines during the 1930s, but both required constant maintenance and repair. The problem of reliable submarine propulsion remained until the late 1930s, when the GM and FM engines were perfected sufficiently to be welcomed by submarine crews.
17. Friedman, 204.
18. Wildenberg and Polmar, 40.
19. Russell Warren, *World War II Torpedo Incidents* (Washington, D.C.: Bureau of Ordnance Publication #305, 1966), 2.
20. Paderfield, 31.
21. *The Torpedo Data Computer, Mark III* (Long Island, NY: Arma Division, American Bosch Arma Corporation, 1952), 2, 3, 4.
22. Doenitz's words were, "Mein Gott! Also, wieder Krieg gegen England!"—My God! So it's war with England, again!
23. Terraine, 218.
24. Blaire, 46.
25. Paderfield, 30.

Chapter 4

1. *NavPers Manual 16160*, 199.
2. Definitions for terms have changed over time. For example, the term "shoot" originally (during the Second World War) replaced the word "fire" because fire meant a conflagration of flames. For that reason the approach officer used the phrase "Final bearing and shoot" as his last periscope observation before releasing a torpedo. During the Cold War and more recently, the term "shoot" relates to a TMA computer solution. It is given by the approach officer, then repeated by the ACC operator to the torpedo room for modern fire control scenarios. Also, generated bearing in modern usage delineates a bearing for the target that has gener-

ated a fire control computer solution in the absence of real-time sonar bearings, and is based on the last updated fire control solution. Thus, the order "shoot on generated bearing" literally means to shoot on the fire control solution's bearing, regardless of whether or not the contact was recently lost. This is used primarily in ASW scenarios where the fire control system solution actually represents a melding of data from multiple sources (sonar, plots, etc.) and the generated bearing is considered the most accurate bearing to the contact that the own submarine has at the time. Even if sonar contact has been maintained throughout the attack, differences in bearings from different sonar arrays (towed, sail, hull, active intercepts, etc.) can result, which is why "shoot on generated bearing" was created.

3. The fleet-type submarine with a full battery charge made the following submerged speeds for the length of time indicated:

    3.0 knots for 48 hours,
    6.0 knots for three hours,
    8.0 knots for one hour,
    9.0 knots for a half hour.

4. Blaire, 89.
5. Ibid., 88. Joe Grenfell and Dusty Dornin were two of the Second World War's legends, with brilliant, quick minds able to grasp rapidly changing relative motions and give clear orders to bring their submarines into firing position.
6. Jim Patton, Capt. USN Ret., "One Mile Equals One Degree in One Minute," *Submarine Review* (October 2008): 55.
7. Ibid.
8. Blaire, 176.
9. The customary doctrine during the 1950s called for M.O.T., aft, forward, in that sequence, for a three-torpedo spread. This spread compensated for errors in speed estimate or changes in target speed. If the target was moving faster than estimated, the torpedo fired forward of the bow would actually hit in the forward part of the ship, the M.O.T. torpedo would hit the stern, and the torpedo aimed at the stern would miss. If the target was moving slower than estimated, the one aimed forward of the bow would miss ahead, the M.O.T. would hit in the bow and the stern shot about the middle of the target. In sum: In a spread of three torpedoes, two would probably hit.
10. Doug Stanton, *In Harm's Way: The Sinking of the USS Indianapolis and the Extraordinary Story of Its Survivors* (New York: Henry Holt, 2001), 93–95.
11. Ibid., 261.

Chapter 5

1. Blaire, 51, 58.
2. George Grider, *War Fish* (New York: Little, Brown, 1958), 55.
3. Blaire, 49.
4. Ibid., 50.
5. Paderfield, 63.
6. The German influence exploder was not reliable. It gave U-boat skippers such a headache that many instructed their torpedomen to remove the magnetic part of the exploder and retain only the contact exploder.
7. Heinz Schaeffer, *U-Boat 977* (London: William Kimber, 1952), 72–75.
8. Ibid., 76.
9. Edgar O'Neil, *A Study of Torpedo Data Computer, T Vorhalt Rechner S-3, German*, Captured Enemy Equipment Number 8266 (Washington, D.C.: U.S. Navy Bureau of Ordnance Publication, July 6, 1945), 3–5.
10. Ibid., 7.
11. Slade D. Cutter, USN, Ret., *Reminiscences of Capt. Slade D. Cutter*, Oral History Program (Annapolis, MD: Naval Institute Special Project, 1985), 126, 127, 128.
12. William J. Ruhe, *War in the Boats: My World War II Submarine Battles* (Washington, D.C.: Brassey's, 1994), 133.
13. William Boyd, *U.S. Navy Bureau of Ordnance in World War II* (Washington, D.C.: Department of the Navy Printing Office, 1943), 105, 106.
14. Ruhe, 138–142.
15. Blaire, 537. Blaire stated on page 331 that in 1942, on his way to the continental U.S. to take command of a new-construction boat, Dornin stopped long enough in Pearl Harbor to establish the first TDC school for young officers.
16. Lloyd Jones, *Personal Archives* (unpublished papers), 125.

17. Friedman, *Through 1945*, 236.
18. Ibid., 236.
19. Ibid., 237.
20. Ibid., 238.
21. Ibid., 234.
22. William R. McCants, *War Patrols of the USS Flasher* (Chapel Hill, NC: Professional Press, 1994), 293.
23. Dudley Morton, Cdr., USN., *USS Wahoo, Third War Patrol Report* (College Park, MD: National Archives, 1945).
24. Eugene B. Fluckey, Cdr., USN, *USS Barb, Eleventh Patrol Report* (College Park, MD: National Archives, 1945).
25. Alex Kershaw, *Escape from the Deep* (Cambridge, MA: Da Capo Press, 2008), 61, 62.
26. Grider, 30.
27. Friedman, *Through 1945*, 234.
28. Blaire, 851, 852, 853.

Chapter 6

1. Paul Johnson, *Churchill* (New York: Penguin Group, 2009), 144.
2. Norman Friedman, *U.S. Submarines Since 1945: An Illustrated Design History* (Annapolis, MD: Naval Institute Press, 1995), 3.
3. Cutter, 122.
4. Friedman, *Since 1945*, 12.
5. Translated as: Grouped Listening Apparatus. German parlance often combines several words into one when adjectives modify a noun.
6. The Navy's Sonar School at Point Loma, San Diego, quickly grew into an ASW training institution of great merit. In so doing, it retrained sonar specialists who were qualified in submarines to use the most advanced techniques and equipment for detection and classification of both surface ships and potentially hostile submarines.
7. Corbin, 129.
8. *Position Indicator Mark 6, Description and Maintenance* (Washington, D.C.: Bureau of Naval Weapons Publication Number 2265), 1.
9. Friedman, *Since 1945*, 18, 19.
10. *Torpedo Data Computer Mark III* (Long Island, New York: Arma Division, American Bosch Corporation Bulletin 27, 1951), 8, 9.
11. Friedman, *Since 1945*, 16.
12. Ibid., 50.
13. The primary target of surveillance for ComSubLant was Murmansk. In the Pacific, ComSubPac concentrated on Petropavlovsk and Vladivostok.
14. Sherry Sontag and Christopher Drew, *Blind Man's Bluff* (New York: Harper Row, 1996), 7.
15. Friedman, *Since 1945*, 8.
16. Ibid., 37.
17. While the primary mission of U.S. submarines during the Korean War was surveillance, a few U.S. submarines participated directly in the conflict. The USS *Perch* (SSP-313), a famous Second World War submarine, transported UDT personnel to coastal locations in their performance of clandestine missions. Other submarines performed photo reconnaissance missions of the Inchon harbor fortifications. During the Vietnam War, U.S. submarines patrolled the coastal water to prevent interventions by Soviet submarines, acted as ASW protection for carriers operating directly in the conflict, and conducted reconnaissance missions in the Tonkin Gulf.
18. Having an all-nuclear-powered submarine force has in recent years presented America with unique tactical challenges. Potentially hostile nations continue to produce diesel-electric submarines that are quiet and difficult to detect. They do not posses the endurance or speed of a modern nuclear submarine, but their tactical advantage in remaining undetected presents a significant problem for American nuclear-powered submarines. As a step in countering the threat posed by quiet-running diesel-electric boats, the U.S. Navy has reached out to its allies that deploy similar diesel technology. The Swedish government allowed its submarine *Gotland*, with its Sterling AIP system, to provide services to American ASW units operating out of San Diego. This arrangement lasted for over a year.

Chapter 7

1. Friedman, *Since 1945*, 27, 28.
2. Ibid., 20.
3. Ibid., 52.
4. Lyle Cummins, *Diesels for the First*

Notes—Chapter 7

Stealth Weapon (Wilsonville, OR: Carnot Press, 2007), 236, 239.

   5. Ibid., 234.

   6. This event was witnessed by the author as a TAD crew member who, being in the operations compartment at the time, was fascinated by the warping of a vertical stanchion near the radio room while *Wahoo* was at crush depth. It was visual confirmation of HY-80 steel's elasticity. As the submarine returned to normal depth, the stanchion straightened to its former condition. The dive was verified later by other crew members, but whether or not the special operations event was logged is unknown.

   7. Norman Polmar and Kenneth J. Moore, *Cold War Submarines: The Design and Construction of U.S. and Soviet Submarines* (Washington, D.C.: Brassey's, 2004), 17.

   8. Friedman, *Since 1945*, 258. Sontag and Drew, in *Blind Man's Bluff*, give a more thorough treatment of this event, which underlines the tensions of America's submarines going in harm's way to gather intelligence on Soviet naval practices. A paraphrased except from pages 34 to 40 is as follows:

   Commander Norman G. Bessac took his submarine *Gudgeon* into the 12-mile limit of Vladivostok. The Soviet ASW ships had discovered the presence of an American submarine and maintained contact with active sonar despite *Gudgeon*'s evasive maneuvers. Bessac stood in the cramped control room issuing orders, as the submarine sought protection from ever-increasing depths.

   After a day of submergence, carbon dioxide levels were high enough that some crew members felt nauseous, others had headaches, and most were otherwise incapacitated. At that point *Gudgeon* had been submerged for approximately 24 hours. The submarine attempted to evade by ejecting canisters of bubble-producing crystals. It was hoped that doing so while turning sharply would shake the surface ships. The Soviet destroyers responded to the escape attempt by dropping practice depth charges which sounded like hand grenades going off very close to the submarine's hull.

   While *Gudgeon* could withstand these small explosions, many in the crew wondered if this were only a prelude to real depth charges. The Soviets made continuing passes over *Gudgeon* with its active sonar pinging against *Gudgeon*'s hull. The submarine continued to seek deeper depths, finally going past its test depth of 700 feet to approximately 850 feet. Aggravating the situation was an obstruction to the outer door of the garbage ejector. This placed sea pressure against only the inner door, which, if violated, would quickly sink the submarine.

   The commanding officer tried other evasive maneuvers, shooting noisemakers from the ejector in the stern room. None of *Gudgeon*'s attempts to evade the Soviet ships had any effect on Soviet determination. Bessac estimated that no fewer than four destroyers were above them. The submarine's Mark 101 fire control system kept torpedoes properly aimed at the multiple targets. As the submarine had now been submerged over 24 hours, fatigue began to force men into their bunks. Lack of oxygen meant that lithium hydroxide crystals were placed on unoccupied bunk covers to absorb carbon dioxide.

   Above *Gudgeon* the Soviet ships moved slowly in a game of pinpointing the submarine and dropping practice depth charges. After 48 hours had passed, with air fouled from lack of oxygen and a near-dead battery, the commanding officer knew he had to take drastic action. He attempted to snorkel, but the Soviets closed with intent to ram. *Gudgeon* went back down to 400 feet while the commanding officer determined that he must surface to save his ship. To threaten the Soviet ASW ships he opened all of the torpedo outer doors. He hoped the sound would threaten the ships and drive them away as he surfaced. The surface alarm sounded, *Gudgeon* came to the surface, and the commanding officer went to the bridge. He sent a flash message to ComSubGruWesPac in plain English that he was in trouble. The Soviet ships lay alongside as *Gudgeon* moved ahead at full speed to vacate the area. The Soviet ship closest to *Gudgeon* signaled by flashing a light, asking, "Who are you?" *Gudgeon* sent back, "U.S. We are going to Japan." The response from the Soviet ship returned in English, "Thanks for the ASW exercise."

   9. Polmar and Moore, 50, 51.

10. Ibid., 55, 56.
11. Ibid., 57.
12. Commander Eugene Wilkinson was the first commanding officer of *Nautilus*. He was relieved by Commander William Anderson. Both commanded *Wahoo* before taking command of *Nautilus*.
13. Polmar and Moore, 59.
14. John P. Craven, *The Silent War: The Cold War Battle Beneath the Sea* (New York: Simon & Schuster, 2001), 24–28.
15. Christley, 57, 59.
16. Friedman, *Since 1945*, 128.
17. Edward Monroe Jones, *Steep Angles and Deep Dives* (Bangor, WA: Submarine Research Center Press, 2004), 95.
18. Edward Monroe Jones, *Undersea Encounters* (Bangor, WA: Submarine Research Center Press, 2006), 169.
19. Ibid., 67.

Chapter 8

1. Edward C. Whitman, *Regulus, America's First Sea-borne Nuclear Deterrent*, www.navy.mil/navydata/cno/n87/usw/issue_11/regulus.html, 3–7.
2. Robert Harmuth, "Up From the Deep" (manuscript excerpt by permission of Mr. Harmuth and published in *Submarine Skullduggery*, Submarine Research Center, 2004).

Chapter 9

1. At 11:42 on January 8, 2005, USS *San Francisco* (SSN-711), under command of Commander Kevin Mooney, struck an undersea mount in the Carolina Islands. Mooney came to command through the route of competency as a nuclear engineering officer. His knowledge of navigation did not include up-to-the-minute knowledge of electronic navigation equipment. He depended on his navigation team for competency in the day-to-day routine of a transit. Running at transit depth and at about 20 knots, the submarine had about 1200 fathoms beneath the keel according to its Position of Intended Movement (PIM). Fully functional were its AN/BQQ-5d transducer, its BQH-1 probe, and its AN/BQR-8 and WOC-2 hydrophones. Its fathometer was fully operational and turned on. The undersea collision killed one crew member and injured others. It caused massive damage to the sonar dome and sonar arrays as well as other internal damage. There were mitigating circumstances, but the root cause of the collision was the failure of the navigation team and the command duty officer to stop the submarine in the face of alarming fathometer indications of a steeply rising shelf. Also, were the transducer to have been energized to verify the fathometer readings, the collision might have been avoided. At the inquest, the navigation team testified that its assumption that the fathometer was faulty was based on its reliance of chart data.
2. Polmar and Moore, 53, 127.
3. The David Taylor Model Basin team was lead by John Craven, who demonstrated his ability in several investigative projects including locating the remains of the *Scorpion*.
4. Polmar and Moore, 128.
5. Roy Burcher and Louis Rydill, *Concepts in Submarine Design* (Cambridge, UK: Cambridge University Press, 1994), 103–195. This reference examined the manifold problems of modern submarine design, many of which were addressed in American efforts resulting in the experiments of the *Albacore* during the 1960s.
6. Ibid., 129.
7. Ibid., 138.
8. Friedman, *Since 1945*, 31.
9. Crush depth is a theoretical sea pressure depth corresponding to the amount of area pressure that can be applied to a hull before it is violated by distortion, warping, buckling or cracking. Test depth is an engineering estimate of a safe operating depth less than crush depth. The ratio of the two varies. The *Tench*-class fleet-type submarine had a crush depth of 450 feet and a test depth of 412 feet. The *Tang*-class boats had a test depth of 700 feet and a crush depth of 760 feet. Hull thickness is only one factor of several determining hull strength. Steel is an alloy made up of several metals other than iron. These may include chromium, nickel, manganese, titanium and a host of others. Carbon content acts to increase brittleness. Thus, a good submarine hull plate is one which minimizes carbon and balances other elements to produce a metal of high yield

ability without compromising compression strength. The key to producing metal hulls suitable to deep-diving submarines is the quality of yield strength in combination with compression strength. A metal hull that has the quality of bending rather than rupturing is a high-yield hull. The second factor in the manufacturing process is the tempering of the steel and shaping of the plates into a final form. The basic concept is that a slow-cooling steel tends to be resilient. A submarine's hull plating is cooled at a specific rate designed to produce the best combination of stress and yield factors. The shaping of the plate in the factory is accomplished with huge hydraulic rollers. Most hull alloys are cold-rolled. As the thickness of the plate increases, the metal resists deformation. The effect of rolling becomes less. The modern mill uses computers to cold-roll submarine hull plates. Each pass through the rollers bends the steel a small amount until, after hundreds of shaping rolls, the plate conforms to the correct hull curvature.

10. Ibid., 58.
11. Polmar and Moore, 131.
12. Friedman, *Since 1945*, 58.
13. Polmar and Moore, 132, 133.
14. Friedman, *Since 1945*, 243.
15. While the *Barbel* was the operational equivalent to the *Albacore*, but conventionally diesel-electric powered with a single screw, the *Skate* was nuclear-powered but retained the conventional *Tang* hull shape with twin screws.
16. Polmar and Moore, 134.
17. Christley, 59.
18. Polmar and Moore, 138.
19. Ibid., 148.

Chapter 10

1. Christley, 65.
2. Friedman, *Since 1945*, 243.
3. Wildenberg and Polmar, 159–162.
4. Polmar and Moore, 155.
5. SOSUS, or Sound Surveillance System, was a ring of land-based stations each having sea-bed stationary hydrophones that were interlinked to a coordinate analyzer. By interpreting the interjecting bearings of a sound source, the position of a transiting Soviet submarine could be radioed to ComSubLant, which then transmitted this information to its submarines in the Atlantic. The ones covering the Denmark strait were in Greenland, Canada, Iceland and Great Britain.

6. Fishing nets were a real problem to American submarines. In June 1968 the *Robert E. Lee* (SSBN-601) headed south from the Firth of Clyde, running submerged in a routine transit. Suddenly, the submarine slowed while noises of scraping and banging along the hull alarmed the captain and crew. The noise ceased and crew members in control believed that whatever had snagged the boat had fallen astern. But the captain was still puzzled. Although the turn count remained the same, the boat was hardly moving. The stern planes were sluggish and the diving officer reported that he could not keep depth. It was apparent to everyone in the submarine's operation compartment that the boat would have to surface. It did so, and as the captain entered the bridge, he looked aft to see a French fishing trawler, the *Lorraine-Bretagne*, which showed a beam aspect. It was a seagoing trawler of about 100 feet. The captain broke rig-for-dive and sent men topside to inspect for damage. They reported that a cable about an inch and a half in diameter was tangled in the stern planes, rudder and screw. It had first been fouled in the sailplanes, had slipped off and had scraped along every missile hatch hinge before getting hung up on the stern. What was not immediately apparent to the captain was the fact that the trawler had been pulled by its beam through the water for a distance of about 3 miles. The French captain pulled his trawler alongside the *Robert E. Lee* and gestured wildly as he pointed to his fouled fishing gear. Eventually, the cables were released, and the French vessel pulled away with its captain still yelling invectives in French, none of which the Americans on the bridge could understand. Jones, *Undersea Encounters*, 111.

7. Sontag and Drew, 141–150.
8. Ibid., 153–169.
9. Polmar and Moore, 268.

Chapter 11

1. Corbin, 129.
2. Polmar and Moore, 285, 286.

3. Friedman, *Since 1945*, 243.
4. Ibid., 16, 243.
5. Polmar and Moore, 274.
6. Jones, *Undersea Encounters*, 73.
7. *Los Angeles*–class submarine construction lasted almost twenty years, from 1976 to 1996. During and subsequent to that period, submarines of that class underwent many modifications to equipment and hull fittings. The most comprehensive change was the introduction of the vertical Tomahawk tubes in the bow. The so-equipped boats were referred to as 719 boats for the first hull number of the series.
8. Friedman, *Since 1945*, 114, 115.
9. SeaLab was an experimental capsule that rested on the sea floor in the depths off La Jolla, California. Its purpose was to gather data on the effects of long-term human habitation in a confined space under conditions of a hostile environment. SeaLab was fitted with locks.
10. Sontag and Drew, 174–186.

Chapter 12

1. Craven, 35.
2. Ibid., 37, 38.
3. While Admiral Raborn exercised his authority with the efficiency and effectiveness gained in various commands during the Second World War, he had to contend with the largely political dominance of Admiral Hyman Rickover on the design and construction of the Navy's submarine ballistic missile program. The balancing act continued until those in Congress who had supported Rickover became aware that, although his contribution to the development of the nuclear-powered submarine could not be overstated, it was time to let others assume the helm of combat submarine design and construction.
4. Ibid., 106.
5. Friedman, *Since 1945*, 199, 200. Lieutenant Charles Allen of the Special Projects Office had estimated that a 5-foot-diameter rocket could throw a 625-pound warhead 1,200 nautical miles, but at a subsequent meeting in 1956, Admiral Raborn redirected efforts toward a smaller missile to comply with Jackson's visualized launch method.
6. Ibid., 201.
7. Ibid., 114, 11.
8. Polmar and Moore, 119.
9. Friedman, *Since 1945*, 206.
10. Polmar, 125.
11. Ibid., 193.
12. Ibid., 194.
13. Friedman, *Since 1945*, 55.
14. Ibid., 22.
15. Food storage for sixty-day patrols was a marvel of computerized organization. For example, food being transferred from a Cisco Company truck to the USS *Alabama* (SSBN-731) at Submarine Base, Bangor, in 2004 was delivered in pre-determined, meal-sized plastic envelopes. Food was craned aboard on pallets through a large-diameter soft patch. The meal packets were placed on a pallet in computerized order of service during the coming two-month patrol. Each dry food parcel was labeled to correspond to others in cool box and freezer. As food was consumed, refuse was compressed and placed in sealed containers that would occupy the vacated dry food storage space. The missile submarines were equipped with garbage ejectors, but these were used only when it was not possible to return refuse to port.

Chapter 13

1. The designator SSN-21 was a working title which would later be amended to a standard hull number that fit the Navy's numerical system. The proposed name of *Seawolf* was retained. It was to be the third submarine with that name.
2. The Type XVI German submarine of the Second World War solved the problem by placing the rudder and stern planes at the rear of the screw, but structural considerations normally outweigh the advantage of such an arrangement.
3. In some ducted propulsors, the ring is fixed to the blades, spinning with them. This system introduces a flywheel problem which slows response time to speed changes and reversing. To overcome this problem impeller, blade adjustable pitch is possible, but this requires intricate engineering much like an adjustable aircraft propeller pitch.
4. One must not carry similarities between aircraft jet engines and propulsors too

far. While their comparative shapes are similar, air is compressible, while water is not. Therefore, the action of a ducted propulsor in a submarine and that of an aircraft's jet engine are totally different. Burcher and Rydill, 117–121.

Chapter 14

1. AMI Report, "Submarine News From Around the World," *Submarine Review* (Winter 2013): 142. The People's Republic of China is reported to have over 300 submarines of various types, all of which are conventionally powered. The *Song* and *Luan* class boats have had problems, and the People's Republic of China has ordered several Amur–1650 SSK-type submarines from Russia.

2. Polmar and Moore, 263–265.

3. Michael Connor, VADM, USN, "Corporate Benefactors Recognition Day, Commander Submarine Forces," *Submarine Review* (Winter 2013): 15.

Bibliography

Alden, John D. *The Fleet Submarine in the U.S. Navy*. Annapolis, MD: Naval Institute Press, 1979.

AMI Report, "Submarine News From Around the World." *Submarine Review* (Winter 2013).

Arma Division Bulletin 12. Long Island, NY: American Bosch Arma Corporation, 1952.

Blaire, Clay Jr. *Silent Victory: The U.S. Submarine War Against Japan*. New York: J.B. Lippincott, 1975.

Boyd, William. *U.S. Navy Bureau of Ordnance in World War II*. Washington, D.C.: Navy Department Printing Office, 1943.

Burcher, Roy, and Louis Rydill. *Concepts in Submarine Design, Cambridge Ocean Technological Series*. Cambridge, UK: Cambridge University Press, 1994.

Califf, Joseph M. *Notes on Military Science and the Art of War*. London: James L. Chapman, 1898.

Christley, J.L. *United States Naval Submarine Force Information Book*. Marblehead, MA: Graphic Enterprises, 2000.

Connor, Michael. "Corporate Benefactor Recognition Day, Commander Submarine Forces." *Submarine Review* (Winter 2013).

Cooper, D.L. "SSN-21 Status: Combat Systems History." *Submarine Review* (Winter 1991).

Corbin, T.W. *The Romance of Submarine Engineering*. Philadelphia: J.B. Lippincott, 1913.

Craven, John P. *The Silent War: The Cold War Battle Beneath the Sea*. New York: Simon & Schuster, 2001.

Cummins, Lyle. *Diesels for the First Stealth Weapon*. Wilsonville, OR: Carnot Press, 2007.

Cutter, Slade D. *Oral History Interviews*. Volume 1. Annapolis, MD: Naval Institute, 1985.

Fluckey, Eugene. B. *USS Barb Eleventh Patrol Report*. College Park, MD: National Archives, 1945.

Friedman, Norman. *U.S. Submarines Since 1945: An Illustrated Design History*. Annapolis, MD: Naval Institute Press, 1995.

_____. *U.S. Submarines Through 1945: An Illustrated Design History*. Annapolis, MD: Naval Institute Press, 1995.

Gray, Edwin. *British Submarines in the Great War*. South Yorkshire, UK: Leo Cooper, 2001.

_____. *19th Century Torpedoes and Their Inventors*. Annapolis, MD: Naval Institute Press, 2004.

Grider, George. *War Fish*. New York: Little, Brown, 1958.

Harmuth, Robert. *Up From the Deep* (unpublished manuscript excerpt). Bangor, WA: Submarine Research Center, 2004.

Humble, Richard. *Undersea Warfare*. London: Hartwell Books, 1981.

Johnson, Paul. *Churchill*. New York: Penguin Group, 2009.

Jolie, E.W. *A Brief History of U.S. Navy Torpedo Development, NUSC*, Technical Document 5436. Washington, D.C.: Navy Office of Printing, 1978.

Jones, David, and Peter Nunan. *U.S. Subs Down Under, Brisbane, 1942–1945*. Annapolis, MD: Naval Institute Press, 2005.

Kershaw, Alex. *Escape from the Deep*. Cam-

Bibliography

bridge, MA: Da Capo Press, 2008.

Krausz, Oliver. *Ruestung und Ruestungserprobung in der deutschen Marinegeschichte—Die Torpedoversuchsanstalt.* Bonn, Germany: Bernard und Graefe in der Moench Verlagsgesellschaft mbH, 1987.

Liddell-Hart, B.H. *History of the Second World War.* London: Cassell Publishers, 1970.

Lightfoot, Bill. *Beneath the Surface: World War I Submarines Built in Seattle and Vancouver.* Newcastle, WA: Greenboard Press, 2005.

Macintyre, Donald. *The Battle of the Atlantic.* New York: Pan Books, 1956.

Martin, Joseph. *Submarine Qualification Notebook* (unpublished document). Bangor, WA: Submarine Research Center Library, 1919.

McCants, William R. *War Patrols of the USS Flasher.* Chapel Hill, NC: Professional Press, 1994.

McCullough, Jonathan J. *A Tale of Two Subs.* New York: Grand Central, 2008.

Monroe-Jones, Edward. *Steep Angles and Deep Dives.* Bangor, WA: Submarine Research Center Press, 2004).

———. *Undersea Encounters.* Bangor, WA: Submarine Research Center, 2006.

Monroe-Jones, Edward, and Lyle Cummins. "Growing Pains in Submarine Design." *Submarine Review* (July 2009).

Morton, Dudley, Cdr. *USS Wahoo, Third Patrol Report.* College Park, MD: National Archives, 1945.

NavPers Manual 16160, the Fleet Type Submarine. Washington, D.C.: Navy Printing Office, 1944.

O'Neil, Edgar. *A Study of Torpedo Data Computer, T Vorhalt Rechner S-3, German.* Captured Enemy Equipment Number 8266. U.S. Navy Bureau of Ordnance, Washington, D.C.: Navy Office of Printing, 1945.

Paderfield, Peter. *War Beneath the Sea: Submarine Conflict During World War II.* New York: John Wiley and Sons, 1973.

Patton, Jim, Capt. USN Ret. "One Mile Equals One Degree in One Minute." *Submarine Review* (October 2008).

Polmar, Norman, and Thomas B. Allen. *Rickover.* New York: Simon & Schuster, 1982.

Polmar, Norman, and Kenneth J. Moore. *Cold War Submarines: The Design and Construction of U.S. and Soviet Submarines.* Washington, D.C.: Brassey's, 2004.

Position Indicator Mark 6, Description and Maintenance. Bureau of Naval Weapons Number 2265. Washington, D.C.: Navy Printing Office, 1955.

Roessler, Eberhard. *Die Torpedo der deutschen U-boat.* Herford, Germany: Koehlers Verlaggesellschaft, mbH, 1984.

Ruhe, William J. *War in the Boats: My World War II Submarine Battles.* Washington, D.C.: Brassey's, 1994.

Schaeffer, Heinz. *U-Boat 977.* London: William Kimber Publishers, 1952.

Sontag, Sherry, and Christopher Drew. *Blind Man's Bluff.* New York: HarperRowe, 2005.

Stanton, Doug. *In Harm's Way: The Sinking of the USS Indianapolis and the Extraordinary Story of Its Survivors.* New York: Henry Holt, 2001.

Sueter, Murray, F. *The Evolution of Submarine Boat, Mine and Torpedo.* London: Grieve, Mathews and Seagrove, 1907.

Terraine, John. *The U-Boat Wars, 1916–1945.* New York: Putnam's, 1989.

Thomas, Lowell. *Raiders of the Deep.* Annapolis, MD: Naval Institute Press, 1955.

U.S. Navy Special Publication 1–X11, "Specifications for the Manufacture of Bliss-Leavitt Automobile Torpedoes." Washington, D.C.: Navy Printing Office, December 1903.

Warren, Russell. *World War II Torpedo Incidents.* Washington, D.C.: Navy Department Bureau of Ordnance Publication #305, 1966.

Wildenberg, Thomas, and Norman Polmar. *The Ship Killers: A History of the American Torpedo.* Annapolis, MD: Naval Institute Press, 2010.

Index

Abelson, Philip A. 128
Aboukir, HMS 18
ACTUV 195
AGSSN 198
Albacore (SS-218) 14
Albacore (SS-569) 134, 143–147
USS *Alert* 21
Archerfish (SSN-678) 151
HMS *Ark Royal* 72
Arma Corporation 48, 114, 115
Armstrong, W.G. 14
ASDS 195, 196

Balderston, Buele, G. 156
Banjo 43, 44
Barbel (SSN-580) 146, 147
Barbero (SS-317 170
Bathythermograph 87
Baton Rouge (SSBN-689) 163, 164
Beach, Ned 82
Behrens, William W. 148
Benjamin Franklin (SSBN-640) 173
Benson, Roy 83
Blandy, Admiral 80
Bliss, E.W. 11
Bliss-Leavitt Company 15
Blueback (SSN-581) 146
Bonefish (SSN-582) 146
Bradley, James A., Jr. 167
Brennan, Louis 8

Cachelot (SS-170) 38
Carbonero (SS-337) 135, 170
Cavalle (SS-244) 119
Chappell, Lucian 83
USS *Cheyenne* 22
Chicago, USS 23–25
Christy, Ralph 46, 83
Churchill, Winston 98
Ciotta, Giovani de 7
CLAM 178
Clamagor (SS-343) 103

Clarke, Vincent A. 28
Cochino (SS-345) 118
COCOMS 184
CONFORM 158
Connecticut (SSN-22) 186
Craven, John 130, 131
HMS *Cressy* 18
Crevalle (SS-291) 79–82
Cusl (SS-348) 135
Cutter, Slade 78, 79, 83, 100
Cuttlefish (SS-171) 38

Dealy, Samuel 85
Dolphin (SS-167) 38
Dornin, Robert 82, 83
DSRV 168

Eberle, Edward W. 37
Ekelund, Joseph 109–111
Electric Boat Company 13, 20, 129, 130, 148, 187
Ericsson, John 7
USS *Essex* 132, 133
Ethan Allen (SSBN-608) 173, 174

Fife, James, Jr. 63, 83
fire control systems, American: A/N BYG 191, 192, 195; CGS Mark 2 177, 178; CCS Mark 2, Block 1C 166, 167; Mark 101 104, 105, 111, 116, 147, 150, 153, 154; Mark 106 117; Mark 113 152–154, 168, 174–177; Mark 117 152; Mark 118 152, 158, 163–165, 176, 178; Mark 134 166
fire control systems, German: T Vorhalt Rechner G-3 74–77
Fisher, Admiral Lord 17
Fluckey, Eugene 83, 88, 91, 94
From, John L. 175

George Washington (SSBN-598) 173, 174
Gleason, Philip 88
Glenard P. Lipscombe (SSBN-685) 151

219

Index

Grayback (SS-574) 170
Grider, George 83, 88, 96
Groves, Lesley R. 128
Growler (SS-577) 135–170
Gudgeon (SS-567) 127
USS *Gulfport* 22
Gunn, Ross 128
Gunn, William 136, 138, 139

Halibut (SS-587) 153, 167–169
Harmuth, Robert 136, 138–140
Hart, Thomas Charles 21, 36, 45, 46, 63
HMS *Hawke* 18, 19
Hendrix, Charles N. 143
Hersing, Otto 17
HMS *Hogue* 18
Howell, John 8, 10

USS *Indianapolis* 66
ISWAS Attack Course Finder 40–42

Jackson, Harry 172
Jimmy Carter (SSN-23) 186

KAST 177, 178
Keeter, Dalton 88
Kern, Donald 148

Lafayette (SSBN-616) 173,174
Lake, Simon 20
Lapon (SSN 661) 154, 155
Leavitt, Frank McDowell 11
Lionfish (SS-298) 71
Lockwood, Charles 80
Los Angeles (SSN-688) 165
Los Angeles (SSN-719) 160, 165

Mack, Chester M. 154, 155
M.A.N. Engine 34, 35, 39
Martin, Joseph 27, 28, 30
MATE 166, 175, 178
McCants, Thomas 88
McKee, Andrew 130, 131
McNish, John E. 168, 169
McVay, Charles V. 66
Miller, Earle 128
MIRV 176
missiles, guided: Harpoon 163; Jupiter 170; Polaris 172–175; Poseidon 176; Regulus 135; Sea Lance 152; SUBROC 152; Tomahawk 163; Trident C-4 176, 177
Morton, Dudley (Mush) 72, 83, 88, 94
MOSS 178
Murray, William B. 134

Nagumo, Chuichi 70
Narwhal (SS-167) 38, 71
Narwhal (SSN-571) 153
Nasmith, Melvin 38
Nautilus (SS-168) 38
Nautilus (SSN-571) 129–132
Nimitz, Chester W. 21

Obry, L 10
Octopus (SS-11) 20
Odax (SS-404) 102
Ohio (SSBN-726) 176
O'Kane, Richard 72, 83, 94, 96
Osborne, James B. 175

Parche (SSN-683) 152, 186
Parks, Lewis S. 78, 79
HMS *Pathfinder* 17
Permit (SSN-594) 152
Propulsor 188–190
Providence (SSBN-719) 164

radar, submarine: SS 85; ST 61, 85
Radford, William F. 170
reactor, nuclear propulsion: S3W 132; S5G 153, 158; S5W 151; S6G 150, 160; S6W 185
Rickover, Hyman G. 100, 129, 130, 148, 160, 183
Roosevelt, Franklin D. 39, 50
ROV 194

Salmon (D-3) 13
Sargo (SSN-583) 131, 132
SAWS 170
SEAL 182, 195, 196
Scamp (SSN-588) 148
Schaefler, Heinz 73
Scorpion (SSN 589) 148
Sculpin (SSN-590) 148
Seadragon (SSN-584) 131, 132
Seawolf (SSN-21) 183–189
Shark (SSN 591) 148
Sieglaff, Barney 83
SINS 174
Skate (SSN-578) 131, 132, 147, 149
Skipjack (SSN-585) 148–150, 172, 173
Snook (SSN-592) 148
Solberg, Thornwald 128
sonar, early submarine systems: JT 43; S.C. Tube 36; SJ 61; Y-tube 28,29
sonar, land based, passive: SOSUS 154
sonar, submarine systems: BQN-134 163; BQQ-2 151; BQQ-5 154, 163, 174;

220

Index

BQQ-6 177; BQQ-7 151; BQQ10(V4) 191; BQR-4 119, 129, 146–148; BQR-20 154, 174; BQR-22 154, 174; BQR-2102, 103 142; BQS-15 163; BQS 20 147, 148, 154, 174; SQS 4 129, 132, 146, 150; TB29A 191; WAA 184
sonar, submarine systems, passive ranging: PUFFS 117, 161
Sturgeon (SSN-637) 151, 152, 158
SUBACS 191
submarines of the United States: *Albacore* (SS-218) 14; *Albacore* (SS-569) 134, 143–147; *Archerfish* (SSN-678) 151; *Barbel* (SSN-580) 146, 147; *Barbero* (SS-317 170; *Baton Rouge* (SSBN-689) 163, 164; *Benjamin Franklin* (SSBN-640) 173; *Blueback* (SS-581) 146; *Bonefish* (SSN-582) 146; *Cachelot* (SS-170) 38; *Carbonero* (SS-337) 135, 170; *Cavalle* (SS-244) 119; *Clamagor* (SS-343) 103; *Cochino* (SS-345) 118; *Connecticut* (SSN-22) 186; *Crevalle* (SS-291) 79–82; *Cusl* (SS-348) 135; *Cuttlefish* (SS-171) 38; *Dolphin* (SS-167) 38; *Ethan Allen* (SSBN-608) 173, 174; *George Washington* (SSBN-598) 173, 174; *Glenard P. Lipscombe* (SSBN-685) 151; *Grayback* (SS-574) 170; *Growler* (SS-577) 135–170; *Gudgeon* (SS-567) 127; *Halibut* (SS-587) 153, 167–169; *Jimmy Carter* (SSN-23) 186; *Lafayette* (SSBN-616) 173,174; *Lapon* (SSN 661) 154, 155; *Lionfish* (SS-298) 71; *Los Angeles* (SSN-688) 165; *Los Angeles* (SSN-719) 160, 165; *Narwhal* (SS-167) 38, 71; *Narwhal* (SSN-571) 153; *Nautilus* (SS-168) 38; *Nautilus* (SSN-571) 129–132; *Octopus* (SS-11) 20; *Odax* (SS-404) 102; *Ohio* (SSBN-726) 176; *Parche* (SSN-683) 152, 186; *Permit* (SSN-594) 152; *Providence* (SSBN-719) 164; *Salmon* (D-3) 13; *Sargo* (SSN-583) 131, 132; *Scamp* (SSN-588) 148; *Scorpion* (SSN 589) 148; *Sculpin* (SSN-590) 148; *Seadragon* (SSN-584) 131, 132; *Seawolf* (SSN-21) 183–189; *Shark* (SSN 591) 148; *Skate* (SSN-578) 131, 132, 147, 149; *Skipjack* (SSN-585) 148–150, 172, 173; *Snook* (SSN-592) 148; *Sturgeon* (SSN-637) 151, 152, 158; *Swordfish* (SSN-579) 141; *Tambor* (SS-198) 50; *Tang* (SS-563) 180–182; *Tautog* (SSN-639) 150; *Thomas Edison* (SSBN-610) 180–182;
Tiru (SS-419) 117; *Trigger* (SS-282) 82; *Tunny* (SS-282) 135, 170; *Viper* (SS-10) 20; *Virginia* (SSN-774) 186–190, 196; *Wahoo* (SS-238) 72; *Wahoo* (SS-565) 126, 127; *Whale* (SSN-639) 153
Suetter, Muray F. 10
Swordfish (SSN-579) 141

Tambor (SS-198) 50
Tang (SS-563) 180–182
target bearing transmitter 56
target motion analysis 117, 120, 153, 154, 166, 175, 177–179
Tautog (SSN-639) 150
telemeter scale, periscope 60
Thomas Edison (SSBN-610) 180–182
Tiru (SS-419) 117
torpedo data computer 43, 47–49, 55–63, 72–84, 111–115
torpedoes of the United States: C-74, C-79 10; Mark 3 11; Mark 4 13; Mark 6 23; Mark 7 11, 15, 27–31; Mark 10 27, 37; Mark 14 31, 43, 46, 47, 80, 152; Mark 18 43; Mark 27 111, 113; Mark 28 111; Mark 37 114, 132, 168; Mark 37NTS 152 ; Mark 48 117, 152, 161, 168, 177; Mark 48ADCAP 152, 164, 177, 192; Nordenfeld 8, 16; Sims Edison 8
torpedoes of Germany: G-7 11, 72
Trigger (SS-282) 82
Tunny (SS-282) 135, 170

UAV 194, 195
UUV 194, 198

Valentiner, Max 20
Vinson, Thomas N. 22–24
Vinson-Traummel Act of 1934 39
Viper (SS-10) 20
Virginia (SSN-774) 186–190, 196

Wahoo (SS-238) 72
Wahoo (SS-565) 126, 127
Walker, John A. 159, 169
Weddigen, Otto 17, 18
Whale (SSN-639) 153
Whitehead, Robert 7, 8
Wilkes, John 63
Wilkinson, Eugene P. 129. 131
Wilson, Arthur, Royal Navy 16

Yamamoto, Isoroku 70

www.ingramcontent.com/pod-product-compliance
Ingram Content Group UK Ltd.
Pitfield, Milton Keynes, MK11 3LW, UK
UKHW041953140426